P9-DUR-169

The Mechanical Bride

Marshall McLuhan

The Mechanical Bride

FOLKLORE OF INDUSTRIAL MAN

The Vanguard Press, Inc., New York

Published simultaneously in Canada by the
Copp Clark Company, Ltd., Toronto

Manufactured in the United States of America
Designer: Ernst Reichl

Preface

OURS is the first age in which many thousands of the best-trained individual minds have made it a full-time business to get inside the collective public mind. To get inside in order to manipulate, exploit, control is the object now. And to generate heat not light is the intention. To keep everybody in the helpless state engendered by prolonged mental rutting is the effect of many ads and much entertainment alike.

Since so many minds are engaged in bringing about this condition of public helplessness, and since these programs of commercial education are so much more expensive and influential than the relatively puny offerings sponsored by schools and colleges, it seemed fitting to devise a method for reversing the process. Why not use the new commercial education as a means to enlightening its intended prey? Why not assist the public to observe consciously the drama which is intended to operate upon it unconsciously?

As this method was followed, "A Descent Into The Maelstrom" by Edgar Poe kept coming to mind. Poe's sailor saved himself by studying the action of the whirlpool and by co-operating with it. The present book likewise makes few attempts to attack the very considerable currents and pressures set up around us today by the mechanical agencies of the press, radio, movies, and advertising. It does attempt to set the reader at the center of the revolving picture created by these affairs where he may observe the action that is in progress and in which everybody is involved. From the analysis of that action, it is hoped, many individual strategies may suggest themselves.

But it is seldom the business of this book to take account of such strategies.

Poe's sailor says that when locked in by the whirling walls and the numerous objects which floated in that environment:

"I *must* have been delirious, for I even sought *amusement* in speculating upon the relative velocities of their several descents toward the foam below."

It was this amusement born of his rational detachment as a spectator of his own situation that gave him the thread which led him out of the Labyrinth. And it is in the same spirit that this book is offered as an amusement. Many who are accustomed to the note of moral indignation will mistake this amusement for mere indifference. But the time for anger and protest is in the early stages of a new process. The present stage is extremely advanced. Moreover, it is full, not only of destructiveness but also of promises of rich new developments to which moral indignation is a very poor guide.

Most of the exhibits in this book have been selected because of their typical and familiar quality. They represent a world of social myths or forms and speak a language we both know and do not know. After making his study of the nursery rhyme, "Where are you going, my pretty maid?" the anthropologist C. B. Lewis pointed out that "the folk has neither part nor lot in the making of folklore." That is also true of the folklore of industrial man, so much of which stems from the laboratory, the studio, and the advertising agencies. But amid the diversity of our inventions and abstract techniques of production and distribution there will be found a great degree of cohesion and unity. This consistency is not conscious in origin or effect and seems to arise from a sort of collective dream. For that reason, as well as because of the widespread popularity of these objects and processes, they are here referred to as "the folklore of industrial man." They are unfolded by exhibit and commentary as a single landscape. A whirling phantasmagoria can be grasped only when arrested for contemplation. And this very arrest is also a release from the usual participation.

The unity is not imposed upon this diversity, since any other selection of exhibits would reveal the same dynamic patterns. The fact that the present exhibits are not selected to prove a case but to reveal a complex situation, it is the effort of the book to illustrate by frequent cross-reference to other materials that are not included here. And it is the procedure of the book to use the commentaries on the exhibits merely as a means of releasing some of their intelligible meaning. No effort has been made to exhaust their meaning.

The various ideas and concepts introduced in the commentaries are intended to provide positions from which to examine the exhibits. They are not conclusions in which anybody is expected to rest but are intended merely as points of departure. This is an approach which it is hard to make clear at a time when most books offer a single idea as a means of unifying a troup of observations. Concepts are provisional affairs for apprehending reality; their value is in the grip they provide. This book, therefore, tries to present at once representative aspects of the reality and a wide range of ideas for taking hold of it. The ideas are very secondary devices for clambering up and over rock faces. Those readers who undertake merely to query the ideas will miss their use for getting at the material.

A film expert, speaking of the value of the movie medium for selling North to South America, noted that:

> the propaganda value of this simultaneous audio-visual impression is very high, for it standardizes thought by supplying the spectator with a ready-made visual image before he has time to conjure up an interpretation of his own.

This book reverses that process by providing typical visual imagery of our environment and dislocating it into meaning by inspection. Where visual symbols have been employed in an effort to paralyze the mind, they are here used as a means of energizing it. It is observable that the more illusion and falsehood needed to maintain any given state of affairs, the more tyranny is needed to maintain the illusion and falsehood. Today the tyrant rules not by club or fist, but, disguised as a market researcher, he shepherds his flocks in the ways of utility and comfort.

Because of the circulating point of view in this book, there is no need for it to be read in any special order. Any part of the book provides one or more views of the same social landscape. Ever since Buckhardt saw that the meaning of Machiavelli's method was to turn the state into a work of art by the rational manipulation of power, it has been an open possibility to apply the method of art analysis to the critical evaluation of society. That is attempted here. The Western world, dedicated since the sixteenth century to the increase and consolidation of the power of the state, has developed an artistic unity of effect which makes artistic criticism of that effect quite feasible. Art criticism is free to point to the various means employed to get the effect, as well as to decide whether the effect was worth attempting. As such, with regard to the modern state, it can be a citadel of inclusive awareness amid the dim dreams of collective consciousness.

I wish to acknowledge the advantage I have enjoyed in reading unpublished views of Professor David Riesman on the consumer mentality. To Professor W. T. Easterbrook I owe many enlightening conversations on the problems of bureaucracy and enterprise. And to Professor Felix Giovanelli I am in debt not only for the stimulus of discussion but for his prolonged assistance with the many publishing problems which have attended the entire work.

Herbert Marshall McLuhan

Contents

The Mechanical Bride

"All the News That's Fit to Print"

The New York Times.

CITY EDITION

Showers ending this morning, cooler later. Fair tomorrow.

Temperature Range Today-Max.,60; Min.,48

Temperatures Yesterday—Max.,69; Min.,55

Full U. S. Weather Bureau Report, Page 53

VOL. XCIX....No. 33,689. Entered as Second-Class Matter, Postoffice, New York, N. Y. NEW YORK, THURSDAY, APRIL 20, 1950. Times Square, New York 18, N. Y. Telephone LAckawanna 4-1000 FIVE CENTS

HOUSE GROUP BARS OVERALL 50% SLASH IN WARTIME EXCISES

Ways and Means Committee Decides to Act Separately on Each Item of List

LEVY ON CAMERAS HALVED

Sentiment Is Strong for Aiding Theatre-Going Public—Total Cuts May Hit Billion

By JOHN D. MORRIS

Special to THE NEW YORK TIMES.

WASHINGTON, April 19—The House Ways and Means Committee tentatively agreed today on a 50 per cent reduction in excise taxes on cameras and other photographic equipment.

Otherwise there were no decisions as the committee tried and failed to obtain unanimous consent for a general 50 per cent cut of all wartime excise rates. A new start is expected to be made tomorrow, when the committee will cast aside the unanimous consent procedure to go over the list again, item by item, and reach determinations by majority vote.

Today's closed-door session, which began the decisive phase in the committee's long deliberations on a 1950 tax bill, was largely aimed at testing sentiment on the question of halving all excises imposed since 1940, except those on liquor and tobacco.

However, unanimous consent could be obtained for application of the formula only to cameras, which carry a 25 per cent levy, and film and other photographic apparatus, taxed at the rate of 15 per cent.

General Cut Held Unlikely

Objection was raised in turn to a 50 per cent slash on each of the thirty other categories in which rates were increased or new taxes levied during the war emergency period. In some cases, it was argued that the proposed cut was too deep, in others that it was not deep enough.

A 50 per cent reduction, committee members were told, would result in estimated revenue losses of $1,156,000,000 annually.

In the light of today's pulse-taking, it appeared unlikely that the committee would agree on such an approach. There is considerable sentiment, however, for an approach that would achieve an over-all 50 per cent cut with the tax on some items being cut more, and that on others less.

Some committee mebers feel, for example, that the theatre-going public should be relieved of most, if not all, of the excise tax. At the same time, they express the opinion that some industries would benefit unjustifiably by comparison from a reduction as high as 50 per cent.

Besides halving the admissions tax, the committee may repeal the entire 20 per cent levy with respect to entertainment tickets selling for 50 cents or perhaps 75 cents.

The decision on photographic apparatus today is subject to amendment after the other items are out of the way. Members reported that, despite unanimous agreement on cuts of at least 50 per cent, some still were holding out hope for a greater reduction in view of the fact that the photo industry was subjected to heavier wartime increases than the others under consideration.

Truman Warning Recalled

After disposing of the excise question, the committee is slated to take up the closing of "loopholes" in other tax laws in an effort to compensate for the revenue losses.

It is widely predicted that excises will be cut by at least $1,000,000,000, considerably more than can be offset by loophole closing. The prospect of a veto consequently is looming increasingly large to the committee. President Truman has warned that he will not sign any bill entailing a net loss in revenue. He recommended that excise reductions be held to $655,000,000.

Representative Robert L. Doughton, Democrat of North Carolina, committee chairman, has predicted to reporters that excise taxes "are going to be cut considerably."

As to the President's recommendation that any reductions in excise taxes be offset by closing the loopholes in the revenue laws, Representative Doughton said that he was "not sure" that this could be done.

Committee members, in their determination to meet insistent demands for excise tax relief, generally appeared to have been unswayed by yesterday's staff report

Continued on Page 30, Column 4

LICENSE REVOKED

Dr. Hermann N. Sander

Associated Press

SANDER IS STRIPPED OF MEDICAL LICENSE

New Hampshire Board Terms His Action 'Reprehensible'—May Restore Him in June

Special to THE NEW YORK TIMES.

CONCORD, N. H., April 19—The State Board of Registration in Medicine revoked today Dr. Hermann N. Sander's license to practice in New Hampshire, but left a loophole for him to apply for reinstatement in two months. The decision of the five-man board was unanimous.

In a sharp statement of more than 500 words, the board charged Dr. Sander with "morally reprehensible action in deliberately injecting air into his patient," Mrs. Abbie Borroto, 59 years old, of Manchester, on Dec. 4, 1949. Mrs. Borroto was incurably ill of cancer.

Dr. Sander, accused by the state of first degree murder by four injections of air into Mrs. Borroto's veins, was acquitted March 9 in a trial that lasted more than three weeks.

Dr. John S. Wheeler of Contoocook, secretary of the medical board, said that it was "not a legal requirement" for that body to leave an opening for reinstatement, but declined to comment further.

Ruling Believed Appealable

The wording of the statement was: "no application of Dr. Sander for reinstatement by this board will be entertained prior to June 19, 1950."

State House sources close to the board were of the opinion that decisions of any state department could be appealed to the State Supreme Court.

Neither Dr. Sander nor his counsel, Louis E. Wyman, had any immediate comment on the decision. The physician's home in Candia was not receiving telephone calls. Mr. Wyman, who was reached by telephone, said he would not discuss the case at least until tomorrow, when he had had a chance to study the statement.

State Representative George A. Myhaver, Republican of Peterborough, said he would ask for a legislative investigation "to bring out why the State Medical Board revoked Dr. Sander's license when he had already been acquitted by a court."

The state board was in session seven hours at the State House before Dr. Wheeler called reporters

Continued on Page 32, Column 2

TRUMAN PREPARES TO LIST ELIGIBLES FOR MAJOR OFFICES

He Assigns 'Little Cabinet' Group to Plan Compilation of a National Register

THIS WILL BE NONPARTISAN

Trouble in Finding Qualified Persons for Top Posts Led President to Take Step

By ANTHONY LEVIERO

Special to THE NEW YORK TIMES.

WASHINGTON, April 19—President Truman proposed today a national register of men and women from which he could select candidates of particular qualifications for appointment to top Government positions, including even Cabinet members.

The cataloging of persons eligible for policy-making positions would be national in scope and would be done without regard to their party affiliations, the White House said. The outlines of the plan emerged after Mr. Truman conferred with a special committee he has organized to get it started.

Mr. Truman assigned one of his own key staff members to get the project under way. He is Donald Dawson, an administrative assistant responsible for personnel procurement, who has the never-ending task of seeking and investigating candidates for important vacancies.

Virtually every top bracket job, including even the now vacant chairmanship of the Atomic Energy Commission conceivably could be filled from the proposed register, as it was envisioned today. Only the Federal judiciary was specifically mentioned as an exception, on the ground that the present method of selecting judges was adequate.

Committee Members Named

Mr. Dawson's committee consists of members of the "Little Cabinet" or officials just below the top level, as Charles G. Ross, White House Press Secretary described them. They held their first meeting with the President this morning. They were, besides Mr. Dawson:

John E. Peurifoy, Deputy Under-Secretary of State; H. Graham Morison, Assistant Attorney General; Philip M. Kaiser, Assistant Secretary of Labor; Eugene M. Zuckert, Assistant Secretary of the Air Force, and Archibald S. Alexander, Assistant Secretary of the Army.

"The catalogue will be confined to posts in the higher echelons," said Mr. Ross. "There are a lot of good people whose light is hidden under a bushel. The aim is to get the names of a great many people who would be available for high posts in the Government."

After the conference in Mr. Truman's office Mr. Ross called Mr. Dawson into his office to outline the plan to reporters. In a way the procedure was unusual, as administrative assistants are supposed to have "a passion for anonymity" and are seldom quoted.

Immediately Mr. Dawson was questioned about the nonpartisan nature of the catalogue and the place of party patronage. It was suggested that the Democratic party would hardly give away important plums to Republicans.

"This is a location process to find people all over the country,"

Continued on Page 23, Column 4

Postal Cuts Startle Officials; Business Sees Political Move

City's 7 Postmasters Uncertain How Soon Changes Can Be Made—Deadline Is July 1—4,300 to 6,450 Face Loss of Jobs Here

By DOUGLAS DALES

Postal officials in this city went into hurried conferences yesterday to study means of carrying out the drastic economy order of Postmaster General Jesse M. Donaldson, which may cost the jobs of 10 per cent or more of the 44,200 post office workers in the city.

The directive, which must be put into full operation by July 1, caught postmasters in the seven separate post offices in the city by surprise. Officials generally were unable to say how soon the various changes could be effected.

The only part that went into effect immediately was the order to discontinue directory service for first-class mail improperly addressed. Fifty thousand letters are normally redirected daily in Manhattan alone.

Some business spokesmen called the order a clever political maneuver timed to support the appeal Mr. Donaldson is expected to make next Tuesday at a Senate committee hearing on legislation on new rates expected to yield $150,000,000 annually. It was charged that the Post Office Department had emphasized the order's effect on home deliveries to obscure its effect on business users of the mails.

The order, which one postmaster called "the most drastic in the history of the postal service," caused considerable alarm among postal personnel, particularly those with a temporary or substitute status.

Philip Lepper, president of the New York Branch of the Association of Letter Carriers, A. F. L., declared that the directive had "thrown panic into the hearts" of

Continued on Page 18, Column 3

O'Dwyer Backs Rises in Pay For Teachers of $150-$250

Mayor O'Dwyer announced yesterday that he would recommend to the Board of Estimate salary increases of $250 a year for high school teachers and $150 for elementary school teachers. Nearly 40,000 teachers would benefit by the increase, which totals $7,000,000.

In a statement issued last evening from City Hall, the Mayor said that after a series of conferences with fiscal advisors and school officials it was decided that "salary increases could be granted within the framework of the present Board of Education budget."

The salary increases, if granted as recommended by the Mayor, would break the single salary schedule for teachers, which has been in effect here since July 1, 1947. It provides equal pay for teachers, regardless of the level on which they teach. Under the schedule, elementary, junior and senior high school teachers start at $2,500 a year and go to $5,125 in sixteen steps. Teachers holding a master's degree or its equivalent receive an additional $200 a year.

Mr. O'Dwyer, in his brief announcement, also said that many teachers would receive regular increments ranging from $156 to $216. It was not immediately known whether junior high school teachers would receive $150 or $250 in pay increases.

A statement from Maximilian Moss, president of the Board of Education, praising the Mayor's salary recommendations, was also released by City Hall. Mr. Moss asserted that the granting of such increases would "earn the heartfelt thanks" of the city's teachers.

The Joint Committee of Teachers Organizations, which represents the bulk of the city's teacher

Continued on Page 26, Column 6

RAIL FIREMEN CALL STRIKE ON 4 ROADS

Men Ordered to Leave Jobs Next Wednesday—Leaders See National Tie-Up Soon

Special to THE NEW YORK TIMES.

CHICAGO, April 19—The Brotherhood of Locomotive Firemen and Enginemen today called a strike against four big railroads for 6 A. M. next Wednesday.

The strike would back a demand for a second fireman on diesel locomotives that has been turned down by a Presidential fact-finding board.

Transportation to and from the Chicago area would be hit seriously by the strike, which was announced by the union after a week-long conference. David B. Robertson, president, said 18,000 men would be called out on the Pennsylvania system west of Harrisburg, Pa., the New York Central west of Buffalo and three of its components, the entire Atchison, Topeka and Santa Fe system, and the Southern Railway.

"We are going to try to settle this on a practical basis after the theorists have got through—attorneys and such," Mr. Robertson said in a denunciation of the fact-find-

Continued on Page 26, Column 4

World News Summarized

THURSDAY, APRIL 20, 1950

Czechoslovakia, calling the United States Information Service a headquarters for espionage and propaganda, demanded yesterday that its offices in Prague and Bratislava be closed and that the American press attaché be recalled. [1:8.]

In Washington, an aroused Senate unanimously approved a resolution for posthumous decorations for the ten men on the Navy Privateer allegedly shot down by Soviet fighters over the Baltic. Indications that Moscow would reject the protest over the incident were seen in a Soviet magazine article demanding punishment for the Americans responsible. [1:6.]

The West will win the "cold war" because "history and morality are on our side" and internal pressures will break down Moscow's control, Ambassador Harriman forecast. [1:7.]

Senate Republicans approved President Turman's approach to consult them on the forming and implementing of foreign policy. [6:5.] The President will make a major foreign policy speech before an editors' convention today. [6:3.] He proposed a national register of qualified persons, regardless of party, from which to draw appointees for top Government posts. [1:3.]

A House committee, unable to agree on a 50 per cent across-the-board cut of excise taxes, reduced the levy on cameras and supplies by that amount. [1:1.] The House trimmed by $1,700,000 the $29,045,030,154 omnibus appropriation bill [22:3.]

President Truman signed the bill for a ten-year program of economic aid to the Navajo and Hopi Indians. [1:2-3.]

Postal officials in this city ceased redirecting improperly addressed letters as the first move to comply with drastic economy cuts ordered by Washington. At least 10 per cent of the postal workers are expected to lose their jobs. [1:4-5.]

Bonn, in the opinion of Western Allied officials, is intensifying its pressure to win further concessions at the Foreign Minister's meeting next month. [5:1.] Chancellor Adenauer said he saw no harm in having led Berliners in singing "Deutschland' Ueber Alles." [4:5.]

The Soviet Union reversed its stand and withdrew support of internationalization of Jerusalem under the United Nations. [13:3.]

State mediators will make a final effort to avert the impending strike of 18,000 Manhattan apartment house workers. [24:3.] Railroad firemen and engineers called a strike against four major roads for Wednesday. [1:4.] In London 1,800 dockers went on a wildcat strike. [9:3.]

Mayor O'Dwyer advocated salary increases of $250 for high school teachers and $150 for those in grade schools. [1:4-5.]

The city spread silver iodide smoke last night as the first step in a new rain-making test. Today is a water holiday. [31:1.]

New Hampshire revoked the license of Dr. Sander to practice medicine but left a loophole for reinstatement. [1:2.]

Index to other news appears on Page 30.

President Signs Bill to Aid Indians; Hails 10-Year Rehabilitation Plan

Special to THE NEW YORK TIMES.

WASHINGTON, April 19—President Truman approved with "gratification" today a bill authorizing an economic rehabilitation program for the Navajo and Hopi Indian tribes that will run a ten-year course.

In a message on the measure, the Chief Executive expressed "my sincere hope that the Congress will promptly appropriate the full amount requested in my 1951 budget to initiate this program."

The ten-year program would cost $88,570,000. In the budget for the fiscal year beginning July 1 the President requested $14,000,000 in cash and $6,000,000 in contract authorizations to start it. The House Appropriations Committee, however, has cut this request to about $11,000,000.

The measure that President Truman signed today was a revised version of the bill he vetoed last Oct. 17. The original bill, Mr. Truman then asserted, contained a provision which subjected the Indians, traditionally regarded as wards of the Federal Government, to the jurisdiction of state courts. He also said that bill threatened their water rights, a vital resource in an arid territory, and raised havoc with tribal inheritance customs.

In vetoing last year's bill Mr. Truman heeded the Navajo Tribal Council and today he had the support of the council in making the measure into law.

"The passage of this act is an important milestone in our Government's administration of Indian affairs. It represents a carefully developed plan for dealing with the unsolved economic problems which have delayed the social advancement of this large segment of our Indian citizens. For these Indian groups it also represents a significant forward step in self-government—a principle to which the

Continued on Page 30, Column 2

SENATE PROPOSES AWARDS FOR FLIERS DOWNED IN BALTIC

Votes 66 to 0 to Request Navy to Decorate Privateer Crew—House Approval Urged

AIRMEN HAILED AS 'HEROIC'

Influential Russian Weekly Asks U. S. to 'Punish' Those Guilty of 'Provocation'

By HAROLD B. HINTON

Special to THE NEW YORK TIMES.

WASHINGTON, April 19—The Senate adopted today, by a roll-call vote of 66 to 0, a resolution directing the Secretary of the Navy to confer appropriate posthumous decorations on the crew of the Privateer that presumably was shot down April 8 by Soviet fighter planes over the Baltic Sea. The resolution was sent to the House for concurrence.

The surprise proposal by Senator Scott W. Lucas of Illinois, Democratic floor leader, touched off several outbursts of denunciation of the Soviet action. Mr. Lucas told the Senate he was offering the resolution as an individual, and not in response to a request from President Truman or from Dean Acheson, Secretary of State.

[In Moscow, The New Times called on the United States to "punish severely" those responsible for "the crime" of the Baltic plane incidents. The tone of the New Times comment made it plain that Moscow would reject the United States protest in terms as pointed as those used in Washington's note Tuesday.]

Resolution Praises Fliers

The Senate resolution praised the Navy crew members for "their outstanding and heroic services in the performance of duty," extended the condolences of the Senate to their families, and directed the Secretary of the Navy to transmit copies of the resolution to each family.

Mr. Lucas explained that he wanted a roll-call, even though he expected there would be no opposition. He said he wanted the record to show that there was bipartisan condemnation of what he termed the "criminal action" of the Soviet pilots. The final tally showed thirty-two Democrats and thirty-four Republicans recorded for the resolution, with no dissent.

Senator Kenneth S. Wherry of Nebraska, Republican floor leader, said that he favored the resolution, but commented that "a lack of bipartisan foreign policy is what has gotten us into our difficulties."

Senator Wayne Morse, Republican of Oregon, favored the resolution, but added that "it behooves the Government to use all existing peaceful machinery, including the United Nations and, if jurisdiction can be established, the World Court," to make clear that the lives of United States citizens would be protected under international law.

He said the world was "sitting on a tinderbox," and that an incident of this kind could turn the "cold war" into a real war. He added that the Russians "think that because there is a 'cold war' on, we won't take any steps to throw us into a hot war."

Senator Harry P. Cain, Republican of Washington, sought to inject a note of caution into the debate, but the Senate was in no mood for it. He asked Mr. Lucas

Continued on Page 3, Column 5

RECALL DEMANDED

Joseph C. Kolarek

The New York Times

HARRIMAN DEPICTS 'COLD WAR' VICTORY

History, Morality, Resources Are on Our Side, He Tells 2,500 State Democrats

Excerpts from Mr. Harriman's speech are on Page 2.

By JAMES A. HAGERTY

W. Averell Harriman, United States Ambassador-at-Large, declared last night that this country and its allies would win the "cold war" with Russia because "history and morality are on our side" and because of the material resources on the side of freedom, with the United States and Canada having half the heavy manufacturing capacity of the world.

Mr. Harriman, who spoke at the $100-a-plate dinner of the Democratic State Committee at the Waldorf-Astoria Hotel, asserted that the nations of Western Europe with the aid of the Economic Cooperation Administration were rapidly gaining economic health and democratic strength.

He predicted that pressures behind the Iron Curtain ultimately would break down the Kremlin's control and said there could be no doubt that the disaffection of Marshal Tito in Yugoslavia had resulted from the success of the Marshall Plan.

"The strength of our economy and the strength of our spirit will be the deciding factors in maintaining freedom and peace," Mr. Harriman added. "On this, I hold three deep convictions:

Spadework on Governorship

"First, that the American people must secure an dbroaden our own well-being at home. Second, that the American people must give inspiration, assistance and leadership, as partners, to the free nations of the world. My third conviction is that, if the American people can do both these things, war can be avoided."

Also speaking at the dinner were Senator Herbert H. Lehman, Mayor O'Dwyer, Paul E. Fitzpatrick, chairman of the party's State Committee; Miss Angela R. Parisi, its vice chairman, and Miss Josephine Bravo, co-chairman of its youth division. William P. Hunt was toastmaster. Twenty-five hundred persons were present, and it was estimated that the committee

Continued on Page 2, Column 2

Surgeon Massages Heart to Save Man, 65, Twice 'Dead' in 4 Hours

A 65-year-old Long Island man who two months ago was pronounced dead on a hospital operating table twice within four hours will be discharged from the institution tomorrow as a recovered patient, it was learned yesterday.

The case, believed to be unprecedented in medical history, was revealed by officials of St. John's Episcopal Hospital, 480 Herkimer Street, Brooklyn. They declined to disclose the name of the patient or the surgeon who twice brought him back to a life he had apparently lost.

On both occasions, it was reported, the "dead man" was revived through manual massage of his heart, after it had ceased to beat and respiration had stopped. This technique had been employed in similar cases before, but hospital authorities said they believed that it had never before been used successfully twice on a single patient.

The patient, later to become famous with the staff as "the miracle man," was admitted to St. John's on Feb. 2. Six days later he underwent an abdominal operation. It was not entirely successful, and doctors ordered a second similar operation for Feb. 14.

The second operation was completed without incident, but directly after it, at about 1:30 P. M., the anesthetist reported to the surgeon that the patient was dead, his heart and respiration having ceased. The doctor immediately made an incision over the heart, reached into the chest cavity, and began to massage the lifeless organ by hand.

This treatment was continued until about 4 P. M., when it was reported that the patient was again living. But, just as he was about to be removed to his hospital room, his heart failed for a second time.

Fortunately, since the operating room equipment and the surgeon

Continued on Page 32, Column 6

PRAGUE ORDERS U. S. TO SHUT LIBRARIES, RECALL AN ATTACHE

Asserts Information Services Were Used to Circulate Untruths, Incite People

COUNTER MOVES WEIGHED

6 Czechs Go on Trial on Charge of Treason—Are Accused of Aiding Washington

Text of the Czechoslovak note accusing Americans, Page 3.

By DANA ADAMS SCHMIDT

Special to THE NEW YORK TIMES.

PRAGUE, Czechoslovakia, April 19—The Czechoslovak Foreign Office today ordered the United States Information Services libraries here and at Bratislava to close by next Saturday noon and ordered the Embassy press attaché, Joseph C. Kolarek, to leave Czechoslovakia "within a reasonable time."

The two moves had been expected since two library employes who had been arrested a few days previously resigned and issued statements April 11 and 12 denouncing Mr. Kolarek's "slanderous campaign" against Czechoslovakia. Two other employes were tried for espionage April 13 and sentenced to fifteen and eighteen years' imprisonment.

A note to the American Embassy cited statements by these former employes to support the contention that Mr. Kolarek had used the library to disseminate "untruthful reports about Czechoslovakia with a view to inciting our citizens against the people's democratic regime." The note charged that he had used his employes for espionage and to gather material for "fictitious reports of incitory character" for the Voice of America.

Prague Cites Lack of Pact

The Foreign Office repeated a charge that Mr. Kolarek, while distributing correctly censored copies of the Embassy's bulletin by mail, added uncensored pages to the copies displayed at the library. It held, furthermore, that the library was operating "without any legal basis such as a special treaty or agreement."

Meanwhile, charged with committing high treason as members of underground espionage groups "directed from the building of the American Embassy in Prague," five men and one woman went on trial before a state tribunal at Pankrac Prison.

The two principal defendants who pleaded "fully guilty" today were Maj. Jaromir Nechansky, 34, a career officer, and Veleslav Wahl, 28, a law student.

Mr. Kolarek, 34, of Baltimore, has been in Czechoslovakia since September, 1945, serving first as assistant and later as chief press attache and information service director. He planned to leave the country next Saturday for a vacation in France before returning to Washington.

Embassy officials said that they would leave comment on Mr. Kolareks' expulsion and closing of the library to Washington.

10,000 a Month Service

Miss Katharine Kosmak, 41, of New York City, who has been directly in charge of Prague and Bratislava libraries since October, 1948, said they had between them served nearly 10,000 patrons monthly since they opened a few months after the war. This meant that the libraries here did more business than those in all other "people's democracies" combined, including the Bucharest and Sofia libraries which have been closed.

Miss Kosmak observed that following the attacks upon the United States service there was only a slight falling off in the number of patrons who made use in Prague of 4,000 books, an extensive supply of periodicals and 675 documentary films available for loan. About 200 persons usually turned up for Monday night record concerts.

Six of the Prague library's eight Czechoslovak employes had resigned before the closing order was received today.

The other four defendants in the treason trial are Milos Sprysl, Jan Dolmalek, Miss Szdenka Vackova and Karel Loris. They were associated, according to the indictment, with espionage centers organized after the Communist coup by the two principals under the direction of the American Embassy secretary, Walter Birge, and other embassy officials. These centers, it was declared, were set up at Most, a mining town in northern Bohemia or Jirlava on the mountainous

Continued on Page 3, Column 2

Front Page

What's the score here? Why is a page of news a problem in orchestration?

How does the jazzy, ragtime discontinuity of press items link up with other modern art forms?

To achieve coverage from China to Peru, and also simultaneity of focus, can you imagine anything more effective than this front page cubism?

You never thought of a page of news as a symbolist landscape?

THESE are only a very few of the questions raised even by the quiet front page of *The New York Times.* Many further questions are raised by the more sensational newspapers. But any paper today is a collective work of art, a daily "book" of industrial man, an Arabian Night's entertainment in which a thousand and one astonishing tales are being told by an anonymous narrator to an equally anonymous audience.

It is on its technical and mechanical side that the front page is linked to the techniques of modern science and art. Discontinuity is in different ways a basic concept both of quantum and relativity physics. It is the way in which a Toynbee looks at civilizations, or a Margaret Mead at human cultures. Notoriously, it is the visual technique of a Picasso, the literary technique of James Joyce.

But it would be a mistake to join the chorus of voices which wails without intermission that "Discontinuity is chaos come again. It is irrationalism. It is the end." Quantum and relativity physics are not a fad. They have provided new facts about the world, new intelligibility, new insights into the universal fabric. Practically speaking, they mean that henceforth this planet is a single city. Far from making for irrationalism, these discoveries make irrationalism intolerable for the intelligent person. They demand much greater exertions of intelligence and a much higher level of personal and social integrity than have existed previously.

In the same way, the technique of Toynbee makes all civilizations contemporary with our own. The past is made immediately available as a working model for present political experiment. Margaret Mead's *Male and Female* illustrates a similar method. The cultural patterns of several societies, quite unrelated to one another or to our own, are abruptly overlayered in cubist or Picasso style to provide a greatly enriched image of human potentialities. By this method the greatest possible detachment from our own immediate problems is achieved. The voice of reason is audible only to the detached observer.

And it is equally so with the popular modern press, despite all its faults. That huge landscape of the human family which is achieved by simply setting side by side disconnected items from China to Peru presents a daily image both of the complexity and similarity of human affairs which, in its total effect, is tending to abolish any provincial outlook.

Quite independently of good or bad editorial policies, the ordinary man is now accustomed to human-interest stories from every part of the globe. The sheer technique of world-wide newsgathering has created a new state of mind which has little to do with local or national political opinion. So that even the frequent sensational absurdity and unreliability of the news cannot annul the total effect, which is to enforce a deep sense of human solidarity.

Certainly if an observer were to consider only the quality of intellectual analysis shown in a particular item or editorial, he would have cause for gloom. Certain habits of mind have led to a natural exaggeration about the value, and even necessity, of "correct views." The same habits of mind lead to the condemnation of modern art because of its lack of a "message." These habits blind people to the real changes of our time. Conditioned in this way, people have been taught to accept opinions and attitudes of the press. But the French symbolists, followed by James Joyce in *Ulysses*, saw that there was a new art form of universal scope present in the technical layout of the modern newspaper. Here is a major instance of how a by-product of industrial imagination, a genuine agency of contemporary folklore, led to radical artistic developments. To the alerted eye, the front page of a newspaper is a superficial chaos which can lead the mind to attend to cosmic harmonies of a very high order. Yet when these harmonies are more sharply stylized by a Picasso or a Joyce, they seem to give offense to the very people who should appreciate them most. But that is a separate story.

There are many places in this book where these issues will recur, but it seemed best to raise them first in connection with the press. They are not questions that can be "answered." They are merely typical of that very common condition of industrial man in which he lives amid a great flowering of technical and mechanical imagery of whose rich human symbolism he is mainly unconscious. Industrial man is not unlike the turtle that is quite blind to the beauty of the shell which it has grown on its back. In the same way, the modern newspaper isn't seen by the reporter except from the point of view of its mushy sensual content, its pulsating, romantic glamour. The reporter doesn't even know there's a beautiful shell above him. He *grows* the shell, unwittingly, subhumanly, biologically. This is not even the voice, but only the feel, of the turtle. This inside point of view would coincide with the practical point of view of the man who would rather eat the turtle than admire the design on its back. The same man would rather dunk himself in the newspaper than have any esthetic or intellectual grasp of its character and meaning. The incorrigible dunker would perhaps do well to skip the next few pages.

The strictly inside or unconscious consumer point of view of industrial folklore is neatly shown in the following item, which appeared in a provincial newspaper:

SEE SELVES ON "VIDEO"

THEN TWO DIE IN CHAIR

> Chicago, April 21, 1950—(AP)—Two condemned murderers saw themselves on television last night and a few hours later died in the electric chair. . . . The doomed men . . . were filmed in death row yesterday afternoon. The film was then put on a 7 p.m. newsreel show and viewed by the men on a set loaned them by the warden.

This situation is a major feat of modern news technique. Hot spot news with a vengeance. What a thrill these men must have got from being on the inside of a big inside story. Participating in their own audience participation, they were able to share the thrill of the audience that was being thrilled by their imminent death.

This is an illustration of the situation of those in the modern world who contribute mindlessly and automatically to the huge technical panorama which they never raise their eyes to examine. In the following pages various sections of that panorama will be centered for conscious scrutiny.

Nose for News

Why does the Hearst press attempt to organize the news of each day into a Victorian melodrama?

Anything queer in a big urban press going flat out for the small town, the small guy, and cracker-barrel sentiments?

Is it a smoke screen or just the fog from a confoosed brain?

As COMPARED with *The New York Times,* note the use of headlines in the Hearst press to build the news of the day into a personal drama keynoted by "Jim Farley's Story."

The New York Times announces "All the News That's Fit to Print." *The Journal-American* proclaims itself "An American Paper for American People." Both these statements prove strange upon examination, but the second would perhaps imply that America is the world.

Note how items like "Soldier's Last Wish Denied," or "Offers an Eye to Blind Mate," when put on the same page and scaled with FDR's "We'll Smoke 'Em Out" (reform of the Supreme Court), provide a sort of X-ray drama of the common passions of the human heart.

In this way even international politics are made a mirror for private passions. Love, hate, deceit, ambition, disappointment, these are the persistent musical accompaniment for a changing set of social and national events.

We see also the paradox of a very big press posing as a brave little man facing giants and ogres. Every day this press would warn or save us from big interests plotting the overthrow of the common man. And when giants are scarce, they must be invented. That is one of the functions of a Westbrook Pegler: Find them and kill them.

By posing as a Jack-the-Giant-Killer, this sort of press can give the ordinary reader an heroic image of himself as capable of similar feats, while it tacitly assumes Barnum's view of the public as sucker. As the noisy champion of the ordinary man, this kind of newspaper invites reader participation in its triumphs. It appeals to the Jeffersonian enmity toward federal centralization and corporations while being itself a vast bureaucratic corporation. It consolidates its Hamiltonian practice of centralism by folksy, Frank Capra scenes and columnists. This urgent appetite to have the cake and eat it, too, is widely prevalent in the myth patterns or emotional tensions of industrial society. It is perfectly expressed in Henry Ford's dream of a rural-village Utopia to be achieved by mass production—the nostalgia for a past which evades the inner logic of the inventions of the world to which it has contributed so much.

It was seen in *Front Page* that the real tendency of disconnected news items assembled from all over the world, and placed side by side, was to evoke the image of a world society. The Hearst press and, as we shall see, *Time* and *Life* try to resist this tendency by swamping with a flood of superimposed emotion the emergent image of the world as one city. For the tight little nineteenth-century mind, nourished on "scientific" doctrines about each nation as an independent organism

JIM FARLEY'S STORY

F. D. R. Was Firm on Packing Court

DAILY, 5 Cents. SATURDAY, 10 Cents. SUNDAY, 15 Cents

No. 22,009 SUNDAY, MAY 9, 1948

SUNDAY MAIL EDITION

5-4 Decision On Labor Act Cheered Him

By JAMES A. FARLEY
Instalment 2

LATE in March of 1937, on his return to Washington from a Warm Springs vacation, the President closeted himself with Vice President Garner, Speaker Bankhead, Majority Leader Robinson and House Leader Rayburn to be brought up to date on the Court fight. On April 1, I had lunch at the White House with the President and Sen. Hugo Black of Alabama. Our conference was largely devoted to the progress of the Court fight.

"All we have to do," the President said happily, "is to let the flood of mail settle on Congress. You just see. All I have to do is deliver a better speech, and the opposition will be beating a path to the White House door."

The President said that the proponents of the plan unquestionably were having the better of the argument; that the program would soon be brought to the Senate floor where it would be passed.

In general, I agreed, but noted that it might take longer than he expected.

Black cautioned that the opposition was most determined and would exercise every means of delay, knowing that their only hope lay in avoiding a vote.

'We'll Smoke 'Em Out,' Said FDR

"We'll smoke 'em out," the President said. "If delay helps them, we must press for an early vote."

Black had expressed displeasure over the appointments of Rear Adm. Emory S. Land and Rear Adm. H. A. Wiley to the Maritime Commission. Black was irked because the appointments were announced without his having been advised, when he had understood that he was to be consulted.

The President soothed him and soon had him smiling and promising to go along with the appointees, whose capacities he had questioned.

On April 12, 1937, I talked with Roosevelt by phone from New York City after the Supreme Court validated the Wagner Act by a five-to-four decision. He was jubilant.

"We did it," he chortled. "I am very, very pleased. You ought to see Homer Cummings, who's sitting with me now. He looks like the Cheshire cat that swallowed the canary. It's wonderful.

Hits 4 Dissenting Judges

"I am convinced more than ever that the proposals for reform of the Court are warranted. It's the same four justices who have dissented all along that are against me this time—McReynolds, Butler, Sutherland and Van Devanter."

The decision did serve to support arguments for the need of a change. None of us had any doubt of passage of the program.

It was in May that the handwriting on the wall, which had been regarded as favorable to the Court plan, was translated into the bitter truth of opposition by Senate leaders. Defeat was certain unless enough Democratic Senators could be persuaded to support the President. There was still hope that a compromise might be effected.

Roosevelt, however, was undaunted. He would not consider compromise. When I told him polls were showing the Senate so evenly divided that Garner might have to cast the deciding vote, he snapped:

"Let him do it."

I counseled him to consider the possibility that the party would be split beyond repair, which provoked the surprising declaration "and good riddance, too."

Barred Any Compromise

At one point he looked out of the window and said, almost to himself:

"This comes from telling them I would not be a candidate again."

He said with all the finality at his command that he would not withdraw as much as an inch and he would not compromise.

The Court packing plan was defeated by a one-inch punch. The paralyzing blow was delivered in the resignation of Justice Van Devanter, staunch member of the "Old Guard bloc."

The knockout blow was the death a few weeks later of Joe Robinson, who kept the plan afloat in troubled Congressional currents by the sheer force of a remarkable personality. Robinson had unflinching support from Byrnes and Harrison.

It was on May 18, 1937, that Van Devanter sent his resignation to the White House. The President accepted it in a friendly note to Van Devanter, adding:

"Before you leave Washington for the Summer, it would give me great personal pleasure if you would come in to see me."

Wouldn't Invite McReynolds

When I saw the letter on the office news ticker, I called the President. I found him unperturbed about the future.

"I wanted you to know I thought you wrote a most interesting and amusing letter," I said, "particularly in the line extending the invitation to him to pay a call before he leaves."

"If I receive the resignation of acertain other judge on the bench, you can be sure he won't get a similar invitation," he said meaningly.

"It wouldn't happen to be a certain Southern gentleman answering to the name of McReynolds?" I asked.

"Still the prophet, Jim. That's exactly the one I had in

Continued on Page 4, Column 1,

JOHN N. GARNER, FRANKLIN D. ROOSEVELT, JIM FARLEY
Democratic Chieftains at a Banquet in Honor of Farley

OFFERS AN EYE TO BLIND MATE

BRAZIL, Ind., May 8 (UP).—Mrs. Dorothy Coward, 37, is praying for a miracle. Her husband has no eyes, but she wants him to see again.

She had offered to have one of her eyes transplanted to her husband, Kenneth, but doctors said it couldn't be done. She still has not given up hope.

"I want so much to give an eye to my husband," Mrs. Coward said. "It is the least I can do in repayment of the happiness he has given me during our 20 years of married life."

STRICKEN 2 YEARS AGO.

Coward became afflicted with glaucoma two years ago and lost the sight of both eyes. His left eye was removed two months ago. His right eye was taken out five weeks later.

Dr. Donald Caseley, director of the Indiana University Medical Center at Indianapolis, said that eye corneas have been transplanted to restore eyesight. He said an entire eye couldn't be given to a blind person.

Friends and neighbors of the Cowards had raised the money to finance the operation.

Mrs. Coward, a grandmother, said she and her husband were "disappointed" at the "unpleasant information," but she still hoped for a miracle.

"They've happened before to other people," she said.

Ship Trapped in Canal As Rival Unions Clash

Special to the N. Y. Journal-American

THOROLD, Ont., May 8.—Thirty-four lake seamen faced possible piracy charges here today, as the seuel to a clash between rival unions.

Members of the Canadian Seamen's Union stormed aboard the coal carrier Glenelg in the Welland canal locks here, to battle with its crew, members of the Canadian Lake Seamen's Union.

Harbor authorities trapped the invaders by releasing the water from the locks and lowering the collier 50 feet to the bottom.

MOUNTIES TAKE 34.

Surrendering to Royal Canadian Mounted Police, the 34 were charged with unlawful boarding of the ship; assault; damaging property, and conspiracy.

In Montreal, officials of Canada Steamship Lines, owners of the Glenelg, said they planned to charge "piracy, with intent to murder," which could carry a penalty of life imprisonment. Authorities here voiced doubt, however, whether such a charge would "stand up."

DYNAMITE PLOT CHARGED.

Simultaneously, J. A. "Pat" Sullivan, president of the Canadian Lake Seamen's Union, charged that the rival union was plotting to dynamite the Cornwall canal, a vital link in Canada's water route to the Atlantic. Harry Davis, CSU president, branded the charge "a downright lie, trumped up to justify bringing in hundreds of gangsters."

Sullivan, formerly president of the Canadian Seamen's Union, resigned that post a year ago, charging that the organization was "Communist-dominated" and later organized the Canadian Lake Seamen's Union.

4 Die as Logs Roll Off Truck

ANNA, Ill., May 8 (INS).—A freak accident caused by a load of logs rolling off a truck brought death to four members of a family and serious injuries to three others.

The dead are Paul A. Flamm, 45, of Cobden; his wife, Frances, 42; their son, Donald, 12, and a daughter, Mary Ann, 5.

Injured were William Flamm, 7; Jean Flamm, 9, and Leonard Flamm, a nephew of Flamm. They are reported in a serious condition at the Anna city hospital.

Witnesses said the accident occurred while the Flamm car drove behind a truck loaded with logs two miles north of Cobden.

A chain holding the logs broke and spilled them into the path of the Flamm car, which was demolished in the crash.

ITALY PAYS U.S. ON WAR CLAIMS

WASHINGTON, May 8 (AP).—Italy has paid the United States $5,000,000 to meet claims of American citizens arising from World War II.

Ambassador Alberto Tarchiani handed a check for this amount to Assistant Secretary Willard L. Thorp at the State Department.

The envoy told reporters with a smile that the payment was not intended to influence the result of American elections.

"I am sure your elections will reflect the will of the people as Italy's did," he said.

Tarchiani referred to Communist charges that American aid and other actions influenced the outcome of Italy's balloting? which brought victory to the anti-Communist Christian Socialists.

The Italian payment is the first to the United States since V-J Day, except for interest on export-import bank loans, officials said. American aid in the same period has amounted to nearly $2,000,000,000.

The payment fulfills an agreement made Aug. 14 concerning financial and economic questions relating to the Italian peace treaty.

2 NAZI SPIES SEIZED DURING WAR ARE FREE

Pair Who Aided Prosecution of 6 Others Sent to Reich

WASHINGTON, May 8 (UP).—The White House has disclosed that two Nazi saboteurs seized here during the war have been permitted to return to Germany. They are living in the American zone there.

President Truman recommended suspension of the sentences of Ernest Peter Berger and George John Dasch provided that they return to Germany to live under conditions specified by the American army commander.

Six other saboteurs who were landed here by submarine in 1942 were executed. President Roosevelt commuted Berger's death sentence to life imprisonment and Dasch's to 30 years because of the assistance they gave the government in supplying details of the conspiracy.

CAPTURED BY FBI.

The eight were rounded up by the FBI soon after they landed. They did not get a chance to carry out their mission of sabotaging key American industries.

Truman acted on recommendations submitted by Attorney General Tom C. Clark. Berger and Dasch served approximately five years and seven months of their sentences.

Berger and Dasch landed from a German submarine on Long Island the night of June 13, 1942, with Richard Quirin and Heinrich Harm Heinck.

A second party of four Nazis landed from a submarine at Ponte Verde Beach, Fla. All eight were seized by FBI agents in Chicago and New York.

After their arrest, Berger and Dasch gave what the White House called "full and complete" identification of all connected with the sabotage plot, and also assisted the goverment in the treason trials of those who assisted the saboteurs.

Red Flier's Bomb Wounds Austrian

VIENNA, May 8 (UP).—A 13-year-old Austrian boy was injured when a Soviet airplane dropped a bomb on a highway in the Soviet zone near Matzen, 20 miles north of Vienna, the Ministry of Interior reported. The government asked the Soviets to explain.

Last year, an Austrian girl was killed by a bomb dropped from a Soviet plane in the same village. The Soviet government then paid an indemnity.

Rogers Best Man As Double Weds

LAS VEGAS, Nev., May 8 (UP).—Cowboy star Roy Rogers and his actress-wife, Dale Evans, stood as attendants at the marriage of Whitey Christensen, Rogers' screen double, and Jane Frazee, Rogers' leading lady, at Hotel El Rancho Vegas.

Brawl Ends Nuptial Party; Groom Held, Bride Weeps

WASHINGTON, May 8 (UP).—Catherine Cecilia Sullivan became a bride but all she could do was cry and say: "What a way to start a marriage."

And, no wonder.

Catherine and James Anthony Manning Jr., were married at St. Stephen's rectory here. Immediately after the wedding, the wedding party—about 100 in all—went to the American Legion Club for the reception.

When the first guests arrived a riot was just getting under way. It was still in the small fight stage. No one knows yet how it started. But guest after guest arrived, saw friends already in the battle, and joined the fray.

Club-swinging police finally broke it up. The groom and about 15 guests were taken to the station. The groom, still in white tie and tails, was charged with assault with a deadly weapon. Police said he slugged Hilton Mace, manager of the club, with a ginger ale bottle.

The bride? She went to the home of a friend. Still crying and saying: "What a way to start a marriage."

Korean Reds Threaten Poll In U. S. Zone

American Troops, Warships Alerted

By RAY RICHARDS
N. Y. Journal-American Washington Bureau

WASHINGTON, D. C., May 8.—American and Russian interests are due to clash violently again Monday in the vital election under direction of the United Nations to establish a democratic constitutional government in South Korea.

Police and U. S. occupation troops are prepared for bloodshed instigated by Red agents, particularly those who have filtered across the boundary from the Russian zone.

In anticipation of riots or an attempted coup, two U. S. warships are anchored in Korean waters and the American 6th and 7th Divisions have been ordered on the alert. In addition, the Air Force is planning a day-long aerial display.

MILLIONS REGISTER.

More than 8,000,000 South Koreans have registered to vote for representatives who will be charged with establishing a permanent government and electing a president.

Syngman Rhee, conservative Korean independent leader, who long has been friendly to the U. S., is expected to be named president, provided the election comes off without Red obstruction.

The scheduled vote follows nearly two years of debate during which Soviet Russia stood against any election ostensibly until the evacuation of all troops from both the U. S. and Russian zones, which are arbitrarily divided by the 38th parallel.

REDS TRAIN ARMY.

The artificial boundary line arose out of military considerations and was decided upon by the joint chiefs of staffs during the war and tacitly approved at the Yalta Conference.

Never officially sanctioned by the U. N., the boundary has taken on many characteristics of the "Iron Curtain" Russia has drawn in Europe.

During two years of occupation

Continued on Page 2, Column 6.

Soldier's Last Wish Denied

Secret Love Won't Get Perfect Rose

RICHMOND, Va., May 8 (UP).—The Virginia Supreme Court of Appeals has left it up to a dead soldier's heirs to decide whether "one perfect rose" would be sent each week to the girl he loved secretly and in vain.

The court ruled that the $3,600 estate left by Valentine Browne Lawless was willed to all his heirs. And the heirs have decided not to send the rose.

The Appeals Court reversed a ruling that the soldier had willed his estate to a brother, Edward Kirman Lawless. This ruling had been made by the Norfolk City Law and Chancery Court.

When Valentine Lawless went to war he made a will which mentioned that some of the money should be spent for a "special purpose." And in a letter to Edward Lawless he told the story of his hopeless love for Mildred Fitzpatrick, who never knew he loved her.

The letter asked Edward to have a florist send "one perfect rose" to Mildred each Saturday before 10 a. m. She was never to be told who sent the flowers. She was only to have the pleasure of receiving them.

Valentine Lawless died in a plane crash in Austria on Oct. 16, 1944, but the only girl he ever loved never got the roses.

She did not know of Lawless' strange request until last Summer, when the case reached the courts. She is now a happily-married 30-year-old housewife, and she said she did not want the roses.

The soldier's sister, Margaret Lawless, said "it just isn't practical" to use the money as Valentine wished.

Grandma, 59, To Graduate

SCHUYLERVILLE, N. Y., May 8 (AP).—A 59-year-old grandmother from nearby Grangerville will be graduated June 28 from Schuylerville Central High School.

Mrs. W. Elmer Shaver enrolled in high school in 1944 after she had reared three sons.

She ranks sixth in the senior class of 39 students, despite an absence of seven weeks this semester because of illness, school authorities said, her average is 87.

Czech Reds War On Protest Voting

PRAGUE, May 8 (INS).—Czechoslovak Communists have launched a drive to eliminate blank ballots in the May 30 elections.

The Central Action Committee called on local committees to organize competition to turn in the lowest number of blank papers.

Since there is only one list of candidates, a blank ballot is the only means of protest voting.

Actress Wife Sues Producer Cushing

LOS ANGELES, May 8 (AP).—Actress Georgette Cushing alleged that her husband treated her cruelly, made her ill and unable to pursue a movie career, in her divorce suit against producer Harry Cook Cushing.

Girl, 12, Wins Car But Can't Drive It

WINSTON-SALEM, N. C., May 8 (UP).—Ernestine Kinzer, 12-year-old Negro girl, can't drive, but she became the owner of a new $3,000 sedan. Her name was drawn as winner from among those who atended an industrial exposition here.

Her father, mother and two brothers don't know how to drive either, but the Kinzers turned down all offers by used car dealers to buy the car.

NO RETAIL ADVERTISING IN THIS EDITION

The advertising messages of New York's leading stores do appear in more than a million copies of the Sunday Journal-American distributed in the New York city and suburban area.

utterly distinct in heredity and environment from any other, it was natural to transform the news of the world into a daily romantic novel filled with cloak-and-dagger episodes and fascinating intrigues hatched in various chancelleries. The news of each day was unified by an underlying plot or dramatized by concentration on great personalities such as Cavour, Wellington, Bismarck, and Gladstone. Each nation had a separate personality of its own.

In America this exciting suspicion about personal plots and dastard motives everywhere led to the popularity of the muckraking press. Even so heroic a figure as Lincoln Steffens rode on this band wagon. Human corruption was a great discovery. Corruption had to go. But after two World Wars it isn't easy to be sure whether the muckrakers made an adequate analysis of the obstacles to the setting up of Utopia.

Far from even looking like accidents, those wars were magnificent displays of what international industry and technology could do. Moreover, they led to an unimaginable acceleration of every phase of technology—especially advancing the universal social revolution which is the inevitable result of the impact of machines on human rhythms and social patterns. The throbbing of the gasoline motor and the rhythm of printing presses have much to do with the everyday thoughts and feelings of ordinary people, whether in Tokyo or New York. They provide us with our "spontaneous" impulses.

Nobody can doubt that the entire range of modern applied science contributes to the very format of a newspaper. But the headline is a feature which began with the Napoleonic Wars. The headline is a primitive shout of rage, triumph, fear, or warning, and newspapers have thrived on wars ever since. And the newspaper, with two or three decks of headlines, has also become a major weapon.

Just as speed of communication and movement makes possible at the same time such diverse facts as stock-market operations, international armies, and news-gathering agencies on a world scale, so it enables the press of any nation to keep mobilized the passions of whole populations year after year until the moment comes for the blow. And it also requires a prolonged stirring of passions by means of the press and allied agencies to launch and to maintain a world war. If there were no such means of communication either in Russia or in the West at the present moment, it would be quite impossible even to dream of a war between them. An amplifying system hitched to one's own heartbeat can, the Russians have found, break down the strongest morale. And the press used as a means of thrill and excitement produces a general emotional situation which leads to a crescendo, and crescendo calls for a catharsis —a blood-bath. The actual outbreak of the Second World War was a visible relief to many after the years of tense waiting.

Where the muckrakers were wrong was in attributing any particular malice to specially placed individuals when it is plain that all the victims of this situation contribute daily to maintain it in thought, word, and deed. Even pacifist agitation or the nation-wide fever of big sports competitions acts as a spur to war fever in circumstances like ours. Any kind of excitement or emotion contributes to the possibility of dangerous explosions when the feelings of huge populations are kept inflamed even in peacetime for the sake of the advancement of commerce. Headlines mean street sales. It takes emotion to move merchandise. And wars and rumors of wars are the merchandise and also the emotion of the popular press.

When people have been accustomed for decades to perpetual emotions, a dispassionate view of anything at all is difficult to achieve. But surely our world, more than that in any previous epoch, calls for detached appraisal. Let us try next to get such a cool view of the Ballet Luce.

A nose for news— and a stomach for whiskey

The city room knows him no more.

He has passed on to some private and personal Nirvana of his own, where every typewriter has all its keys and a bottle waits at every four-alarm fire.

And the only epitaph he would have wished is this . . . *"He was a good reporter."*

His greatest, and most unconscious, characteristic was an insatiable curiosity. He seethed with questions. Nothing was as it seemed, and he picked frantically at surface facts until the shell broke and the muck, or the treasure, underneath was exposed to his greedy mind.

▶ With or without the vine leaves in his hair, his sense of news verged on the occult. He knew bishops and gunmen, politicians and pickpockets, and treated both the great and the sham with the same casual impertinence. His mind was a brimming pool of assorted facts, which he turned on and off like a tap.

Under a glass-hard exterior, he had a heart as soft as mush. He rooted fiercely for the underdog, perhaps because he was so much the underdog himself.

He got paid very little—and when other people talked of the "profession of journalism" his was the loudest laugh.

▶ Sometimes he grew out of it. Sometimes he became a famous columnist, a noted author, or even an Editor. But mostly he grew old at 45. And when he saw a new youngster in the City Room he figured the best thing he could do was to take him across the street and say to him: "Kid, what the hell are you doing around here? Get out of it. It's a lousy business . . ."

But the youngster never took his advice. Year after year thousands of new youngsters decided there was only one thing in the world they wanted to be—a newspaperman. And the American press grew up.

The old-time reporter has passed from the scene. But he left behind him a legacy of incalculable value to the nation. For he established the tradition of good reporting as the foundation of a free press.

What happened? Who did it? Where? When? Why?

▶ As long as these questions can be asked by good reporters free to write the truest and frankest answers they can find, freedom will have survived.

True, since the days of the old-time reporter, both men and minds have changed. The reporter of today is a better man than his predecessor. He *has* to be. He is better-educated, better-paid. Neither he nor his editor can get away with the cheap sensationalism of yesterday's Yellow Journalism—and neither of them insists on any special license to get drunk. The reporter's passport today is respected everywhere, and he is expected to live up to the code of his profession.

▶ Too, America's appetite for news has grown sharper. It takes some 25,000 local reporters and 1,888 daily newspapers to gratify it. Altogether, 300,000 men and women are engaged in telling you what is happening in the world, with all the trimmings you're accustomed to—comic strips, women's pages, photographs, society notes, advice to the lovelorn, columnists, cartoons, editorials, crossword puzzles.

But whatever the extra values newspapers and magazines may offer today, one thing remains the same . . . *the heart of a free press is still the good reporter.* It is still the man with the nose for news, as peculiar and authentic a possession as the eye of a painter or the ear of a musician.

▶ Perhaps good reporting is the reason, above all other reasons, why the Newsmagazine has come to occupy such a high place in the brain and heart of the nation.

For the Newsmagazine has, as grist for its weekly mill, all that has been found out by all the world's good reporters. Sometimes these good reporters are TIME's own correspondents or legmen. Sometimes they work for one of the great Press Associations. Sometimes they are obscure people whose nuggets have been buried on page 10 of some little-read publication. Sometimes they are men and women in TIME's home-office, who—at one end of a wire—probe a reporter three hundred or three thousand miles away until a few confused facts become a well-ordered, living story.

The world is the good reporter's hunting ground. No man can tell where a nose for news may pick up the scent. Stories may break in the White House, the Holland tunnel, the Balkans, the South Pole, Number 10 Downing Street, or 1913 Central Avenue, South Bend.

▶ No man can anticipate TIME's stories. The Newsmagazine is as unpredictable as the warring, struggling, creating, cock-eyed human race, whose historian it is. Only this is certain . . .

In today's world the true adventures of your fellow humans, gathered and told by good reporters, make more absorbing reading than anything in the world of make-believe.

This is one of a series of advertisements in which the Editors of TIME hope to give all the readers of LIFE a clearer picture of the world of news-gathering, news-writing, and news-reading—and the part TIME plays in helping you to grasp, measure, and use the history of your lifetime as you live the story of your life.

The Ballet Luce

Why do newsmen pose as the last romantics? Or is it the first romantics?

Why is it their plangent duty to achieve cirrhosis of the liver?

Is the newspaper world a cheap suburb of the artists' bohemia?

Why the air of cynical omniscience and detachment cloaking the frenzy of the crusader?

Where did you see that bug-eyed romantic of action before? Was it in a Hemingway novel?

THIS ADVERTISEMENT for *Time* features an old-fashioned reporter bursting from a saloon to cover some violent episode. The copy tells us that:

> He seethed with questions. Nothing was as it seemed, and he picked frantically at surface facts until the shell broke and the muck, or the treasure, underneath was exposed to his greedy mind. . . . He knew bishops and gunmen, politicians and pickpockets, and treated both the great and the sham with the same casual impertinence. . . . Under a glass-hard exterior he had a heart as soft as mush. . . .
>
> *What happened? Who did it? Where? When? Why?* As long as these questions can be asked by good reporters free to write the truest and frankest answers they can find, freedom will have survived.

What kind of insight into human relations or international affairs is likely to be won by a man whose eyes bug out when he hears a fire-engine? This type is a custodian of freedom? Note that hard-boiled impertinence ("treated the great and the sham with the same casual impertinence") is also a basic *Time* formula. *Time* still cocks its adolescent snoot at "bishops and gunmen" with the same excited fervor today as in the cock-a-hoop decade when it first appeared. The saloon-era reporter may have disappeared, but the malady lingers on in the pages of *Time*.

One matter Englishmen don't think in the least funny is their happy consciousness of possessing a deep sense of humor. Even in the good old days you could joke about their empire, but to suggest that there was something odd about their *insisting* on their sense of humor was not advisable. As long as England was a recognized top dog, it was easy for her clubmen to emit a jolly old guffaw at the ways of those who weren't. Much humor consists of this sense of confident superiority. It is certainly so with *The New Yorker*, for instance. Snobbery based on economic privilege constitutes the mainstay of its technique and appeal. Just notice the kinds of people it holds up to ridicule. Take a quick guess at their salary scale. Like *Punch*, it is read by top dogs, but especially by the much greater public of underdogs who wish to share top-dog emotions. From the first, *Time* was conceived on similar lines. *Time* readers were somehow taught to think of themselves as "different." They are in the know. They are not like other people. They are an exclusive little coterie of millions and millions of superior people. Just why a man who observes these unintentionally amusing aspects of *The New Yorker* and *Time* should be regarded as unable to read and enjoy them is not so easy to see. The old romantic notion that you shouldn't understand what you enjoy is still with us. Dale Carnegie would not recommend that anybody "knock" at these props of our complacency.

Time, however, is an important factor in contemporary society. Its shape and technique constitute a most influential set of attitudes which are effective precisely because they are not obviously attached to any explicit doctrines or opinions. Like the clever ads, they do not argue with their readers. They wallop the subconscious instead. It has already been suggested that the over-all effect of the press today has been to develop the image of the world as a single city. This effect is not intentional. It is the by-product of the sheer techniques of news-gathering and presentation.

Less crudely than the Hearst press, for example, *Time* resists this anonymous and impersonal tendency of the communication techniques of our day. *Time* is nothing if not personal. Consider the old *Time* boast: "As if by one man for one man." Does this suggest a highly colored and selective approach? A strong tinge of the totalitarian in the formula? Surely it is not the formula for a world society but for clique control and indoctrination. In the intensity of its tone of private gossip and malice, in the eagerness with which it distributes thwacks to its guests (people of the week) and audience alike, *Time* resembles the various "quiz" programs. In these programs representative persons from the audience are pushed and shoved and humiliated by masters of ceremonies. And this sado-masochist mechanism of punch and get punched will be found everywhere from Winchell to the kids' comics. Inevitably it depends on readers and entertainers who are sunk in a subrational trance. Such patterns can only persist in a dream state of some sort, to which it will be replied: "Oh, but *Time* writers and readers are very wide-awake people, indeed. Their I.Q.'s would stand well above the average."

Let us grant this at once. What remains to be recognized is that a very able person may often choose to freeze or anesthetize large areas of his mind and experience for the sake of social and practical success or the pleasures of group solidarity. Nothing is more familiar, for instance, than the spectacle of the eminent scientist with the emotional patterns and reading preferences of a bloodthirsty child.

Briton Hadden, co-founder of *Time,* seems to have been the principal forger of *Time* style and attitudes. Hadden, says his biographer Noel Busch, regarded *Time* readers as the same sort of admiring group that had surrounded him when, from the nursery, he edited *Glonk. Time* is also a nursery book in which the reader is slapped and tickled alternately. It is full of predigested pap, spooned out with confidential nudges. The reader is never on his own for an instant, but, as though at his mother's knee, he is provided with the right emotions for everything he hears or sees as the pages turn.

And it is not opinions or thoughts that *Time* provides its reader as news comment. Rather, the newsreel is provided with a razzle-dazzle accompaniment of Spike Jones noises. Politics and affairs have been reduced to music. In *Time* trombones and trumpets take up the task of comment on the tale of the tribe.

In their original prospectus Hadden and Luce announced their dissatisfaction with the untidy modern press which made too many demands on the busy man who had no time to appraise the multifarious news items laid out before him. Therefore they proclaimed their intention of producing a magazine "on a new principle of COMPLETE ORGANIZATION" (their caps). Twenty-five years later the formula was phrased: "as if by one man for one man." Strictly heart to heart.

The political meaning of *Time* style and technique are made fully explicit in the following words from Noel Busch's biography of Hadden:

> *Time,* by treating them [events] all as though seen by the same person, made them a continued story. Instead of resembling a ragged mob shuffling down the side street of perception, the march of events became a glittering parade, with flags waving, bands playing and the ranks keeping step.

If a goose-stepping reader could be persuaded to dwell on that passage in connection with *Time,* he would learn more than there is space to comment on here. But note the "continued story" technique of nineteenth-century and Hearst journalism, deliberately receding from the spontaneous cubism achieved in *The New York Times* front page. Again, in place of the simultaneous and multiple vision of the front page which provides a bird's-eye view, note *Time's* "all as though seen by the same person," which amounts to the breathless outpourings of a private diary. And that is also Winchell's snoop technique with Mr. and Mrs. North America.

But the urgency with which *Time* insists that events must march in glittering parade to brassy music is surely expressive of the inevitable state of *Time* readers as a crowd of enthusiastic kids lining the curbs as *Time* marches on. Power, glitter, and mass hypnosis engendered by regular ranks. Such, rather than insight or intelligibility, is the object of all this technical brilliance. General gaiety is maintained by the *Time* salute to the parade of events. The editors stand at mock attention on the reviewing platform, thumb on nose. The seal of haughty schoolboy sophistication.

Life has changed the proportion of its ingredients in

very recent years. The initial layout consisted of heavy doses of pictorial violence, mayhem, and death plus equally heavy rations of strip tease (in ads and news alike), plus a wodge of pseudo-science in the form of pictorialized "wonders of modern science." Girlie art remains the heavy staple, but violence and mayhem have been somewhat reduced and religious art given a place beside pseudo-science. The twenty million or more *Life* readers are not given the same encouragement to think of themselves as a tight little club of knowing sophisticates as are *Time* readers.

But *Fortune* is conducted as a major religious liturgy celebrating the feats of technological man. Gone are the nursery politics. Here is the real thing, the inner sanctum. A Bayreuth festival in the most megalomaniac style. Paeans of praise to machine production interspersed with numerous scenes of luxurious and exclusive playgrounds for the *gauleiters* of big business.

It is plain that the Ballet Luce embraces, in a carefully calculated way, the arts of communication and control as at present these have been ordered to tease, soothe, and flatter a mass public. Perhaps we should be thankful that Mr. Luce and his advisors are content to enjoy the irresponsible manipulation of these arts and techniques as entertainment without directing them to the achievement of direct political power. But the effect of the Ballet Luce is political, for all that. A mindless, helpless, entranced audience emerges from the scene of this potent entertainment. "COMPLETE ORGANIZATION," even for entertainment purposes, has its political consequences. And when news is written "as if by one man for one man," there is always the possibility that another sort of man may pop himself in place of the present amiable operator at the controls.

The Revolution Is Intact

Are you the shy type? Then say it with tanks.

You thought Salvador Dali had a monopoly on surrealist savagery? He looks like Disney from here.

Just take a peek at our suburban dream through this convenient horse collar.

You didn't know what a hero's last words should be? Let the movie magazines tell you.

ACCOMPANYING this full-page ad for *Modern Screen* was the following text:

> It was one of those things you wouldn't think would happen to a picture of Betty Grable.
>
> But it did happen. Somewhere in the South Pacific.
>
> We heard about it when Miss Grable, with tear-filled eyes, showed one of our Hollywood reporters a letter she'd received from a soldier's buddy. A letter enclosing that worn and torn, bullet-punctured picture of Betty.
>
> "Dear Miss Grable," the letter said, "we were moving up in an armored job—we came up where a few kids had been holding off some Japs—just as we arrived, we saw a soldier double up—heard him

say 'Goodbye, darling . . .' We got every one of the fifteen Japs, and then we hustled to move this kid, but it was too late . . . we pried open his hand, and it held this picture of you—the bullet had gone through it . . ."

Maybe that picture had been torn out of our magazine. We don't know.

But we do know that a *lot* of people see *Modern Screen* every month, overseas and at home.

This month, *millions* of people will look for the exclusive life story we run in each issue . . . and they'll read about the incident of the bullet-pierced picture in our new life story of Betty Grable.

They'll read intimate, private-life items about Betty—anecdotes never before released for publication. They'll see pictures of Betty in many of her great roles—as "Sweet Rosie O'Grady"—as "Pin-up Girl" —and as *herself* . . .

—the girl who is now Mrs. Harry James . . . the girl who works tirelessly, as do other great film stars, for "her boys" at Army camps and canteens and benefits . . . the girl with the "pearl-and-gold" freshness who can talk to anybody and make them love her—yes, and the girl who cried when she got the letter and the picture we've shown you on this page.

We're sure you'll like our October issue of *Modern Screen*. Please *share* your copy—lend it to your friends if their newsstands run short. Although we're printing 1,300,000 copies, these just have to be enough, in these times, to go around.

This blurb accompanying the ad is delivered with the slick aplomb and automatic tones of profound human interest and understanding so necessary to the moving of emotion and merchandise. The meaning of war and the glory of death, we are to suppose, are nobly expressed by this "episode." What is more moving than to think that this soldier fought and died for the fantasies he had woven around the image of Betty Grable? It would be hard to know where to begin to peel back the layers of insentience and calculated oblivion implied in such an ad. And what would be found as one stripped away these layers, each marked with the pattern of sex, technology, and death? Exactly nothing. One is left staring into a vacuum such as is created by the techniques for "developing your executive ability" and found in the philosophies of revolution described in a recent book, *Zero*, by Robert Payne.

The European nihilists were conscious, logical, articulate. But the new world is supplied with another type, unconscious, illogical, and inarticulate, that gets even bigger effects of the same sort. The nihilist, says Mr. Payne, must destroy because of the vacuum and self-hatred within him. He is born now, of the violent meeting and woundings which occur when different cultures converge. In short, he is born of the social conditions of rapid turnover, planned obsolescence, and systematic change for its own sake.

Out of this situation there arise those vampire dreams that send ads like these from the agencies. These dreams meet a somnambulist public that accepts them uncritically. Otherwise, how explain the absence of reaction in the name of the human dignity which they destroy? An alert and conscious public would have repudiated this ad emphatically. The magazine would have ceased publication. The papers which carried the ad would have been glad to have gotten off by the gesture of firing large sections of their staffs. But, instead, the dream grows.

While junior was dreaming of Mrs. Harry James in the Pacific, his mother was dreaming of similar romance at home. A news item from San Francisco, February 24, 1946, was captioned

MATRONS ASK MOVIES GIVE
LOVE THRILLS FOR "OVER 40"

A group of San Francisco matrons rebelled against the emphasis on young love today and asked Hollywood to provide a few thrills for women "frankly over forty."

The organization, known as the Senior League . . . submitted Charles Bickford as the adult answer to Van Johnson. . . .

"We demand that actors like the red-haired Bickford, who is virile, violent, but seldom victorious with the cinema ladies, be given the chance to make filmic love to actresses like Bette Davis, Irene Dunne and Greer Garson."

The ad and the news item fit like a glove, suggesting the futility of any sort of direct action or any simple solutions to such a state of mind. It is too early to be "constructive" when the habit of inspection and diagnosis has been reduced to the present low point. The very people who yell in a chorus of down-beat to "accentuate the positive" are precisely those most deeply engaged in the promotion of nihilistic dreams.

Deep Consolation

A CURRENT twenty-five-center with the usual erotic cover is entitled *Bury Me Deep*. The *New Detective Magazine* for November, 1949, with a similar splash of pictorial sex, offers such lush fare as "I.O.U.—One Grave," "Half Past Mayhem," "Two Can Die," "Dying Room Only," "Murder On My Mind," "Wrong Way Corpse," and "Dead Men Talk."

How dry I am?

I cried until they told me it was watertight.

The more the burier, said Digby O'Dell?

More stiffs are turning to the watertight brand?

The titles do not belie the riot of cadaverous fleshiness of the entertainment inside the covers. A corpse enters at once in "Half Past Mayhem":

> She was a flabby, grey monolithic woman in her seventies, with a cold blue eye and vast wealth, and she had taken pleasure out of using her wealth like a club. . . . It's a messy affair.

Exuberance of human gore and obstructed flesh, when linked with sex, gunplay, and fast action, provide a widely popular dish.

In striking contrast to such appeals stands the timid world of mortician beauty doctors and mortuary advertising. It is seldom that these people dare to break out with such enthusiastic copy as "Cash In on Cremation" or "If you aren't buried here you haven't lived." The present ad is typical of the uncertainties and confusion which attend the commercial management of death and burial. In contrast to the lusty confidence of the big industry of fictional violence and blood (to say nothing of news reports of the real thing), there is an utter absence of assurance in the funeral department. There isn't much in the pattern of daily life to provide an attitude toward death beyond what amounts to little more than a brush-off. Select a coffin as you would a car. Glorify "the dear one" as you would a debutante. And, as for the cost, sock the bill home "while the tears are in their eyes." People who live with their gaze on commodities of their neighbors must be taught to die in the same way.

At the bottom of this ad there is inserted a landscape swept by storm, and underneath it the casket is seen to be secure and *dry*. To buy the loved one such a casket is "the finest tribute . . . the most trusted protection." The thoughts of the woman at the window are recorded in the copy:

> There's a deep consolation . . . serene through shower or heavy rain . . . for those who know the casket of a dear one is protected against *water* in the ground by a Clark *Metal* Grave Vault.

This sentiment also fits glovelike over the mortician chapel with its hush, its deep carpets, banks of flowers, and sweet organ music.

All that music, perfume, science, hygiene, and cosmetics can do is done to create an evasive, womblike world of comfort and soft sympathy. "Home was never like this." Death is thus brought within the orbit of the basic attitudes of a consumer world and is neutralized by absorption into irrelevant patterns of thought, feeling, and technique. The solid comforts and security missed in this life are to be enjoyed in the next.

One of the most important sections in Siegfried Giedion's *Mechanization Takes Command* concerns the mechanization of the meat industry. He notes that in the 1830's "systematic teamwork was introduced in the killing and dressing of hogs. The assembly-line attitude is present before it can be applied in mechanized form to complicated machine processes." This kind of perception of the interrelation of disparate activities is indispensable to modern man living in an era of specialization, change and expansion. It offers not only a principle of intelligibility but also of order and control, and permits the correction of errors which can lead to unwanted consequences. Giedion goes on to observe the abattoir where "killing itself cannot be mechanized. It is upon organization that the burden falls. . . . The death cries of the animals are confused with the rumbling of the great drum, the whirring of gears, and the hissing sound of steam. Death cries and mechanical noises are almost impossible to disentangle." In this passage one has only to substitute "life" for "death" to have a description of any of the great scenes of modern business and industry, a fact which current art and literature did not fail to record long before the event, to the dismay of the public. It would seem to be a principle that the failure to face and evaluate unpleasant facts under conditions of art and controlled observation leads to a subsequent avalanche of the disagreeable.

When we see the scientific techniques of mass killing applied with equal indifference in the abattoirs, in the Nazi death camps, and on the battlefields, we can afford to ask whether our habit of bringing death within the orbit of our "life" interests and industrial procedures is altogether sound. In fact, this tendency would seem to play a vivid spotlight on much that is radically unsound in our daily patterns of existence. There is a kind of trancelike dream logic in extending the methods and attitudes of one sphere of action to another. But is it consistent with the purposes of conscious or even of continued existence?

The present ad is merely one more example of this dream logic, enabling us to see how death now tends to get the same treatment as sex (see "Love Goddess Assembly Line"). But this treatment does violence to actuality. Something seems to rebel inside us which sets up a wild oscillation that produces two kinds of unreality: at one extreme the wide interest in "Half Past Mayhem," and at the other the narcotic mortician world of deep consolation.

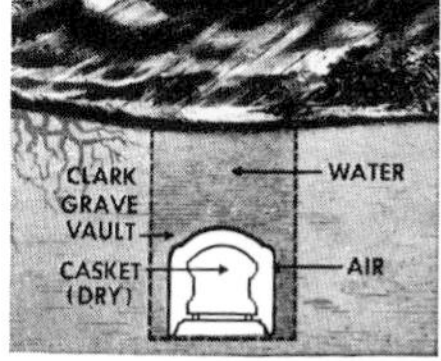

Placed over the casket, the Clark Metal Grave Vault is scientifically designed to use the pressure of air in the dome to keep seeping water from the rains and melting snows from reaching the casket.

Your funeral director will gladly show you stately, beautiful Clark Vaults within your means. All made of enduring metal instead of porous material. And available in styles armored with 25 to 35 lbs. of *zinc* by Clark's *exclusive* process to insure up to 2 to 5 times as long-lasting protection as the same vault uncoated.

Write for FREE 28-page booklet, *"My Duty." Tells what to do when you are asked to "take charge." Over a million copies distributed. The Clark Grave Vault Co., Dept. E-117, Columbus, O.*

Copyrighted, 1947

THE FINEST TRIBUTE . . . THE MOST TRUSTED PROTECTION

Charlie McCarthy

Successor to the little-man dramas of early Chaplin?

One must talk with two voices to be understood today?

Do I have to be a split personality just because I'm a wooden dummy?

Are the bureaucratic Bergens turning us all into Charlies?

We still have our freedom to listen?

"I'LL MOW YOU DOWN!" Truculence, jaunty irreverence, dandified elegance, light-hearted lies, and pathetic boastfulness, mounted on a bubble of illusion—Charlie has combined these into a symbol for more than a decade. The Bergen-McCarthy axis hinges on a good many issues. And in this respect the character and function of the popular myths of technological man appear quite plainly as cluster images of many interests and anxieties that go into action to produce a comic catharsis or relief.

Thus, the Bergen-Charlie relationship is a strained one. Charlie is endlessly exploring the extreme limits of what he can get away with. And his supreme hope and threat is that he will simply get away. Dramatic illusion can scarcely go farther than in those exchanges between Bergen and Charlie when Charlie announces that he is about to sever relations with boss Bergen. He is about to vamoose with Bergen's girl friend or radio guest.

Bergen plays the role of the disillusioned but firmly patient papa with Charlie. The note of the aggrieved, long-suffering, and only-too-understanding foster parent is always in Bergen's voice. It is the voice of bureaucracy, just as surely as Charlie's cocky nasalities register the tones of rebellious individualism that is now a mere shadow or dummy of the real thing.

That is the essential Bergen-McCarthy drama: real authority versus the ghost of freedom. There is no mistaking those muted and forbearing tones of Bergen for anything but power. His quiet, neutral patience with the raucous and querulous McCarthy embodies the relationship between the average man and the impersonal agencies of social control in a technological world. And the situation of Charlie the dummy is a very accurate reflection of the paradox of the individual of Big Town. The more he becomes drunk with the power that flows through and around him, the more he is recalled to his helpless dummy status. The louder his rebellious ravings, the more the mouthpiece he.

The rest of the program fits this pattern by allowing Charlie to ride sadistically over a number of carefully selected victims. The wise parent allows the rage of the child to vent itself on useless objects. And so Charlie (with whom the listener is sympathetically identified) is allowed to triumph not only over Bergen but over a variety of program guests and regulars who represent the success and prestige denied to him, the straw man, the essential stooge. This explains the spite which is spent on professors and experts with "cultivated voices." They are indispensable victims of Charlie's deep inferiority and envy and must be ridiculed constantly. Spite for the "professors" and coquetry for the feminine celebrities constitute the unvarying formula of the show.

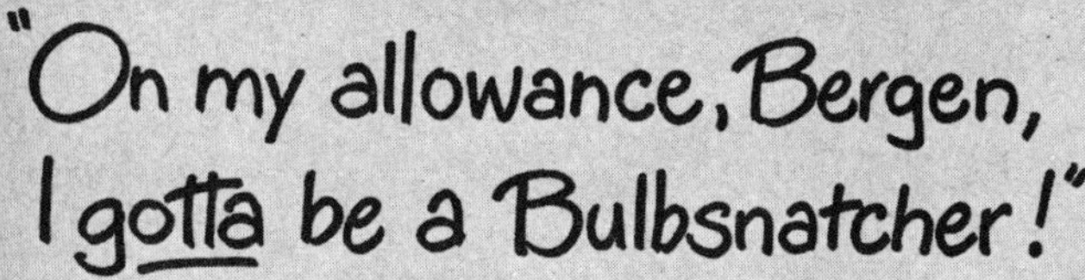

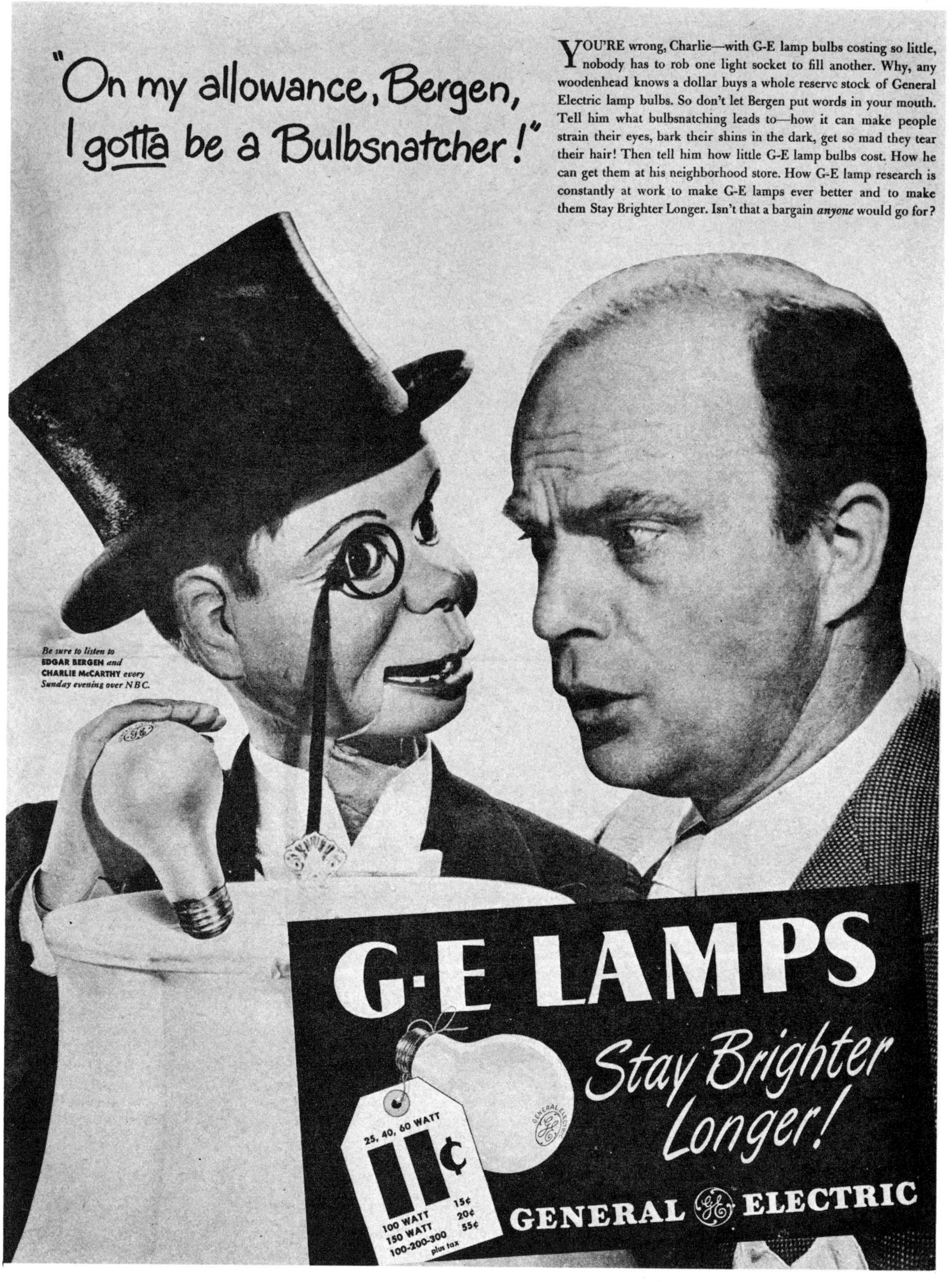
"On my allowance, Bergen, I gotta be a Bulbsnatcher!"
YOU'RE wrong, Charlie—with G-E lamp bulbs costing so little, nobody has to rob one light socket to fill another. Why, any woodenhead knows a dollar buys a whole reserve stock of General Electric lamp bulbs. So don't let Bergen put words in your mouth. Tell him what bulbsnatching leads to—how it can make people strain their eyes, bark their shins in the dark, get so mad they tear their hair! Then tell him how little G-E lamp bulbs cost. How he can get them at his neighborhood store. How G-E lamp research is constantly at work to make G-E lamps ever better and to make them Stay Brighter Longer. Isn't that a bargain *anyone* would go for?
Be sure to listen to EDGAR BERGEN *and* CHARLIE McCARTHY *every Sunday evening over* NBC.
G·E LAMPS
25, 40, 60 WATT
11¢
100 WATT 15¢
150 WATT 20¢
100-200-300 55¢
plus tax
Stay Brighter Longer!
GENERAL ELECTRIC

(The same spite toward the experts appears in most quiz programs.)

An instructive parallel to the Bergen-McCarthy drama is the Uncle Remus-Brer Rabbit saga. Writing in *Commentary* for July, 1949, Bernard Wolfe presents Uncle Remus as the dummy on the knee of Joel Chandler Harris. Seated on the knee of dummy Remus is a little white boy who is told of the savage triumphs of Bre'r Rabbit. And Mr. Wolfe explains how by this indirect means the Negro could dare to express his anger. That the benign and helpless Rabbit should repeatedly appear in the role of savage executioner, killing off all his powerful enemies, is a drama that needs no commentator.

Dummy Remus (the conventional benevolent darkie of the white man's wish), reporting the savage triumphs of the weak and helpless Rabbit to the little white boy on his knee, is not very remote from the Bergen-McCarthy situation. But the Bergen-McCarthy drama is more direct. The "kindly" boss and the underpaid victim act out a weekly parable of the big, absent-minded technological world and the robots who are its very conscious victims. For that paradox is also registered in this drama. Bergen appears less conscious than Charlie of the actual state of affairs, and it is Bergen who seems to be the robot.

The big planning and executive agency—Bergen—appears to be mindless and unfeeling. The supposedly mindless robot—Charlie—appears to be acutely sensitive and conscious. It is in the unannounced interplay of perceptions like these that the power and appeal of this show consist.

The Bergen-McCarthy "myth" is typical of industrial folklore in that it centers and organizes a variety of thoughts and feelings born of the relations between man and the machines he has made. But there is a wide range of mental states engendered in the same man-machine relationship—mental states not embraced in the Bergen-McCarthy "myth"—which have found equally popular expression in unexpected ways. Many of them, naturally, are prone to overlap. The exhibits in this book are selected in an effort to suggest their character and extent.

The Sage of Waldorf Towers

Mr. and Mrs. North America, get a load of my tommy-gun rattle, rat-a-tat-tattle.

Wrap me in the flag after the battle and bury me under the prairie?

Look, Mom, I'm . . . Is there anybody alive in the audience?

Let's go to the cleaners?

BUDD SCHULBERG in *What Makes Sammy Run?* occasionally cites a mythical sage whose cell of contemplation is in "The Waldorf Towers." The wisdom with which this hotel hermit is accredited rings with the authentic note of a very ripe cantaloupe, as for example:

> We don't know we've had a good time till the waiter at the Troc hands us a check for 200 bucks.

Walter Winchell has the same knack of hitting the soft-cantaloupe note when the tragic side of life comes to bat in his column, as in the days when he printed the verses of Don Wahn:

> *This is a world of never-ending strife.*
> *Dreams are a one-way passage out of life.*

For the extremely mechanized, whose core of human perception lies under layers of callousness unremittingly acquired since diaperhood, it naturally takes a terrific wallop to turn on the tap of human tears.

When the telegraphic rattle of Walter Winchell announces: "Mr. and Mrs. North America, let's go to press," the harsh rat-a-tat-tat of the vocal delivery is very expressive indeed. It is the voice of the symbolic "gunman" reporter of the big night spots. The Winchell imitators always miss this breathless tension which establishes his role as the mock executioner. Reputations, marriages, and romances wilt and vanish under his spate of wordy gunfire.

Nothing could exceed the note of ferocious back-fence intimacy in Winchell's gossip delivery. He raises the social page of the home-town newspaper to "screaming heights" of big-town significance. The small-town paper is edited on the correct assumption that its readers want most of all to see their own names and to read of their own weddings, funerals, travels, and lodge meetings. These people find their own lives interesting. But Winchell has brilliantly transferred this formula to please those who find their own lives very dull. For these people it is the doings, real or imaginary, of a group of invisible yet deliciously wicked society folk which provide the thrills that make life worth while. *Time, Life,* and the Hearst press, among other publications, commonly provide a sort of home-town diary of the fascinating carryings-on of these dazzling dolls of Big Town. In addition, Winchell's introspection taught him that the envy embedded in this popular interest in the rich and great called for a heavy note of savagery. That is why Winchell functions both as reporter and executioner on the Broadway beat.

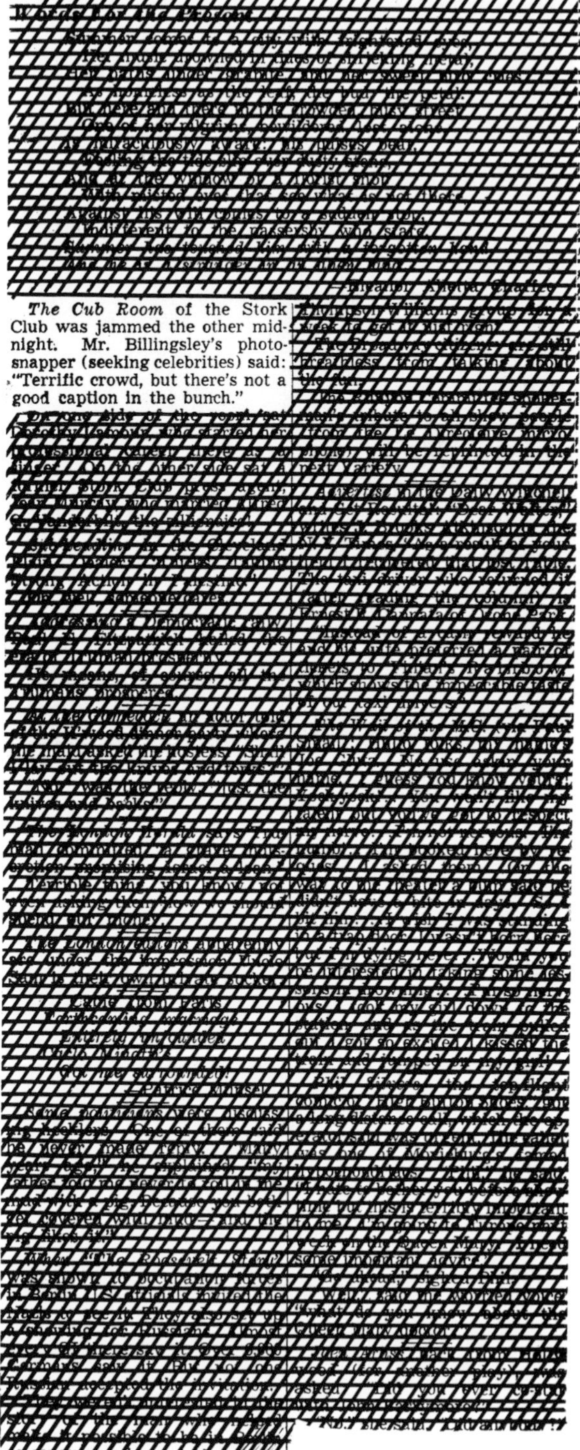

Walter Winchell

In New York

The Cub Room of the Stork Club was jammed the other midnight. Mr. Billingsley's photo-snapper (seeking celebrities) said: "Terrific crowd, but there's not a good caption in the bunch."

"Our American concept of radio is that it is of the people and for the people"

Freedom to LISTEN – Freedom to LOOK

As the world grows smaller, the question of international communications and world understanding grows larger. The most important phase of this problem is *Freedom to Listen* and *Freedom to Look*—for all peoples of the world.

Radio, by its very nature, is a medium of mass communication; it is a carrier of intelligence. It delivers ideas with an impact that is powerful . . . Its essence is freedom—liberty of thought and of speech.

Radio should make a prisoner of no man and it should make no man its slave. No one should be forced to listen and no one compelled to refrain from listening. Always and everywhere, it should be the prerogative of every listener to turn his receiver off, of his own free will.

The principle of *Freedom to Listen* should be established for all peoples without restriction or fear. This is as important as *Freedom of Speech* and *Freedom of the Press.*

Television is on the way and moving steadily forward. Television fires the imagination, and the day is foreseen when we shall look around the earth from city to city, and nation to nation, as easily as we now listen to global broadcasts. Therefore, *Freedom to Look* is as important as *Freedom to Listen,* for the combination of these will be the radio of the future.

The "Voice of Peace" must speak around this planet and be heard by all people everywhere, no matter what their race, or creed, or political philosophies.*

David Sarnoff

President and Chairman of the Board,
Radio Corporation of America.

**Excerpts from an address before the United States National Commission for UNESCO.*

FREEDOM IS EVERYBODY'S BUSINESS

Freedom to Listen

In his testimony to the Senate Committee on Interstate Commerce (December, 1945) the president of the National Broadcasting Corporation ridiculed the proposal to separate business control from program control:

> This is to forget that "he who controls the pocketbook controls the man." Business control means complete control, and there is no use arguing to the contrary.

But the present ad, with its home-town flavor, would seem to belie this. It suggests the peace and quiet of farm and village life, which, in turn, evoke the Jeffersonian creed of political independence founded on the economic independence of small cultivators and craftsmen. In his *Notes on Virginia* (1782) Jefferson wrote:

> Those who labour in the earth are the chosen people of God. . . . Corruption of morals in the mass of cultivators is a phenomenon of which no age nor nation has furnished an example. . . . Dependence begets subservience and venality, suffocates the germs of virtue, and prepares fit tools for the designs of ambition.

This vision of human integrity based on a noncommercial way of life remains the core of the American dream. As such, it haunted Henry Ford. As such, it is constantly tapped by the advertising agencies and the movie industry in order to sell products. In this ad it serves to lull suspicion. Here it is the juicy bone held out to quiet the growling of the house dog. Home-town sentiment, the Pilgrim Fathers, Paul Revere, Valley Forge, and so on, provide an ample stock of juicy bones for the ad agencies. In the same way, the David Harum brand of cracker-barrel wisdom thrives in soap opera, and the folklore of the frontier pours from the ad agencies in horse-opera variants. As the industrial market extends its power and control over thoughts and earnings alike, it swathes itself increasingly in the archaic garments of pre-industrial man.

It would seem that there is some sense of compulsion among the marketeers to assume the appearance of Little Red Riding Hood's granny. But this fear of detection is groundless. The modern Little Red Riding Hood, reared on singing commercials, has no objection to being eaten by the wolf. "Freedom to Listen," in a world where effective expression via newspaper or radio is reserved only for a tiny minority, is freedom to put up or shut up.

The ordinary person senses the greatness of the odds against him even without thought or analysis, and he adapts his attitudes unconsciously. A huge passivity has settled on industrial society. For people carried about in mechanical vehicles, earning their living by waiting on machines, listening much of the waking day to canned music, watching packaged movie entertainment and capsulated news, for such people it would require an exceptional degree of awareness and an especial heroism of effort to be anything but supine consumers of processed goods. Society begins to take on the character of the kept woman whose role is expected to be submission and luxurious passivity. Each day brings its addition of silks, trinkets, and shiny gadgets, new pleasure techniques and new pills for pep and painlessness.

Vogue is a perfect expression of this state of mind and body. It often plans whole months for its readers, giving exact instructions for what to see, say, eat, read,

---

We're listening. Who hired that big mouth?

The rustic scene accentuates the positively phoney?

Is somebody's formula showing?

Come on, kiddies. Buy a radio and feel free —to listen.

or wear for each hour of the day. It deals with its readers as a Sultan with his harem, just as *Time* deals with its readers as a Sultan with his eunuchs. *Vogue* and *Time,* like the radio, are major political forces shepherding their flocks along the paths of comfort and thrills.

Mr. Charles Siepmann, in *Radio's Second Chance,* explores behind the radio façade, exposing many of the shams and frauds of pretended freedom in this third estate of the public domain. Morris Ernst's *First Freedom* did the same for radio, and also for press and movie, centralization. Concentration of power and control is a universal trend in these fields, with monopoly resulting in monotony. And both authors agree that decentralization would result not only in greater richness and variety of product but would best promote the social conditions for enterprise and opportunity. Wide legal experience in these fields permits them to make specific proposals for attaining freedom and variety of expression.

But these writers are typical of many reformers in having isolated only a very small segment of facts for analysis. The present book intends to illustrate, tentatively, a technique for handling a much wider set of facts and related situations. The reformer looks at the effect of industrial techniques on the passive citizen and shudders. He overlooks the fact that industrial technique was born of a pre-industrial appetite—in the Newtonian age—for mechanical order and power. That passionate dream of unlimited monopolistic power still carries over into the new age of relativity physics. But the dream of relativity physics is not of centralism but of pluralism. It is not centralist but distributist in the matter of power and control. And to see this new vision at work side by side with the old one is to permit the reformer a sure method of diagnosis and therapeutic suggestion. It permits the reformer to co-operate with the same forces that have produced the disease, in order to point the way to health.

Thus, as passivity becomes extreme in the bulk of society, a sizable segment of citizens detaches itself from the dream-locked majority. As vulgarity and stupidity thicken, more and more people awaken to the intolerability of their condition. Much can be done to foster this state of awareness, even though little can be done directly to change the policies of those in control today of the media of communication.

In fact, Mr. Siepmann provides much evidence to show that, even if policies of entertainment and communication control were changed, no improvement would follow at present. Why? Because there are no standards of admitted excellence. "The Federal Communications Commission has failed, in the eleven years of its history, to define any such elementary standards." Few can agree on what is good entertainment or what is a sound educational program for the airways.

That should suggest to the reformer that his discontent with administrative policies is a very superficial affair indeed. The level at which change and awareness are needed is much deeper. The superhighways of thought and feeling which have been stretched across the contemporary mind are even more menacing than financial or bureaucratic concentrations of power. They can scarcely be expected to encourage the development of spontaneity or sensitive taste. And while standards of excellence, like criteria of freedom, are not merely an affair of private but of social growth, they can exist only in individual minds.

No standard of taste can be defined by a vote unless the voters are persons of trained perception and judgment. Lacking such recognized standards, the program sponsors feel entirely justified in equating public interest in radio with low sales resistance. Programs are tailored to evoke and to maintain just those states of mind which can be induced in the largest possible audience that can be led to buy a specific product. Since this policy is bad for the audience, it is also bad for business in the long run. It creates apathy through monotony, and boredom through excessive sensation. Horizons narrow. Imagination flickers out. Markets contract, as the movie industry had begun to discover even before television. But business does not take long views. It has to have quick turnovers. However, this is not a situation peculiar, for example, to the radio, movie, or book industries. And real reform can come only by awareness of the widest bearings of one situation on another. With this awareness there comes the gradual formation of a surer taste, and a stronger sense of what standards are relevant to any particular situation.

Thus, for example, it is not listening-freedom to be able to turn on or turn off the unweaned whimperings of hit-parade crooning. It is, relatively, freedom to be able to "place" them for what they are in relation to the range of human experience. It is not listening-freedom to hear or not to hear a Gunther giving the inside trot talk on global conditions, but it is, relatively, freedom to be able to understand the extreme limitations of such reportorial techniques. Freedom, like taste, is an activity of perception and judgment based on a great range of particular acts and experiences. Whatever fosters mere passivity and submission is the enemy of this vital activity.

Book of the Hour

The great white snow purifies prurience?

Why doesn't somebody write of a last-minute gamble for happiness in a cattle car headed for Buchenwald?

Why isn't there a gadget for pouring great literature through the window of the subconscious during sleep? Or is this it?

What is that rising noise? A new sex machine or a collective yawn?

THE PROCESS by which dress fashions produce uniformity while pretending to cater to a wild passion of the public for diversity and change is equally true in the book industry. For example, the current effort to make almost every reprint cover look lustier than the next has brought them all to a dead level of fleshliness. The same amorphous monotony is characteristic of their contents. The promoters have hung onto the whistle pull until the steam has gone from the boiler, and mighty blasts on the tooter herald the arrival of just another pip-squeak.

Naturally the authors are easily inveigled into the same tactics, eager to sell their souls for a pot of message. Authors of promise (promise to pay) are now built up for the public by the same means as movie stars. If a heavy groove has been scooped out of the public mind by the frequent passage of kindly killers and "bitch heroines," the book clubs will encourage one of these stars to try for the jackpot with something even deadlier and bitchier. Techniques for walloping the public, learned from Proletcult, Hollywood, and radio, are tried out in books. And books commissioned as surefire "slugs" in the book-club machines are also written with an eye on Hollywood.

Increasingly the reader is treated as the sluggish male is treated by the sex-hungry cave woman in the shirt ads. Is it not strange that amid the unmitigated torrent of sadistic sex novels works of reflection are tolerated only if they are gentle, sympathetic, and "warmly human"? The writer who ventures to entertain an idea must abase himself masochistically before the reader before daring to state it. Sinuous writhings and self-abasements mark the prose styles of the twentieth century. The reader is to be habitually soused with sex and violence but at all times protected from the harsh contact of the critical intellect. This comment leads one smack up against a door marked "Peter Pan, Inc.," behind which sit the amalgamated forces of Henry Luce, the Comic Books, and the syndics of the book clubs.

The Vixens, by Frank Yerby, is advertised in *The New York Times* as:

> a flaming novel of New Orleans in the frenzied days of carpetbaggers, scalawags, and Klansmen. . . . Here a man who was a legend in the city came home a traitor, to marry an insane beauty and fall in love with the bewitching Creole hellion. . . .

Across from this ad is a notice of "a small-child's Bible":

> Each story has a full-color illustration that makes real for the child the reverence and beauty of the story.

Milk for babes but meat for men. Beside these let us put the book-club ad which, under the pictures of the usual "notables" who are "to choose the masterpieces which offer the greatest enjoyment and value to the *pressed-for-time men and women of today*" is pleased to inform us as follows:

> Perhaps you have often wondered how these truly great books "got that way." First, because they are so readable. . . . And of course to be interesting they had to be easy to understand. And those are the very qualities which characterize these selections: readability, interest, simplicity.

After reading these easy books,

> You will have lost any personal concern about an inferiority complex and any fear about being the equal of others whose formal education is greater than your own.

This poisonous bilge is gulped down by many school teachers and earnest parents who are eager to provide an "atmosphere of cultured refinement" for their children.

Books also are now receiving the Hopkins Televoter treatment previously devised for movies. Albert Sindlinger has a New Entertainment Workshop based on his experience as a Gallup Poll vice-president. An author's manuscript is boiled down to a one-hour reading which is recorded and played to various segments of the population across the continent. They, in turn, record their impressions (swell, so-so, bad) by a flick of the wrist, and a gadget pumps their responses together and digests them. "People who scoff at poll-taking," says Sindlinger, "are scoffing at democracy." So he spends his time treating the people as a pulpy mass of very raw material that is to be tested constantly for what it can stand in the way of dunking and duping. As much time goes into the search for a title for some indigestible cold lard as in launching a starlet with the kind of name that will twang your synapses. Sterling North, gaping at these wondrous totalitarian techniques for mashing the public into process cheese, observes that they are a means of consulting "the collective wisdom of the American people." Which gives the cube root of pink toothbrush, at least.

Mabel Seeley's *Woman of Property* is presented with this little tag:

> "Money meant more to her than decency." Doomed to poverty and hard work, Frieda suddenly decided to get money . . . dressed her hair like the rich girls did . . . became a beautiful and desirable somebody. . . . she married again and again! She betrayed her best friend, lied, cheated, stole and deceived everyone . . . but was she alone to blame? Read this thrilling novel about a woman you will never forget.

For *Unconquered*, the tag is also fetching:

> "I bought this woman and I mean to keep her." . . . "A magnificent story of love, treachery, bravery—of everything that could make up the most fascinating, enjoyable novel you ever read."

It has been made into a film at the cost of $5,000,000 and with the assistance of 4,000 actors.

Some of the smaller print in the present exhibit concerning *The Great Snow* refers to the two sisters who

> under the impact of shattered nerves and shattered morals trade their loves in a last desperate gamble for happiness. . . . Cobb watches with distress his timid and frigid wife's surrender to her sister's lover—sees her grasp anxiously for the warm sharing of passion —but lets himself be drawn into a love affair with his sister-in-law.

Of course, the great white snow outside endows these actions with symbolic purity of intention: "Faithless under my own roof, before my children's eyes . . ." cries sensitive Nolla. And excitable Clifton Fadiman yells, "Terrific zip," and Christopher Morley whispers: "Loaded with beauty and pain. . . . It took me and troubled me with its villainous charm. Only a testament so frankly carnal could be so strong in spirit."

Let the kids' comic books do their worst, they will fall far short of the pretentious infantilism of these serious efforts of reputed adults who govern the affairs of the trade routes of contemporary fiction.

The Web of Days, by Edna Lee: "Seductive as Scarlett, ambitious as Amber. This fascinating tale of flaming love and terror."

Del Palma, by Pamela Kellino (Mrs. James Mason):

> She loved him with another woman's body . . . one of the tensest, most passionate romances you have ever experienced.

Notice that last word. There is obviously no longer any question of mental appraisal in fiction. Such stories are not a means of holding up human actions for the

This sensationally different best-selling novel

Now... yours FREE!

as a new member of The Fiction Book Club

It's Man Against Nature! Man Against Woman!

For twenty days and nights the great snow falls. It imprisons in one house Ruston Cobb, his love-starved wife, his voluptuous devil-may-care sister-in-law, and her artist-lover. When nature-in-the-raw breaks loose—it's a fight for life and love! Hidden emotions burst forth . . . conventional morals break down . . . almost anything can happen . . . and does!

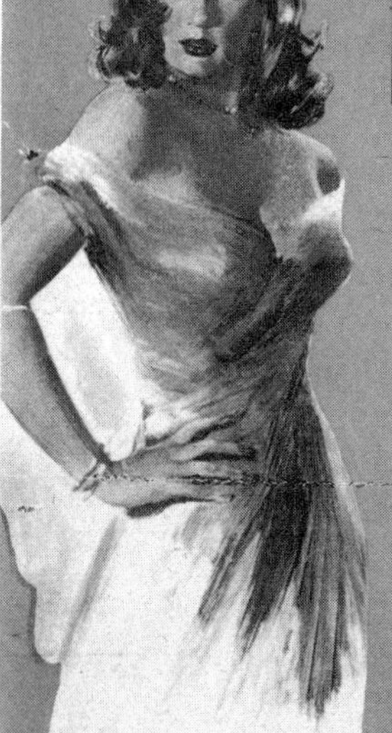

THEY TRADED LOVES

in a last-minute gamble for happiness!

the passionate, revealing story of two beautiful sisters who forgot about consequences and defied conventions when they thought the great snow meant each day might be their last!

"Here's a tale of conflict—man with nature—man with woman. This is a story to remember," says the Cleveland Plain Dealer. And how you'll agree as you race through the pages of "THE GREAT SNOW"—yours free as a new membership gift from The Fiction Book Club.

You'll share what starts out to be just an amusing weekend at the Cobb's country mansion and then find yourself trapped by the worst snowstorm in history with Ruston Cobb, his neurotic wife, an effeminate son, a wholly-average daughter, a passionate and possessive sister-in-law and her drifting artist-lover.

It is Ruston Cobb's story and the tense drama of his exciting fight for survival, but it is also the intimate picture of two sisters (different as dusk from dawn) who under the impact of shattered nerves and shattered morals trade their loves in a last desperate gamble for happiness.

In an atmosphere of violence and jealousy, Cobb watches with distress his frigid and timid wife's surrender to her sister's lover—sees her grasp anxiously for the warm sharing of passion—but lets himself be drawn into a love affair with his sister-in-law. Yet before fate plays its final cards all four are to find new meaning to life and a happiness they thought would never be theirs.

Discover for yourself what happens in "THE GREAT SNOW." Sweeping the country at $2.75 in the publisher's edition—this sensational best-selling novel is now yours FREE as a membership gift from The Fiction Book Club. But hurry, please! This offer is limited! Mail gift coupon below TODAY.

"Who says we mustn't . . ."

scoffs reckless Beryl. "Not the man who makes the keys for my apartment. Locksmiths laugh at love, you know." Beryl's gay banter belies her hungry yearning for the only man she's ever loved or wanted—her sister's husband. You'll thrill to unforgettable drama as fate throws them into each other's arms as they seek their salvation together in the surprising climax of "THE GREAT SNOW." It's yours FREE—as a new member of The Fiction Book Club. Mail coupon NOW!

"TERRIFIC ZIP" says Clifton Fadiman.

★ "LOADED WITH BEAUTY and pain . . . savagely ingenious. It took me and troubled me with its villainous charm. Only a testement so frankly carnal could be so strong in spirit."—Christopher Morley.

★ "A JOY TO EYES grown weary reading tons . . . of novel writing."—Harry Hansen.

★ "IT KEPT ME UP far beyond a sensible bedtime."—Chicago Tribune.

★ "TRULY REMARKABLE NOVEL—nothing can keep "THE GREAT SNOW" from rating near the top of the year's best fiction, whatever the remaining months may bring."—Minneapolis Tribune.

"Why did I do it . . ."

. . . "Faithless under my own roof, before my children's eyes . . ." cries sensitive Nolla to herself. But when she thinks each day may be her last, does she have the right to this last chance at happiness—with her own sister's fiance? You'll discover the answer to these intimate questions in this dramatically powerful story—"THE GREAT SNOW." Send for this great best-selling novel—it's yours FREE as a membership gift from The Fiction Book Club—if you act AT ONCE!

Send No Money! Mail Coupon!

YOURS FREE... "The Great Snow"

The best-selling novel everybody's talking about!

The FICTION BOOK CLUB (Dept. 182), 31 West 57th St., NEW YORK 19, N. Y.

I want to take advantage of your sensational introductory offer to send me free the outstanding best-seller "THE GREAT SNOW," and at the same time (and also FREE) make me a fully privileged member of The Fiction Book Club. I understand that each month I will be offered a new and popular best-seller at only $1.39 (plus a few cents postage). This means savings to me of up to $1.61 on each book from the regular price of the publisher's edition. However, I can accept or reject monthly selection as I please. My only agreement is to purchase 6 of the entire year's offerings. Rush my free copy of "THE GREAT SNOW" and begin club service with current selection: that great best-selling novel, "The Vixens."

NAME ________________
Please Print Plainly

ADDRESS ________________

CITY __________ STATE __________
Zone No. (if any)

OCCUPATION __________ AGE (if under 21) ______
(Slightly higher in Canada. Address 266 King St. West, Toronto) NYN-4

Membership Is FREE in the FICTION BOOK CLUB

. . . and you get all these Money-Saving advantages too!

You will be sent immediately FREE your copy of the best-seller "THE GREAT SNOW" when you mail the coupon. You'll also become a member of The Fiction Book Club with your choice of the club's monthly best-seller selections and you'll get these four big advantages, too:

1. You Save Up to $1.61 on Every Book!

Fiction Book Club contracts for big special editions — prints from original plates and in return for mass distribution, authors accept lower royalties. These savings are passed right on to you. You save up to $1.61 on every book you get. And you get the best-seller—"THE GREAT SNOW"—FREE as an introductory gift!

2. You Get Outstanding New Books!

Selections are made only after a careful study of current books from all publishers. From these reports of top-quality novels at $2.50 to $3.00, our editors select the best available books that are "the cream of the crop." No guesswork. No opinions. Fiction Book Club selections are always outstanding best-sellers...books by leading authors...brand-new, full size, beautiful books you will be proud to own.

3. You Pay No Special Dues or Fees!

No trick obligation clauses. You simply agree to accept any six of the twelve outstanding books offered in a year. You do not have to accept every book offered—just those you want after you have read a detailed description well in advance.

4. You'll Find Plan So Simple and Easy!

If you decide you don't want the book simply notify us not to send it. Otherwise simply do nothing, and it will be mailed to you. For each monthly selection YOU decide you want you pay just $1.39 plus a few cents postage.

SO ACT NOW!

Get your FREE copy of "THE GREAT SNOW"—the book everybody's talking about and all the conveniences and savings of free Fiction Book Club membership! But hurry—offer is limited! It's first come—first served. Mail coupon NOW to The Fiction Book Club, 31 West 57th St., New York 19, N. Y.

First Selection!

That blazing best-seller The **VIXENS**

$2.75 in the publisher's edition. Only $1.39 to Club Members.

She wouldn't share her man with any woman—not even his wife!

No wonder this passionate vixen was the talk of the French Quarter in its most scandalous days! And when the irresistible Denise Lascals meets that reckless renegade Laird Fournois, the result is as explosive as a torch set to gasoline. "You'll consume it with little gasps of excitement."—Cincinnati Enquirer. "Better than 'The Foxes of Harrow' . . ."—Chicago Sun.

MAIL COUPON NOW! HURRY...OFFER LIMITED!

critical evaluation which strengthens the powers of reasonable living. They are things to be felt in the viscera. They deliver a direct wallop to the nervous system, unmediated by reflection or judgment. The net result of the cult of literary violence, supported as it is by other media and excitements, has been to reduce the reading public to a common level of undiscriminating helplessness. Overstimulated, it has begun to get sluggish, too. The crescendo of sex and sadism already makes it yawn a bit. Sales aren't what they should be. But the disease is in excellent health.

One unintended effect of trying to dragoon everybody into a single monster book club has been to splinter the public into numerous fragments. Each club trying to corner the whole public has, by its particular bill of fare, witlessly caused an anti-club segment to be formed. And the more the clubs have tried telepathically to find and control the window to the public subconscious, the more they have created blind spots and indifference. So that there are today more reading publics than in Dickens' time, when a much smaller public bought a million copies of more than one of his books. Sir Walter Scott would have thought he had done very poorly to sell only 100,000 copies of a quality of novel which a book club today couldn't puff to near that figure. Commercially, in short, the high-pressure methods have proved self-defeating.

But though book sales are not spectacular, there can be little doubt that the taste of the public has been leveled down until it is taken for granted that a President and his stenographers will read the same books. The literary taste of English ministers of state and of the aristocracy has long been synonymous with what in America corresponds to book-club standards. Just as the appeal to sensation and the romantic values of action have resulted in America in the all-leveling effect of boredom and indifference, equally in England and America the literary qualities of Churchill, extrovert of the inside story, are heralded as worthy of the highest flights of the copy-writer's manual. Boredom with sex and sadism has not prevented us from accepting these stereotypes of fiction as a basis of camaraderie between the sage and the slick chick. And the monotony which has settled on books as a result of their rivalry in sensation has been handed on to their readers. As Groucho Marx summed it up to the blonde on his knee: "Read any good books lately?"

Roast Duck with Jefferson

Want to eat dead duck with Jefferson?

Have you had your literary hypodermic today?

You know what you like? You have all four feet on the ground?

Then you'll like a wodge of this.

How much behaviorism is needed to make a big mental proletariat behave?

Here is a sample

XXXVI. Caesar to Cleopatra: From the daily letters.

Oh, yes. I obey the Queen of Egypt. I do everything she tells me to do.

The top of my head has been purple all day.

Visitor after visitor has looked at me with horror, but no one has asked me what was the matter with me. That is what it is to be a Dictator: no one asks him a question about himself. I could hop on one foot from here to Ostia and back and no one would mention it—*to me*.

At last a cleaning woman came in to wash the floor. *She* said: "Oh, divine Caesar, what is the matter with your head?"

"Little mother," I said, "the greatest woman in the world, the most beautiful woman in the world, the wisest woman in the world said that baldness is cured by rubbing the head with a salve made of honey, juniper berries, and wormwood. She ordered me to apply it and I obey her in everything."

"Divine Caesar," she replied, "I am not great nor beautiful nor wise, but this one thing I know: a man can have either hair or brains, but he can't have both. You're quite beautiful enough as you are, sir; and since the Immortal Gods gave you good sense, I think they didn't mean for you to have curls."

I am thinking of making that woman a Senator.

of the sheer delight, the wit, the warmth, the thrill of pleasure that make THE IDES OF MARCH incomparable reading

"A fascinating book, and while it owes some of its fascination to the period with which it deals, a great deal of its charm is entirely the author's who manages to depict with high effectiveness a number of vivid, glowing and powerful personalities who meet in crowded conflict in the last few months of a great man's life."

—MAX RADIN, *N.Y. Herald Tribune Book Review*

THORNTON WILDER'S

new novel

THE IDES OF MARCH

$2.75

THE AD for *The Ides of March* may not open a door into the world of the Caesars, but it certainly does into contemporary fiction and letters. Thornton Wilder has a respectable place in that world. And since "good wine needs no bush," his publishers proudly present a page of his novel as an ad. It reads:

> XXXVI *Caesar to Cleopatra: From the daily letters.*
>
> Oh, yes. I obey the Queen of Egypt. I do everything she tells me to do.
>
> The top of my head has been purple all day.
>
> Visitor after visitor has looked at me with horror, but no one has asked me what was the matter with me. That is what it is to be a Dictator: no one asks him a question about himself. I could hop on one foot from here to Ostia and back and no one would mention it—*to me.*
>
> At last a cleaning woman came in to wash the floor. *She* said: "Oh, divine Caesar, what is the matter with your head?"
>
> "Little mother," I said, "the greatest woman in the world said that baldness is cured by rubbing the head with a salve made of honey, juniper berries, and wormwood. She ordered me to apply it and I obey her in everything."
>
> "Divine Caesar," she replied, "I am not great nor beautiful nor wise, but this one thing I know: a man can have either hair or brains, but he cannot have both. You're quite beautiful enough as you are, sir; and since the Immortal Gods gave you good sense, I think they didn't mean for you to have curls."
>
> I am thinking of making that woman a Senator.

Of course, this is baby talk. But that's not the point here. The formula for all this brand of "historical" writing is to put the public on the inside; to let them feel the palpitations of royal and imperial lovers and to overhear their lispings and cooings. It can be argued that a man has to live somewhere, and that if his own time is so cut up by rapid change that he can't find a cranny big enough to relax in, then he must betake himself to the past. That is certainly one motive in the production of historical romance, from Sir Walter Scott to Thornton Wilder. But mainly this formula works as a means of flattery. The public is not only invited inside but encouraged to believe that there is nothing inside that differs from its own thoughts and feelings. This reassurance is provided by endowing historical figures with the sloppiest possible minds. The great are "humanized" by being made trivial.

The debunking school began by making the great

appear as corrupt, or mean and egotistical. The "humanizers" have merely carried on to make them idiotic. "Democratic" vanity has reached such proportions that it cannot accept as human anything above the level of cretinous confusion of mind of the type popularized by Hemingway's heroes. Just as the new star must be made to appear successful by reason of some freak of fortune, so the great, past or present, must be made to seem so because of the most ordinary qualities, to which fortune adds an unearned trick or idea.

This technique for taking the teeth out of the "democratic" envy of the great or rich also gets a good deal of support from the rapid leveling down that has taken place with respect to the mental habits of public figures. Today the big extroverts in any field would on the whole make poor company for a well-read boy—though there are some of them who merely conceal intelligent interests and insights which would, if known, destroy the confidence of their associates. This urgency for the concealment of intelligence is felt today as acutely among leaders as formerly among intelligent girls on an average date. Thus, of *Release From Nervous Tension, The Book-of-the-Month Club News* says: "Dr. Fink not only knows his stuff, he knows how to write . . . with humor, relaxed and easy." That is the formula. If you have anything to say, smile. Reassure people that there's nothing menacing or serious, nothing difficult to come. And when presenting the great, be sure to make it plain that they, too, were "dopes." There is merely an apparent exception to this formula in the "savagery" of a Philip Wylie or in the onslaught on science in Anthony Standen's *Science Is a Sacred Cow.* When Wylie dances up and down on "Moms," or Standen takes the cow by the horns, we are given, not insight, but a Danny Kaye sort of act which passes for moral edification. Acts of this sort are occasionally promoted into popular successes, because they illuminate nothing. Standen, for example, sees none of the lethal psychological and social effects which arise not from science but from its popularization.

One of the most approved methods for hacking the great down to pygmy size is well shown in an ad for *Van Loon's Lives* which began:

> Tonight, without leaving the comfort of my armchair, I will journey through space and time into the minds of more than forty of the great men and women in history. . . . I will drink beer with Elizabeth the Great and share a roast duck with Thomas Jefferson. . . . Dante will come to dine with me . . .

Not only is the reader invited to stay in his own armchair, he is assured that he will remain locked inside his own viscera. Biography has thus been reduced to being assimilated via the alimentary tract.

Exactly in the spirit of this widespread brand of romantic history and biography is *Modern Screen's* series of dream dates with the stars and their wives. In its February, 1946, issue it was:

> If You Had A Date With Lana Turner: Assuming that just the thought of beauing Lana around for a night doesn't bowl you over in a deep swoon, here's how she'd act, talk, look. Also, here are pointers on what she expects of her swain.

Since there's no need to reassure the swooner that Lana is human flesh and blood, the stress of the piece is on culture, elegance, and refinement:

> The butler would answer the door, ask you to wait in the library, and offer you a cocktail. . . . You'd have a feeling of respect for a girl who, at twenty-four, owned a home like that.

But natch. Well, we're in the library now:

> It would be then that you'd get your first inkling that Lana, off the screen, is a much more serious-minded person than you had expected her to be. You'd see such books as *The Fountainhead, The Prophet,* and Tagore's *Fireflies,* and they would look like books that had been read many times. . . .
>
> She loves conversation and would be very interested in what you were doing, a trait most unusual in Hollywood. . . . Then, perhaps, the conversation will change to music . . . her preference is for symphonies.

The excerpt from The *Ides of March* by which the publishers wish to illustrate "the sheer delight, the wit, the warmth, the thrill of pleasure" that make it such "incomparable reading" actually provides the reader with no more valuable an experience than the dream date of *Modern Screen.* It is important to grasp the interlocking character of the mechanisms employed in these seemingly separate spheres of writing, if only in order to step outside the trance world which they both presuppose and perpetuate.

Crime Does Not Pay

Suppose crime did pay?

Crime thrills for the law-abiding and sex thrills for the impotent?

Is crime literature an escape valve or a driving shaft in the life respectable?

How much armchair violence is necessary to the good life?

Is it crime that keeps us good?

"Crime does not pay" is as much a maxim of the weasel ethics of a calculated hedonism as "honesty is the best policy." A reader testifies:

> I was reading a comic book in study hall, which is not permitted, when a teacher caught me. When he saw the name of the magazine I was reading, he let me finish it, because he enjoys it himself. . . . I can hardly wait for the next issue.

To discourage the reading of such books, why not have regular examinations on their contents in school hours, or, better, full discussion concerning their obsession with a narrow range of themes, their endless stress on violent action and the infliction of suffering and death?

At the end of one of the real-life cases in an issue is featured the sardonic figure of Crime wrapped in a shroud and seated beneath the hanging corpse of Sloper. Crime croaks:

> How can you make anything out of such material? Either they're girl-crazy, or stir-crazy, or cop-crazy, or just plain crazy! When am I going to find a normal criminal?

To which the editors add:

> Never, Mr. Crime! Normal people know that Crime Does Not Pay!!

At the beginning of the Sloper Case, Crime, the dramatic chorus, also has his little piece to say:

> If you ask me, *nobody* and *nothing* makes trouble like women—that is, for boys in *my* profession! Ever since Eve, they've been turning man's paradise into chaos with their bewitching beauty, their venomous vengefulness: A smart operator needs a dame like he needs a hole in the head! Didn't Billy the Kid? . . . Didn't Dillinger bleed his life out in a Chicago alley, because he kept a date with a red-head? Beware, Felix Sloper, Beware—Death wears a dimple—Death is a dish whose smiles can make your heart stand still forever!

Now, that's got some of the old Elizabethan gore in it. It's much more clear headed than the ad for *The Great Snow* (See "Book of the Hour"), and it proffers a crude morality which puts the best-seller goo to shame. Kids crave morality until they are old enough to see the deeper justice of mom and pop trading loves with week-end guests in a last bid for happiness.

But, for all that, there is something queer about the twin co-ordinates of this comic-book world.

There is, for example, the matter of calculating chances and probabilities as a basis for virtuous revul-

MORE THAN 6,000,000 READERS MONTHLY!
CRIME
ISSUE
NO.63
10¢
DOES NOT PAY
The ORIGINAL and BEST!
ALL TRUE CRIME STORIES
CANADIAN EDITION • CHARLES BIRO AND BOB WOOD, EDITORS
THE MAGAZINE WITH THE WIDEST RANGE OF APPEAL!
DEDICATED TO THE ERADICATION OF CRIME!
RRRRRRRING
RRRRRRRRINGGG
CHARLES BIRO
INTER-AMERICAN SAVINGS BANK
WHY DIDN'T HE COME OUT WHEN HE HEARD THE ALARM? NOW ALL FRISCO IS HEADING THIS WAY! WHY SHOULD I MOTH AROUND A HOT POTATO LIKE HIM? I WAS A NITWIT TO GET MIXED UP WITH A STUMBLE-BUM LIKE HIM IN THE FIRST PLACE!
THE FOUR GRAND THAT TRIXIE'S HOLDIN' AN' THE FEW BUCKS I GOT WILL GET US TO MEXICO IN FAIR STYLE! TRIXIE, TRIXIE, TRIXIE! WAIT-DON'T GO WITHOUT ME! TRIXIE!
RRRRINGG
BANG! BANG!
U.S. BON
2760

sion from crime. Thus, in this magazine there is a separate tale called "A Lesson in Murder," which begins:

> One hundred police working on a case can make a thousand mistakes before they strike on the right solution, but the criminal, working against these hundred police, cannot afford to make a single error.

So far as human daring and courage go, this stacking of the cards is a challenge. And the kids feel it as such. The criminal is the hero because he is fighting against hopeless odds. Against this kind of daredevil there is no use in talking up the mealy-mouthed righteousness of the respectable businessman. Not so far as adolescent generosity is concerned. The public heart goes with the criminal just because the official head is against him. Therefore, until some sort of moral heroism returns to the scenes of ordinary life, the kids will want to shoot it out with the cops.

The second dubious feature of this crime sheet is the notion of "normalcy" as a criterion of virtue. Of course, it is just as riddled with ethical nonsense as "business normalcy" is shot through with economic absurdity. The normal (virtuous) man, according to this doctrine, is he who always has a clear idea of the risks involved in asocial behavior. (See "What It Takes To *Stay* In.") So long as he keeps his appetites in the legally defensible channels, excess is success.

The moral value of magazines and programs of the "Crime Does Not Pay" genre is questionable. To a notable degree they reveal the techniques used by criminals and point to ways of avoiding the flaws leading to their capture. More dubious still, they cannot help but play up the criminal as the underdog who never had a chance anyhow.

Added to this there is the fact well known to the public and announced in *Quick* (May 8, 1950) apropos of the Senate investigation into gambling:

> U.S. Crime Does Pay—Millions a Year.

Some sections of the public are cynical enough to suspect that the really big criminals can afford to pay not only for legal defense but even for some of the legislation they need.

Writing in the *New York Herald Tribune* (January 25, 1948), John J. O'Neill gave an account of Professor Joseph B. Rhine's views on the possibility of E.S.P. (Extrasensory Perception) as a means of wiping out crime. E.S.P. turns out to be even more pretentiously totalitarian than the Hopkins Televoter mechanism. Using mechanically controlled telepathic powers to probe into the subconscious of individual and society alike, it follows, in the view of Professor Rhine, that:

> Crime on any scale could hardly exist with its cloak of invisibility thus removed; graft, exploitation and suppression could not continue if the dark plots of wicked men were to be laid bare . . .

Neither crime nor human consciousness could exist in the scientific circumstances Professor Rhine outlines in his book, *The Reach of Mind.* A single mechanical brain, of the sort developed at the Massachusetts Institute of Technology by Professor Norbert Wiener, when hitched to the telepathic mechanism of Professor Rhine, could tyrannize over the collective consciousness of the race exactly in comic-book and science-fiction style. The means envisaged for this purpose are complex, but the kind of wish for unlimited power over men which evokes such means is moronic. From the point of view of civilized values, it is obvious that, as our powers of crime detection have advanced, the power to define vice or virtue has declined. In the same way, as market-research tyranny has developed, the object and ends of human consumption have been blurred. Know-how has obliterated the why, what, and when.

The dream of E.S.P. has stirred the minds and hopes of the top brass of the executive world much as the comic books stir the passions of the very young. If any measure in addition to that of ridicule and satire could be effective in recalling such adult minds to a sense of the true proportions and dignity of human life, it should be invoked at once.

To put the matter simply, we no longer have a rational basis for defining virtue or vice. And the slogan "Crime Does Not Pay" is the expression of moral bankruptcy in more senses than one. It implies that if crime could pay, then the dividing line between virtue and vice would disappear.

Know-How

As THE ad implies, know-how is at once a technical and a moral sphere. It is a duty for a woman to love her husband and also to love that soap that will make her husband love her. It is a duty to be glamorous, cheerful, efficient, and, so far as possible, to run the home like an automatic factory. This ad also draws attention to the tendency of the modern housewife, after a premarital spell in the business world, to embrace marriage and children but not housework. Emotionally, she repudiates physical tasks with the same conviction that she pursues hygiene. And so the ad promises her a means of

---

How much more Know-How is needed to make human life obsolete?

Is there any known gadget for controlling a rampant Know-How?

The lady in the ad has found a mechanical substitute for moral choice?

King Midas knew how to change everything into gold. Where did all that popcorn come from?

doing physical work without hating the husband who has trapped her into household drudgery.

To purchase gadgets that relieve this drudgery and thus promote domestic affection is, therefore, a duty, too. And so it is that not only labor-saving appliances but food and nylons ("your legs owe it to their audience") are consumed and promoted with moral fervor.

But gadgets and gimmicks did not begin as physical objects, nor are they only to be understood as such today. Benjamin Franklin, protean prototype and professor of know-how, is equally celebrated for both his material and psychological technology. In his *Autobiography*, still a central feature of Yankee moral structure, he tells, for example, how he hit upon a system of moral bookkeeping which would enable any man to achieve perfection in several months. The trick is to select only one fault at a time for deletion, and by concentration and persistence the moral slate will soon be clean. Related to this system was his discovery of various techniques for winning friends and influencing people which are still as serviceable as ever.

Some of the contents of the summer issue of *Woman's Life*, 1947, which are listed on the back cover as follows, illustrate Ben Franklin's know-how mentality very well: "How To Hold a Man," "Eight Ways To Ruin a Compliment," "How Are Your Home Manners?" "Ways To Meet New Men." "Plan Your Charm," "If You Want To Be in Movies," and so on through the know-how hall of mirrors. On the other side of the cover is advertised a book by Louis E. Bisch, *How To Get Rid of "Nerves,"* which lists such chapters as "How To Avoid Nerves When Married," "How To Avoid Boredom," "How To Make Your Wishes Come True."

Books on how to relax would seem just about to cancel out books on how to build up nervous tension for success drive.

A recent book by Ira Wallach, entitled *How To Be Deliriously Happy*, provides know-how for the whole range of success drives, recommending that if you are in debt, go deeper. If you think you are inferior, look at yourself in a mirror bordered with eagles. Say to yourself you are taller than Napoleon. Which all adds up to the simple formula implicit in all formulas for living and success philosophy: "Love that strait jacket."

Locked in one of these mechanical strait jackets, a man may feel safe and strong, but he can exercise very little of his human character or dignity. And it is possible to understand this passion for mechanical strait jackets today by considering it in relation to similar human behavior in totally diverse circumstances. In his *Hero With a Thousand Faces*, Joseph Campbell compares our modern dilemma with that of primitive men:

> For the primitive hunting peoples of those remotest human milleniums when the sabertooth tiger, the mammoth and the lesser presences of the animal kingdom were the primary manifestations of what was alien—the source at once of danger and of sustenance—the great human problem was to become linked psychologically to the task of sharing the wilderness with these beings. An unconscious identification took place, and this was finally rendered conscious in the half-human, half-animal, figures of the totem-ancestors . . . through acts of literal imitation . . . an effective annihilation of the human ego was accomplished and society achieved a cohesive organization.

It is precisely the same annihilation of the human ego that we are witnessing today. Only, whereas men in those ages of terror got into animal strait jackets, we are unconsciously doing the same *vis à vis* the machine. And our ads and entertainment provide insight into the totem images we are daily contriving in order to express this process. But technology is an abstract tyrant that carries its ravages into deeper recesses of the psyche than did the sabertooth tiger or the grizzly bear.

Concentration on technique and abstract system began for the Western world, says Werner Sombart in his *Quintessence of Capitalism*, with the rise of scholastic method in theology in the twelfth century. The monks were also the first begetters of methods of abstract finance, and the clockwork order of their communal lives gave to the tradesmen of the growing towns the great example of systematic time economy. The puritan both retained the scholastic method in theology and gave it expression in the precision and austerity of his secular existence. So that it is scarcely fantastic to say that a great modern business is a secular adaptation of some of the most striking features of medieval scholastic culture. Confronted with the clockwork precision of scholastic method, Lewis Mumford could think only of the mechanical parallel of a smoothly working textile plant. The object of this systematic process is now production and finance rather than God. And evangelical zeal is now centered in the department of sales and distribution rather than in preaching. But the scientific structure and moral patterns of the monastic discipline are still intact, so that anybody seeking to understand or modify the religious intensity of modern technology and business has to look closely into these antecedents.

The know-how of the twelfth century was dedicated to an all-inclusive knowledge of human and divine ends. The secularizing of this system has meant the adaptation of techniques not for knowledge but for use. Instead of an intelligible map of man and creation, modern technology offers immediate comfort and profit. But it is still paradoxically permeated with a medieval spirit of religious intensity and moral duty, which causes much conflict of mind and confusion of purpose in producers and consumers alike. So that the Marxists urge that technology be finally cut loose from religion as a means of resolving these conflicts; but this is merely to repudiate the parent while idolizing the offspring. More common and hopeful is the effort to modify the social and individual effects of technology by stressing concepts of social biology, as Lewis Mumford and others do. But in this conception there is the dubious assumption that the organic is the opposite of the mechanical. Professor Norbert Wiener, maker of mechanical brains, asserts that, since all organic characteristics can now be mechanically produced, the old rivalry between mechanism and vitalism is finished. After all, the Greek word "organic" meant "machine" to them. And Samuel Butler in *Erewhon* pointed out how very biological modern machines had become: "The stoker is almost as much a cook for his engine as our own cooks for ourselves." And as a result of our obsessional care for these objects, he goes on, they daily acquire "more of that self-regulating, self-acting power which will be better than any intellect." Consequently we have now arrived near the day of the automatic factory, when we shall find it as natural for an unaided factory to produce cars as for the liver to secrete bile or the plant to put forth leaves.

Fortune (November, 1949) offers "A Key to the Automatic Factory" in pointing out that "the computers that direct guns might also direct machines." How persistently the face of murderous violence associates itself with know-how! It is hard to say why the public target of such a factory should be any happier than the recipient of a bomb or shell. And it has long been plain that the executives of production and selling have been thinking in military terms, smashing public resistance with carefully planned barrages followed by shock troops of salesmen to mop up the pockets. It will take more than a change of vocabulary to eradicate this lethal aspect of know-how, for it is not easily separated from its origins or its uses. The public may smile at the suggestion that it need be perturbed at being the target for a barrage of corn flakes or light bulbs. But this industrial ammunition has the character of exploding in the brain cortex and making its impact on the emotional structure of all society.

The symbolist esthetic theory of the late nineteenth century seems to offer an even better conception than social biology for resolving the human problems created by technology. This theory leads to a conception of orchestrating human arts, interests, and pursuits rather than fusing them in a functional biological unit, as even with Giedion and Mumford. Orchestration permits discontinuity and endless variety without the universal imposition of any one social or economic system. It is a conception inherent not only in symbolist art but in quantum and relativity physics. Unlike Newtonian physics, it can entertain a harmony that is not unilateral, monistic, or tyrannical. It is neither progressive nor reactionary but embraces all previous actualizations of human excellence while welcoming the new in a simultaneous present.

This conception is suggested, particularly in "Front Page," as effectively present in several features of industrial folklore. But it is especially evident in the best modern art, poetry, and music, to which the merely technological man finds himself so poorly attuned.

Standing on the threshold of the technological era, Jonathan Swift wrote a prophetic account of its human dangers in the third book of *Gulliver's Travels.* At the same time, John Locke, godfather of the American Constitution, pointed out that the dangers of know-how lie in the ease with which it distracts us from the obvious: "He that was sharp-sighted enough to see the configuration of the minute particles of the spring of a clock, and observe on what its elasticity depends, would discover something very admirable; but if eyes so framed could not at a distance see what o'clock it was, their owner would not be benefited by their acuteness."

Anybody who turns his scrutiny on the typical behavior of men absorbed in the dream of technology will find himself making that point over and over again. Know-how is so eager and powerful an ally of human needs that it is not easily controlled or kept in a subordinate role, even when directed by spectacular wisdom. Harnessed merely to a variety of blind appetites for power and success, it draws us swiftly into that labyrinth at the end of which waits the minotaur. So it is in this period of passionate acceleration that the world of the machines begins to assume the threatening and unfriendly countenance of an inhuman wilderness even less manageable than that which once confronted prehistoric man. Reason is then swiftly subdued by panic desires to acquire protective coloration. As terrified men once got ritually and psychologically into animal skins, so we already have gone far to assume and to propagate the behavior mechanisms of the machines that frighten and overpower us.

Much hope, however, still emerges from those parts of the scene where rational self-awareness and reasonable programs of self-restraint can be cultivated. Combatants merely infect one another. But the friendly dialogue of rational beings can also be as catching as it is civilizing.

Executive Ability

Daniel Starch and Mr. Milquetoast, or "Made for Each Other"?

Do you have a personality? Our executive clinic will get rid of it for you.

Let us make you over into a bulldozer?

ADS OF THIS TYPE, that appeal to the drive, pep, and resourcefulness which it is assumed have made us what we are, can be seen from many points of view. For example, it can be picture-framed by a Pond's ad for the "special outside-inside face treatment" which is captioned: "That hidden, magic self within you can transform your world." On many people the cumulative effect of such magic seems to be to reduce them to a coma. In this coma they remain avid customers for the success manuals and beauty treatments which by themselves constitute a large line of merchandise—a line not to be despised even when set beside the big-thriller industry of fantasy, violence, mayhem, and murder consumed by men of action.

It would seem, however, that there is no fantasy about Dr. Daniel Starch. His picture should reassure the reader that he is dealing with a man who stands for no nonsense. The picture and the name suggest that Dr. Starch is just the writer to put a bit of gumption into the Milquetoasts who get pushed around at work.

"A few typical suggestions of this powerful book" include "using the method of science to find out how men became executives." And the ad goes on to say:

> You will want, especially, to mark the paragraphs which tell *how to get your thinking started,* how to keep it out of the *fog,* how to keep it from becoming lopsided—and how to turn your thoughts into *action.*

It would seem reasonable that the executive who can usually afford a secretary to correct his spelling and grammar could also afford today an electronic brain to do his thinking. He would then run far less risk of bogging down in any unpractical or kindly human thoughts such as keep ordinary men in the lower-income brackets. In Norman Mailer's *The Naked and the Dead,* the General, faced with a critical battle, is admiringly described as follows:

> When he reached that telephone line, the decisions would have to be almost immediate. He reviewed the personalities of his line officers, remembered the distinguishing characteristics, if there were any, of different companies, even individual platoons. His acute memory reissued a spate of incidents and strength figures: he knew effectively where every gun and every man on Anapopei was placed and all the knowledge passed in an undigested flow through his head. At the moment he was an extremely simple man. Everything in him was functioning for one purpose, and from experience, with a confident unstated certainty, he knew that when demanded of him all the

HOW TO DEVELOP YOUR EXECUTIVE ABILITY

A FEW TYPICAL SECTIONS OF THIS POWERFUL BOOK

Using the Method of Science to Find Out How Men Became Executives
How Executives Organize Their Thinking
How Executives Turn Thought Into Action
The Best Way to Start
The Way New Ideas Are Actually Created
How Executives Tackle Their Work
Turning Bad Breaks Into Opportunities
How Executives Fit Themselves for Responsibility
How Executives Handle People
The One Way to Get a Man To Do What You Want
A Philosophy to Keep You Going Ahead

THE difference between earnings of $3,000 a year and $30,000, between $5,000 and $50,000, and between $7,500 and $75,000 is often due to the difference in EXECUTIVE ABILITY between individuals!

What is the difference between the qualities *you* possess and those found in men who are earning $25,000 and more a year? What makes so many men *followers*—and so few *leaders?*

Can top-notch executive ability be developed, or must one be born with it? If you are groping in a "blind alley" job—or if you feel that you are "weak" in whatever executive position you hold—here is a book you owe it to yourself to read.

Send for it on 10 days' free trial—no money in advance. If it doesn't give you the answers you have been seeking, the trial will cost you absolutely nothing.

DR. DANIEL STARCH

Dr. Starch is widely known as one of America's foremost authorities on business research. For many years a Professor at the Graduate School of Business Administration, Harvard University, he is President of Daniel Starch & Staff, in which capacity he has conducted research on management problems for many of the country's largest concerns.

150 EXECUTIVES HELP YOU

For many years as head of his own large company of business research experts, Dr. Daniel Starch—the author of this startling book—has had intimate contact with many types of businessmen. Applying the principles of research, Dr. Starch has taken 150 present-day executives "apart." Fifty of these men are top executives of America's leading enterprises and are paid salaries of $80,000 to $200,000 a year; 50 are from the $7,000 to $20,000 bracket, and 50 are in the $4,000 to $5,000 class. Dr. Starch has classified their similarities and their differences, has cataloged their backgrounds, their training, their processes of thinking, their methods of getting things done. And in his fascinating book "How to Develop Your Executive Ability," he shows you what makes them "tick"!

FOUR BASIC PRINCIPLES

Business everywhere is seeking men who can lead others—for upon leadership rests the destiny of any enterprise. The world is full of followers, but competent leaders are still too few. One of Dr. Starch's greatest discoveries is that top-notch executives are not "born" that way—they are *developed on the way up!* And now, instead of acquiring executive ability through one's own experience alone, by the "trial and error" method, anyone with intelligence can learn the secrets which all BIG executives know and use.

In "How to Develop Your Executive Ability," Dr. Starch clearly explains the four basic qualities which you *must* possess if you are to lead others. These are: *ability to handle people, the ability to think, the ability to drive your ideas through to completion, and the ability to assume responsibility.*

But Dr. Starch does not merely point out these essential qualities of executive leadership. He does not preach or deliver "pep" talks! He shows, in down-to-earth, brass-tacks fashion, exactly HOW you can acquire these qualities. He gives "case histories" which are so interesting and so instructive that you will not want to close the book until your eyes rebel! Moreover, if you are like most readers, you will want to *mark* passage after passage for re-reading over and over again!

EXACTLY WHAT TO DO

You will want, especially, to mark the paragraphs which tell you *how to get your thinking started*, how to keep it out of the *fog*, how to keep it from becoming *lopsided*—and how to turn your thoughts into *action*. You will want to re-read the secrets of turning "bad breaks" into opportunities, how to *invite* and *delegate responsibility*, how to get people to carry out your orders and instructions willingly—how to handle men and women who make mistakes, who "stall," who "alibi"—and how to reward loyalty, faithfulness, ambition. Dr. Starch tells you what *you* must *do* and *be* to deserve confidence, obedience, cooperation, respect!

MEANT FOR YOU

Whether you have reached the top rung of the ladder or are a minor executive—and especially if you are still taking orders from "too many bosses"—by all means let us send you a copy of "How to Develop Your Executive Ability." It is the *one* book you cannot afford to miss, in fairness to yourself. If you are earning $3,000, $5,000, $10,000, or even $25,000 a year your opportunities for advancement are too great to allow inertia and indecision to stand in your way.

Never before has there been such a need for competent executives—for men who can lead the way to greater progress and greater achievement. Never before have there been so many opportunities to move ahead on every industrial front. And never before has there been a book that so clearly sets forth the specifications required to reach the goals now in sight for businesses of every description—manufacturing, distributing, retailing, servicing! That is why we willingly offer to send you a copy of "How to Develop Your Executive Ability" on 10 days' FREE trial.

The book contains 260 pages, printed in large, clear type, durably bound in cloth. Mail coupon NOW—before you turn this page!

READ WHAT OTHERS SAY

"I certainly found your book very stimulating. Many of the principles are so fundamental. The job is to put them into practice, constantly."—L. B. Steele, *Sales Mgr. in Charge of Advertising and Promotion, Cellophane Div., E. I. du Pont de Nemours & Co., Inc., Wilmington, Del.*

"A book for which there is a great need. Its scope is vastly greater than the title suggests. Should be read and re-read by business executives and by anyone who aspires to a position of responsibility in any field."—Prof. Dale Houghton, *Dept. of Marketing, School of Commerce, New York University, New York City.*

"The most complete, most important book that a business or professional man can buy. Should be a textbook in every college in the United States."—Marvin Robinson, *Wichita Falls, Texas.*

"Got so darn interested that I ended up reading it aloud to my wife. It is not only full of meat, but so interestingly written that I am going to loan it around the store and I am sure it will produce some good results." — Carroll M. Swezey, Pres., *Swezey & Nevins, Inc., Patchogue, L. I.*

"I am buying ten copies for distribution to members of our staff."—P. S. A., *New York City*

EXAMINE IT 10 DAYS FREE

Send No Money—Pay Nothing on Delivery

Read It on This DOUBLE Guarantee!

Send for this book NOW—it may show you the way to double, triple, or quadruple your earnings! You take absolutely no risk. We do not ask you to send money in advance. You will not be obligated to pay on delivery.

Simply mail the coupon at right, and "How to Develop Your Executive Ability" will be mailed to you at once, to read FREE. If you like it, mail your remittance to us in 10 days. If not, return the book. And, as a final evidence of our confidence in what this book will mean to you, we say: even *after* you have paid for the book, you can still get your money back upon its return within 30 days. This *double* guarantee protects you in every way. Mail the coupon NOW—your future may depend on this one act!

Personal Improvement Guild, Dept. T223, Rockville Centre, New York

FREE EXAMINATION, DOUBLE-GUARANTEE

PERSONAL IMPROVEMENT GUILD, Dept. T223
ROCKVILLE CENTRE, NEW YORK

Please send me a copy of "How to Develop Your Executive Ability." Within 10 days I will return it and owe you nothing, or if I find it to be a valuable guide to development of my executive ability, I will remit $3.00 plus shipping charges. Furthermore, I reserve the right to return the book within 30 days for refund, even after I have paid for it.

Name Mr. Mrs. Miss ______________________ (Please PRINT name and address carefully)

Street and No. ______________________

City ____________ Zone ______ State ______

☐ To save postage, check here and enclose only $3.00, and we pay all postage and handling charges. Same 30-day return privilege for full refund still applies of course.

information would crystallize into the proper reactions. If he built up enough tension his instincts would not fail him.

Norman Mailer had only to draw on any of the behavioristic success manuals in order to produce this portrait of the army executive whose tasks and decisions so closely resemble those of the business executive. The more complexly mechanical the job, the simpler the man becomes and the more he has to rely on sheer automatism of response: "If he built up enough tension his instincts would not fail him." How big an ulcer is needed to rally the necessary quantity of instinct for executive success?

Mailer's General is literally a big nobody. He is big because he is geared to a war-machine of which he is the central nervous system. He is successful to the degree to which he can reduce his personal nervous equipment to the level of that machine. Success in this renders him a robot, a nobody, a vacuum. That is inevitable in modern circumstances. The successful executive has to strip himself of every human quality until he is nearly mad with boredom. Then he can work, work, work without distraction. The work is the narcotic for the boredom, as the boredom is the spur to work.

The success manual is for men what the "love-goddess assembly line" is for women, namely, a technique for leveling all personal differences and distinctions. The ads for "magical new beauty in one minute" match those for "increasing your income by thousands of dollars in fifteen minutes a day." Both cults make for the production of masses of replaceable human parts. And both have come to insist more and more on automatic simplicity in the formula.

The Dr. Daniel Starch ad is really a very old model. Two of the newer models are worded as follows:

$50,000 a Year For Looking Out the Window

This is a Funk and Wagnalls ad which explains that whereas an executive was formerly paid to be dynamic he is now paid to *think*. "He employs a definite technique to clear his mind and his desk of distracting detail."

Another ad is for a book called *Get What You Want*, by psychologist Lester F. Miles, and is headed:

Some People Work So *Darn* Hard Trying To Get Ahead When They Could Succeed in Life So Much Faster This *Easy* Way!

One big business executive quoted in the ad said frankly, "I don't like the idea of seeing all these things in print. There are some things I believe people should learn *the hard* way." The unconscious irony in his argument is, perhaps, this: that the simpler and more available the technique for outsmarting your neighbors and colleagues, the more "democratic" it is. Yet the more equality there is in the race for inequality, the more intense the race and the less the inequality which results from the consequent rewards. That means less and less distinction for more and more men of distinction. And that makes for less incentive to enter the race.

These comic contradictions which riddle every feature of success and advertising clack today naturally produce serious uneasiness in many people who can't separate them from democratic ideals. If the ideals are to survive, they might well be dissociated from the very agencies that talk them up so ably as a smoke screen for other activities.

Heading for Failure

THIS AD has been selected as hinting at a new social pattern emerging in our industrial world. Mr. A earns $25,000 a year "but he's heading for *failure*." Mr. B earns $100 a week "and he's heading for *success*." Mr. A may seem to have everything. "Two big cars. A fine home. A lovely wife. Happy children with their rosy futures seemingly certain." But really he is just like the happy grasshopper in the fable who made no provision for the future. Mr. B, on the other hand, not only knows where he stands today but "where he is going tomorrow." Like the ant in the same fable, he's preparing for the winter of old age.

Here, in fact, is a modern fable which relates to the age-old see-saw between bureaucracy and enterprise. Historically speaking, periods of enterprise and individual initiative have been brief and rare in comparison with the periods dominated either by state or monopolistic bureaucracies. In our own time, the big monopolistic enterprises which have mushroomed from individual speculation have rapidly taken on the character of bureaucracies, and the labor unions have merely encouraged by these big monopolies in land, labor, and capital to recognize the changes they have themselves brought about in society.

For example, patterns of individualism of the Western nineteenth century fostered the desire of each married couple to have a house of its own. For a farmer, that's one thing; for a city worker, it's another. For the latter it means a constant supply of ready cash. As his family grows and marries, it means an extension of housing units and a mounting ratio of expense per unit as public services expand over larger and larger urban areas. Megalopolis is both humanly and economically wasteful.

Within recent decades this increasing cost has brought about the contraction of the housing unit to the point where two or three children are now almost a luxury. Full-time housemaids are even greater luxuries. And so the baby-sitter, for example, has within fifteen years come as a new institution reflecting the disappearance, first of grandparents, parents, or other relatives from sharing the life of a household, and, finally, the disappearance of the housemaid.

Supplied as we now are with many millions of houses too small to be shared by aging relatives, and having acquired a deep reluctance to have them under the same roof even when that is possible, there has come with some suddenness the situation in which those deprived of income through age are yet compelled to have the ready cash necessary to maintain a separate and isolated life in a small urban house. In the rigid, specialized structures of modern production and distribution, retirement is absolute. The opportunities for earning a small income from the exercise of some skill at home is almost nil. Indeed, most men are glad not to be tossed onto the scrap heap at fifty. And an ordinary man seeking a job after forty has no chance of fitting into any of the big firms. Again, an extreme of individualism has swiftly brought on the need for "security" plans and bureaucratic administration, just as the rigidity of big-business control of the market brings about timidity and lack of imagination in developing new markets and industries. Certainly the big monopolies have driven the imaginative individuals to the cover of safe bureaucratic jobs. In its survey of "The Class of '49," *Fortune* (June, 1949) found that this class was "admirably adjusted to the now tightened job market." Employers reported that they had never met a class so "eager to make itself useful to business." And big business has in many

---

You want to feel secure? Well, nothing recedes like success.

This way to the American way of life?

Is the future a 10,000-story bureaucracy beside a suburban cottage?

The Yanks are Kremlin?

EARNS $25,000 A YEAR...

YOU'D SAY that Mr. A has *everything*. Two big cars. A fine home. A lovely wife. Happy children with their rosy futures seemingly certain. Yet . . . the picture could change *overnight*. His family's security could be *swept away* . . . because he has not planned properly for tomorrow.

MR. B, at $100 a week, is already earmarked for success. For he knows where he stands today . . . what's more, he knows where he is going tomorrow. With an eye to the future he has drawn his own *Analagraph** plan . . . a plan that provides amply for his family's tomorrow . . . yet permits comfortable living today.

Don't guess about your future... *Analagraph it!*

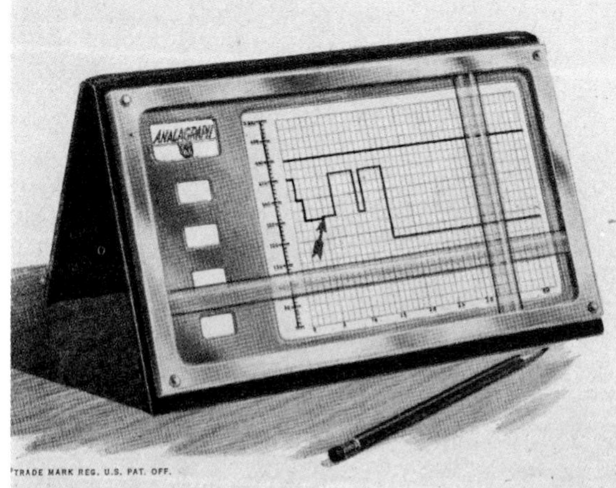

■ Why leave *your* family's future to chance? With the *Analagraph* . . . created by The Mutual Benefit . . . you can *see* what's ahead. And it takes only 30 minutes to chart a plan that lets *you* enjoy good living today . . . and spells security for your loved ones' tomorrows.

■ You chart your own goals . . . protection for your family . . . education for your children . . . a debt-free home . . . funds for retirement.

■ The *Analagraph* is exclusive with The Mutual Benefit. It is offered as part of our service without cost or obligation. Write today for the interesting new booklet, "The Analagraph—What It Can Do For You".

P.S. *Where estate problems are complex, your Mutual Benefit representative will cooperate with your legal adviser and the trust officer of your bank to assure maximum security for you and your family.*

THE MUTUAL BENEFIT LIFE INSURANCE COMPANY

ORGANIZED IN 1845  NEWARK, NEW JERSEY

*TRADE MARK REG. U.S. PAT. OFF.

cases "developed closer ties with the campus, often with grants and scholarships." Neither the new graduates nor the old tycoons are in a mood to take any chances.

As a new pattern in industrial life, this means that less and less will individuals seek "creative values" in "the romance of business" and selling. Competitive drives and ambitious impulses will be transferred increasingly to leisure and home occupations. Business and political life will take on mainly the character of diversion and entertainment for the passive public. So far as business and politics are concerned, the public is likely to become a mere audience, increasingly passive, like the shareholders of a corporation. In fact, all these tendencies have gone very far already. So that when two great stars of the competitive Hollywood game, Rita Hayworth and Ingrid Bergman, should both have elected feminine passivity at the very peak of their success, it is symbolic. In *Quick* (May 22, 1950) Bergman is quoted as saying: "I have no plans to go back to movie work. I have given up all artistic ambitions. I just want to play this passive part of mother and wife. This is the first time someone has taken care of me. . . . This new feeling of being taken care of is wonderful." The entire consumer public is in a Bergman mood today, tired of the pep talks of Dr. Daniel Starch and ready for the wonderful new experience. But what a failure of American enterprise and imagination! Among all her passive male fans in America not one, it seems, had ever got the idea of taking care of Bergman. Rossellini has passed judgment on our economic system.

Technology means constant social revolution. So much so that Marx argued that the machine would win all his battles without political assistance. A century ago the socialists began their attack on the family unit and Proudhon pointed out that their arguments really came to one, namely, that the family cost too much. By the end of the nineteenth century, industrialists and businessmen had already adopted this argument in practice by offering jobs to women. Why should half the population exist in a semi-leisured state when it might be put to work and thereby bring down the scale of men's wages? That, we can now see, was the *economic* logic in feminism. The woman of leisure might wear long skirts, but the working woman was put into adolescent short skirts and told in big press campaigns that the age-old tyranny of men was at an end. Today she is told every few months to shorten or lengthen her dresses in accordance with market exigencies, and she obediently does so. And by this type of operation all superfluous cash is removed from people who might otherwise find means to provide for their later years without analagraphing their future."

Plain Talk

In "The Answer" section of this ad we are told that: "In the business and social world, the ability to express ideas with clarity . . . accuracy . . . and force is the most highly prized gift of all." In the "Sparkling Chapters Like These" division are listed such chapters as

---

Plain talk or double talk?

Words and wisdom shall never meet?

Do you want ideas or plain ideas?

Is this a book for Freudened Fräuleins?

Another promotion—*what's he got that I haven't got?*

It isn't brains. Or education. Or social position. And I'll give him credit, it isn't *pull*. We went to the same university together; if anything, my marks were better than his. And don't say it's clothes or personality. I'll match mine against his any time. But when the promotions are handed out, he's the one who gets them. When somebody throws a party, he heads the invitation list. He makes twice what I earn, maybe more. Yet we started together from scratch. *What's he got that I haven't got?*

THE ANSWER: In the business and social world, the ability to express ideas with clarity . . . accuracy . . . and force is the most highly prized gift of all. Few possess it, but it is a gift that anyone, through a little study, can claim as his own. You can quickly and easily learn to make it *yours* with an amazing, instantly successful new book called:

EXAMINE IT 10 DAYS **FREE**

By RUDOLF FLESCH

WEEKS before it was published, people whose profession is word-business were talking about this book. Authors, editors, advertising men, teachers, clergymen, radio and screen script writers, public relations experts, labor leaders, business executives—all looked forward to its publication with high expectations. Their interest is easily explained: Rudolf Flesch is the first man to have *scientifically* analyzed English for the purpose of making it work more effectively.

In THE ART OF PLAIN TALK he reveals these secrets to you. He shows you how to cut out vague, colorless language and replace it with phrases that carry a punch. No wonder his book sold out immediately on publication!

How It Came to be Written

Psychologists have long been interested in finding out how quickly people understand what they read. But until Dr. Flesch pioneered in adult education, most research was confined to textbooks for children. Flesch went to work on the problem in Columbia University's Readability Laboratory. Out of his research came a book (his doctor's thesis) called *Marks of Readable Style*.

Spontaneous word-of-mouth publicity broadcast its unique help to those who write for a living. Almost overnight it became the bible of the profession.

Tested Where Results Count

Columbia Broadcasting System uses Dr. Flesch's findings to pre-test radio scripts. Readable News Reports uses his formula to simplify newspapers, has applied it to United Press copy. Book publishers use his "yardstick" to measure the readability of manuscripts.

Meanwhile Dr. Flesch's publisher backlogged one batch of orders after another. When paper again became available, long-patient customers clamored to have the book reprinted. Dr. Flesch said no.

He had written *Marks of Readable Style* as a technical, scholarly treatise—little thinking it would become a popular handbook for writers. It bothered him that a book about *making prose readable* should not be the essence of readability. Documented with statistical formulas, the text was too tough for his taste. So he sat down and applied his own discoveries to the original manuscript. The result is THE ART OF PLAIN TALK.

A Brand New Kind of Book on How to Express Yourself

THE ART OF PLAIN TALK is not a grammar nor a volume of "usage." It is not a rehash of vague generalities. Instead it shows you specifically how to avoid dullness when you write and speak . . . how to present what you have to say so that it will be clearly, emphatically understood . . . how to put wings on your words . . . how to present your ideas effectively *and make them stick*.

Dr. Flesch shows you how to choose words and build sentences. You'll learn many odd things about language—about full words, empty words, crowded words, live words. Among other things you'll cease to be a slave of stuffy grammarians and their sterile traditions.

In writing the book, Dr. Flesch gives a wonderful example of the skill he proposes to teach: his book is fun to read. Peppered with wit, it is filled with startling and amusing translations of muddy prose into straightforward English.

At the end of each chapter Dr. Flesch supplies exercises to rehearse and drive home significant facts. The key to the whole book is the simple yardstick formula Dr. Flesch has devised. With it anyone can test his use of words against established standards for any audience.

Praised by People Who Know

THE ART OF PLAIN TALK has received an overwhelming reception. Here's an example. It's part of a full-page editorial written by the President and Publisher of *Printers' Ink*:—

"I have just finished a book that ought to be read by all advertising writers, sales correspondents, editors and business-paper writers.

"Its name is THE ART OF PLAIN TALK. Its author is Rudolf Flesch. Dr. Flesch (yes, he's a Ph.D.) has worked out a formula for rating readability. It applies equally to advertising copy, business-paper articles and even to editorials like mine. It is a humbling kind of book, because even as I write this I am conscious I am violating a dozen of Dr. Flesch's principles.

"He doesn't ask you to strip your writing to bare essentials. He doesn't believe that Basic English solves all writing problems. He recognizes that few of us write to be read only by morons.

"He does believe that a lot of writing is unnecessarily difficult to read. He believes in simple, direct writing. He allows for frills but tells you how to make them readable.

"You don't have to apply his particular mathematical formula. But if you read this book you will get many tips that will help you correct your faults (we all have them) and yet retain whatever individuality and freshness your style has.

"I think I'll go all the way over the dam and say that I believe this is the most useful and important book to business writers that I have ever read."—*C. B. Larrabee.*

SPARKLING CHAPTERS LIKE THESE

- Plain Talk Is an Art
- Let's Start with Chinese
- Listen to Plain Talk
- Sentences Come First
- Gadgets of Language
- The Grammar of Gossip
- Here's Your Yardstick
- Live Words
- Crowded Words
- Empty Words
- The Glamour of Punctuation
- Turnabout Rhetoric
- Follow the Language
- Short Cuts
- Talking Down and Reading Up
- Can Science Be Explained?
- The Trouble with Textbooks
- What Price Copy?
- How to Read the Federal Register
- The Juvenile Touch
- One Language After Another
- The Future of Plain Talk
- Appendix: How to Use the Yardstick Formula
- Index

THE ART OF PLAIN TALK

READ WHAT EXPERTS SAY:

"Brilliant . . . vivid, startling, amusing . . . how to get your meaning over to other people through the written or printed word . . . a remarkably interesting and remarkably valuable book for almost any reasonably thoughtful person."—Dorothy Canfield Fisher, *Book-of-the-Month Club News*

"At last I've discovered a man who knows how to write about 'how to write': Rudolf Flesch. THE ART OF PLAIN TALK has finally applied to writing problems a method of analysis that makes sense."—Mark Wiseman, *Advertising and Selling.*

"The rumors speak the truth. I've been raving about THE ART OF PLAIN TALK, chiefly because it has been making me over."—Harry A. Overstreet.

"THE ART OF PLAIN TALK offers specific, eye-on-the-word criticism of bad writing. (Dr. Flesch practices what he teaches.) It offers much good advice about the art of learning to write so that people understand you."
—*Christian Science Monitor*

"At last! A sensible book on language . . . one of the clearest and most sensible and helpful books in the last ten years."
—*Indianapolis Times*

"If I had to recommend one golden book on writing, for beginners as well as for those who ought to know better, this would be the one. This man knows how to write and how to teach. THE ART OF PLAIN TALK is a delight to read . . . salted down with common sense."—Aaron Sussman, *Saturday Review of Literature.*

AT ALL BOOKSTORES

MAIL THIS COUPON TODAY

10 DAYS' FREE EXAMINATION

HARPER & BROTHERS, 51 E. 33rd St., N. Y. 16

Gentlemen: Please send me THE ART OF PLAIN TALK for 10 days' free examination. At the end of that time I will remit $2.50 or return the book postpaid.

Name__________

Address__________

City______ Zone______ State______ 3602A6

SAVE! If you enclose payment, publishers will pay postage. Return privilege guaranteed.

"Gadgets of Language," "The Glamour of Punctuation," and "Turnabout Rhetoric." Until you have read this book people may have laughed when you opened your big mouth, but now you can learn in no time "how to put wings on your words" and how to present your ideas and "make them stick."

Small wonder that "the experts" are in a dither about the work. Harry A. Overstreet reports: "It's been making me over." C. B. Larrabee says that it sent him "over the dam." Presumably, with the art of plain talk mastered, you can expect to explain Kafka in ten simple words or the newest industrial process in two or three phrases. As for the booby traps of language that worry the genteel Sherwin Cody School of remedial English teachers, you can prance around them with abandon. On a dull day, why not pause, one hand on the door, and dazzle the boss with a pellucid little monologue on some abstruse subject? Let him have a little plain talk from time to time.

There is no end to the making of books and promises on the theme that:

> The *Big Jobs* usually go to men who are able to express themselves . . . but never to those who are always groping for words.

All this seems to have little relation to the laconic and ungrammatical stammerings of those strong, silent tycoons of yesteryear. Surely all this talk about how to talk is intended for a pygmy tribe of desk clerks, or, at best, for minor bureaucrats. Can't the big man hire a dozen professors of English as his private secretaries? Hasn't he anything to do besides avoid the pitfalls of English? Are all those thoughts which he turns into the masterful actions of production and distribution just translations of puny little words?

Vocational-guidance investigation has turned up the curious fact that executives of whatever educational background do show an aptitude for words that is more than usual. Here is unexpected confirmation of the ancient Ciceronian claim for eloquence as training for practical life. Before Cicero, the Greek Sophists had taught how to make men wise and powerful by making them eloquent. But they saw no split between words and wisdom, as this ad does. Man, they said, was distinguished from the brutes by his aptitude for speech. Speech and reason were one, and the development of either involved the other. Therefore an encyclopedic program of studies was necessary to produce eloquence. And eloquence was power, wisdom, and political prudence at the same time.

This curiously unified and extensive program remained the basis of classical education until 1850. And it was only as the professors adopted the specialized bent of our times that they lost their bearings and influence. Today it is not the classroom nor the classics which are the repositories of models of eloquence, but the ad agencies. Whereas the older concept of eloquence linked it to public responsibility and ceremony and a unified program for enlisting the passions on the side of reason and virtue, the new school of eloquence is virtually demagogic in its headlong exploitation of words and emotions for the flattery of the consumer.

Just about the time when the classical program of studies collapsed, Macy's was experimenting with the hypnotic power of words. In the *New York Herald* for January 5, 1859, it carried a long Gertrude Stein sort of dry-goods poem which in part ran as follows:

COME, COME, TIME, TIME
        COME, COME, TIME, TIME
                THE TIME HAS COME
WHAT IS TO BE DONE? IS THE QUESTION
WHAT IS TO BE DONE? IS THE QUESTION
                WHAT SHALL BE DONE?
                WHAT SHALL BE DONE?
MARK EVERY ARTICLE
MARK EVERY ARTICLE
                                WAY
WAY
                WAY DOWN
TO SOME PRICE WHICH WILL MAKE IT
TO SOME PRICE WHICH WILL MAKE IT
                SELL AND GO QUICK,
                SELL AND GO QUICK,
                SELL AND GO QUICK,
        LADIES
Ladies, all this has been done in a most thorough manner.

OUR GOODS SHALL BE SOLD CHEAP!
OUR GOODS SHALL BE SOLD CHEAP!!
                IN THIS GREAT SELL OUT.
                IN THIS GREAT SELL OUT.

Fifty years before Gertrude Stein developed an artistic prose for the recording of the mental gropings of the very young and the very stupid, Macy's copy writers had mastered the same persuasive art of plain talk. Books such as *The Art of Plain Talk* are perhaps still behind Macy's ad of 1859 and way behind Gertrude Stein in the techniques either of following or of controlling the childish mental processes of those locked in the mass dream.

The Great Books

And how to know them? The customer is always right.

One hundred and two ideas a minute? It's only 1951.

Want to get into the big poker game of the ages? Fill out the form below.

War a great idea but not Peace?

Latch onto our big idea index for deep consolation?

THE SERVICES of Dr. Hutchins and Professor Adler to education are justly celebrated. They have by their enthusiasm put education in the news. It is therefore ironic that the present *Life* feature (January 26, 1948) should have so mortician-like an air—as though Professor Adler and his associates had come to bury and not to praise Plato and other great men.

The "great ideas" whose headstones are alphabetically displayed above the coffin-like filing boxes have been extracted from the great books in order to provide an index tool for manipulating the books themselves. By means of this index the books are made ready for *immediate use.* May we not ask how this approach to the content and conditions of human thought differs from any other merely verbal and mechanized education in our time?

In the matter of insistence on the supremacy of technique at the expense of nutriment, the University of Chicago is the child of Harvard, as Harvard is the child of German know-how. Professor Adler's bookshelf is the natural successor of President Eliot's five-footer. Both anguish and starvation of mind are the normal condition of those engaged on the assembly lines of Harvard graduate study, forcing the constant importation of talent. This inability to supply its own staff is a well-known paradox about Harvard, but the Harvard methods and pursuits differ little from those of any other graduate school. The pressure is higher there, but, humanly and intellectually speaking, Chicago is almost as badly off in its unconscious and uncritical assimilation to the rigid modes of a technological world.

> But to hope that even the best training in criticism can cope with the constant storm of triviality and propaganda that now beats upon the citizen seems to me to expect too much of any educational system.

This is deafeatist enough, but it comes naturally from an educator whose system and technique in education is itself an unintentional reflection of the technological world in which he lives. It would seem that the very first thing that would occur to an educator today is the fact that for the first time in history there exists an unofficial program of public instruction carried on by commerce through the press, radio, movies. Carried on by the state, the upshot would be no different. This public instruction is paid for by a tax of billions of dollars levied on the public *via* advertising and entertainment. It has mainly neutralized the much smaller program of official education with its much smaller budget and much less well-paid brain power.

Compared to this volume of education, the University of Chicago is tiny indeed. Yet what does Dr. Hutchins

THE INDEXERS POSE WITH THE FILE OF GREAT IDEAS. AT SIDES STAND EDITORS ADLER (LEFT) AND GORMAN (RIGHT). EACH FILE DRAWER

have to say about it? As a contemporary, radical, revolutionary, humanistic educator, he suggests that we concentrate on the great books. But it is quite hopeless, he admits. A last-stitch stand of denuded minds.

This book, on the other hand, proposes and illustrates some of the uses of this unofficial education on which Dr. Hutchins turns his back in dismay. That unofficial education is a much more subtle affair than the official article as sponsored by Dr. Hutchins. More important still, it reflects the only native and spontaneous culture in our industrial world. And it is through this native culture, or not at all, that we effect contact with past cultures. For the quality of anybody's relations with the minds of the past is exactly and necessarily determined by the quality of his contemporary insights. Thus the failure to come to grips with the particulars of contemporary existence also becomes a failure to converse with the great minds *via* great books. That is why it can be said that the medievalism of Dr. Hutchins and Professor Adler turns out to be no more than a pictur-

CONTAINS INDEX REFERENCES TO A GREAT IDEA. IN CENTER ARE THE WORKS OF THE 71 AUTHORS WHICH CONSTITUTE THE GREAT BOOKS

esque version of the academicism that flourishes in every collegiate institution.

Why has it not occurred to Dr. Hutchins that the only practical answer to the "storm of triviality and propaganda" is that it be brought under control by being inspected. Its baneful effects are at present entirely dependent on its being ignored. In launching such a part-time program of uninhibited inspection of popular and commercial culture Dr. Hutchins would find himself on a radical tack at last. Why shouldn't the young in school and college be invited to scrutinize widely selected examples of this unofficial education? Their studies and their lives would be considerably enlivened thereby. Best of all, this procedure would help to promote that unprecedented self-awareness which harmonious life in an industrial society requires. The study of the great books would then be pursued with a fuller sense of the particularity of cultural conditions, past and present, without which there is no understanding either of art, philosophy, or society.

Galluputians

Calling all Airedales?

Why not the one woman in five who must surely shave once in a while?

How does the Galluputian sort of statistical contour fascinate the Lilliputian mind?

Want to know where you fit in so you can be outstanding? Do you feel a need to be distinctive and mass-produced?

To A LARGE degree opinion polls function as educational rather than fact-finding agencies. This is illustrated in Professor Kinsey's *Sexual Behavior of the Human Male* when he says on page 681 that many who are perturbed by their own sexual habits or histories "may be put at ease when they learn what the patterns of the rest of the population are." Most people are terribly ill at ease unless they are "in line" with their fellow men. The polls are a graphic means of showing people where that line is.

The advertisers have been using this technique for a long time. "More people are switching to . . .", or "2 out of 3 have pink tooth brush," and so on. The present ad uses a supposed poll finding not to frighten but to flatter the customer. Since in point of fact almost every man shaves daily, via this ad he can have the pleasure of thinking himself the rugged one in seven whose fast-springing bristles simply have to be mowed every few hours.

In a *P.M.* interview with Gertrude Stein (July 21, 1946) on the subject of Gallup Polls, she noted:

> We were cut off here for a long time from America, and when we did get in touch with America again we learned some funny things. The funniest was this Gallup Poll . . . when a man can take a poll and tell what everybody is thinking, that means nobody is really thinking any more. . . . Over here, the people have outlived industrialism. In America, industrialism still drowns the people, drowns them until they are dead poor. I told those G.I.'s to learn to think as individuals.

On November 3, 1948, when the pollsters were proved wrong in forecasting a Dewey victory over Truman, nobody failed to notice that there was congratulation even among some Republicans. It was vaguely felt to be a victory for men over the machines. This spontaneous outburst of joy suggests that there is a very widespread and suppressed anxiety about the human effects of the pollster-geist operations. Underlying the bravado and public hyperbole of all these activities of the poll-control men, the ad agencies, and Hollywood producers, there is a sense of guilt. Most of these people somehow feel that they are trapped in antisocial situations which are too big for them. Cynicism becomes their private refuge. But publicly they have to produce an ever slicker, tougher, tighter, and more effective kind of ballyhoo.

In his *Public Opinion*, Walter Lippmann analyzed the fallacies inherent in our notion of government as a sort of automatic mechanism geared to the ballot box. This analysis is also confirmed by the close connection between opinion polls and consumer surveys. Both kinds of investigation are carried on by interested parties to reduce the gamble in their activities. A political machine wants to have exact knowledge of how to weight its electoral program. A big business will alter its product and its advertising only in order to reach a specific market. So both of them call in the social statistician. The statistician employs the method of laboratory analysis of small samples of human blood and tissue. While it is difficult to obtain a sample of social blood or tissue, it is no exaggeration to say that the pollsters with their questionnaires are out for blood. When they get their sample, they analyze it and turn the results over to their masters, who then decide what sort of shot in the arm the public needs.

For present purposes it is not important to decide whether the polls are socially desirable or not. It is more to the point to see how they are related to other things. Thus, the idea current in education that the child must be "adjusted" to its environment provides a mechanical notion of human training and relationships which gears very neatly with the impulse behind the pollsters. They are engaged in seeking the means of adjusting products to consumers and consumers to products, whether the article is corn flakes or legislation.

This educational gearing is seen strongly at work in Professor Kinsey's surveys, with their economist-like normalcy charts and statistics. And survey techniques inevitably throw up images of normalcy that reflect the ways of those who make few demands of themselves. As the cabdriver tends to be the opinion-pollster hero, the truckdriver becomes the ideal of the sex-pollster. Thus the "villain" of Professor Kinsey's book is the college man whose incidence of sex frequency is so inferior to that of the man whose education ends at grade school. (The college man is not very useful to the opinion pollster, either.) Kinsey clearly prefers the sex mores of the lower educational levels, where the great Niagara of genital gratification, as shown in his charts, rotates no fewer than seven dynamos. He lists these as sexual "outlets," betraying his mechanical and excretory notion of sex in that term. The "outlets" are, by his enumeration: "masturbation," "nocturnal emission," "petting," "coitus," "homosexual," "animal coitus," and "spontaneous." These humming dynamos vary in size, but, it seems, if they were powered only by college graduates there would be nothing to write a book about.

After many pages devoted to illustrating that those in whom "the onset of adolescence" occurs first are those whose incidence of sex frequency remains highest for the greatest length of time, he suddenly changes the subject in order to prove that the sex life of the past generation was much like our own. Now, this digression of Professor Kinsey's engaged his feelings so deeply that he failed to notice that he had inadvertently wrecked his main thesis. He was so eager to discredit those who argue that, sexually speaking, we live in a degenerate age that he says that the testimony of a previous generation is useless. There is no scientific value in questioning older people about the sex mores of their youth. Especially is this true of his sex heroes of the early onset and high frequency, because, he insists, they are "often in very poor condition physically and mentally by the time they reach 45 or 50 years of age."

This is a rare bit of luck so far as the lay reader is concerned. For it is seldom that he has any means of knowing when "science" is withholding vital data. Professor Kinsey's book is a *carte blanche* for maximal genital activity. As popularized science, that is its entire drift. It is only incidentally that Professor Kinsey reveals the cost of footing this bill. If there should prove to be some ultimate usefulness in such a poll as Professor Kinsey's, it will be in spite of his ardent advocacy of the view that "the best things in life are free." The Kinsey report is only one example of how the public can be rendered helpless by popularized science.

Sexual Behavior in the Human Male is a penny arcade peep show given the chrome treatment of scientific charts and figures. It is like those slot machines for registering your "dynamic energy" or those quiz machines for determining your "Emotional Maturity Quotient" by answering such stark scientific inquiries as: "Do you undress in front of your husband or wife?" Or "Do you get a strange feeling when people stare at you?" The "normal" person is the one with the slugs that fit those slots.

It is only by observing the interrelations between these families of "scientific" devices that it is possible to evaluate the separate activities of Professor Gallup or Elmo Roper. By keeping everybody in a panic through daily invitations to "See how you stack up with your fellow man on the following issues," the individual can be torn between the fear of being a misfit and the passion for the distinction conferred by purchasing a mass-produced item. That sets us right in the center of the drama of a consumer economy once more. And it is the impulses released within that economy which throw up the statistical imagery of the Galluputians. Their "science" appears as the conditioned reflex of that economy rather than as a contribution to human knowledge.

Market Research

We are told that the audimeter in the ad is "installed in a radio receiver in a scientifically selected radio home. By recording every twist of the dial, every minute of the day or night, the audimeter obtains precious radio data not available through any other means." These meters are, of course, installed with the consent of the scientifically selected radio-owner.

Ethical and social values quite to one side, an instrument of this sort chimes with a good many other facts of our world. It is obviously the commercial counterpart of the secret microphone installed for political reasons. It is the mechanical sleuth which eventually pieces together the radio habits of a household into a single chart-image. It gives the *inside* story which is typical

---

How about a little old wooden horse to work for *us* in your home?

All we want, folks, is the cube root of your special neurosis. For your greater listening freedom, see?

Don't look now, but I hear somebody hooking this gadget to an electronic brain—for the good of mankind, of course.

Wouldn't this be a good time to read Lewis Carroll's ballad about the Walrus and the Carpenter?

THE NIELSEN AUDIMETER

. . . the graphic recording instrument installed in a radio receiver in a scientifically selected radio home. By recording every twist of the dial, every minute of the day or night, the Audimeter obtains precious radio data not available through any other means. Audimeters are of 3 different types (only one illustrated here).

Figure 4

Figure 5

Installed in a typical radio receiver—the Audimeter operates silently and unseen.

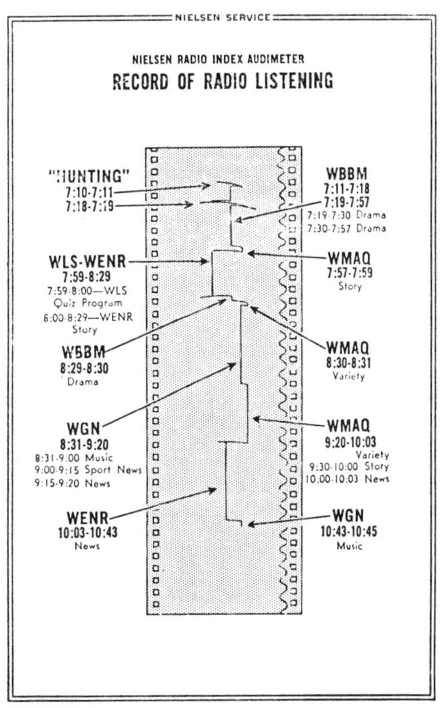

Figure 6

of X-ray photographs, boudoir journalism, and cubist painting alike. For, as in cubist painting, the spectator is placed in the center of the picture.

Professor Whitehead tells us in his *Adventures of Ideas* that whereas Newton gave us the picture of an atomic universe, Leibnitz "explained what it must be like to be an atom. . . . Leibnitz tells us how an atom is feeling about itself." Of course, there is no logical connection between Leibnitzian monads, modern intercellular photography, and Winchell's inside stories. That is to say, there is no abstract and necessary conjunction between such groups of facts. In the same way there is no logical connection between Bergson and Proust. But they certainly belong in the same world. Put side by side, they throw a good deal of light on each other.

The long-established anthropological techniques for observing life in primitive societies, as explained by the popular Margaret Mead in *Male and Female*, are extremely interesting. The object is for the anthropologist to become just like the audimeter in the present ad. To be inconspicuous and yet to have a central position commanding as many views as possible. No Pinkerton snoop-sleuth ever had a more bizarre assignment than Dr. Mead imposed on herself in order to get to see and feel, from the inside, exactly how a primitive society functions. To these techniques of observation is added the psychoanalytic insight that the most valuable data are yielded by individuals or groups involuntarily, in moments of inattention. It is that latter consideration which makes popular culture so valuable as an index of the guiding impulses and the dominant drives in a society.

As market research takes on the character of social engineering and education, it draws attention to the fact that an industrial society must have exceptional awareness of its processes. A small mechanical miscalculation always costs money and often costs lives. We have long been familiar with the need for exactitude and awareness in mechanical, commercial, and military operations. But we are just beginning to learn how all these operations themselves have been affecting the quality of individual and social life for the past century and a half. Until a few years ago liberal economic theory scoffed at the possibility of social deterioration and impoverishment as long as economic advance was statistically evident. In exactly the same spirit of unimaginative isolationism there is the fact recorded by Siegfried Giedion in *Mechanization Takes Command*, namely the irritation and incredulity of a physicist when confronted with parallels between the techniques of his science and those of modern art.

Since current art and science alike show that we have entered a new era, it is now especially important to recognize the intellectual limitations of the past era of mechanization. Market research today is a useful instance of new methods being employed in the old mechanical spirit. Dr. Margaret Mead, on the other hand, is using the same methods with that full sense of responsibility and respect for the vital interests and the harmonic relations of an entire society. Market research and opinion polls are not carried on in this spirit but rather with an eye to local and particular interests.

Descartes, as much as any one person, can be said to have initiated the stress on mechanization and rationalism which fostered the era of Newtonian physics and the allied notions of a self-regulating market and social institutions. He was explicitly motivated by a passion for exactitude and universal consent. He expressed his disgust with the age-old disagreements of philosophers and suggested that universal agreement was only possible in mathematics. Therefore, he argued, let mathematical laws become the procedure and norm of truth. Scientists and philosophers such as A. N. Whitehead and J. W. N. Sullivan are agreed that it was to this procedure that we owe our present mastery of the physical world and our equal helplessness in managing social and political affairs. Because mathematics can only provide descriptive formulas for practical material purposes. Entirely different methods are necessary if we are to escape from an inhuman specialism and to discover the means of orchestrating the arts and sciences in the fullest interest of individual and social life. Such new methods are utilized by Siegfried Giedion in *Mechanization Takes Command*. In his section on "The Assembly Line and Scientific Management" he notes that "the growth of the assembly line with its labor-saving and production-raising measures is closely bound up with the wish for mass-production." Similarly, at the beginning of a whole era of mechanization there stands Descartes with his passionate wish for a universal mathematical unity in thought and society.

In looking at the folklore of the industrial society that resulted from these wishes, we are justified in seeing a wish-fulfillment on a huge scale as surely as the psychologist is justified in deciphering wishes in the dream symbols of his patients. Of course, the wish and its fulfillment are not just logically, but analogically, connected. Our world of mechanized routines, abstract finance and engineering is the consolidated dream born of a wish. By studying the dream in our folklore, we can, perhaps, find the clue to understanding and guiding our world in more reasonable courses.

Emily Post

ROCK OF BEHAVIOR, norm of conduct, guide for the perplexed from the cradle to the gravy. Her name itself is a greater asset than anything she says and is better than anything a Harry Conover agency could have contrived to inspire the relevant kind of public interest.

The descendants of uncourtly and anti-frilly Puritans could be expected to take their social life with a degree of deliberate rigor and implacable precision. These qualities are amply provided by Emily Post. A commercial society whose members are essentially ascetic and indifferent in social ritual has to be provided with blueprints and specifications for evoking the right tone for every occasion. The same spirit rules the erection of historical sets in Hollywood. Accuracy without vitality or spontaneity. Creative confidence can only be permitted in neutral social territories dominated by the adolescent or by Greenwich Village. Here manners and taste have free play. But where money transactions are somehow at stake, panic enters the socially spotlighted host or hostess. "It's got to be just right if it kills us." And both rectitude and ostentation are best secured by adherence to a mechanical and arbitrary code. So that the socially immature cling aggressively to the books of Emily Post with the same baleful discomfort as the mentally exempt latch onto *Reader's Digest.* Hope for this situation increases daily with the self-consciousness and uneasiness of those still umbilically attached to such guides.

How well Posted are you? Latch onto refinement, bud.

Does your butler yearn for a mustache?

Are you shaky about the logistics of birth, marriage, and death?

Do you want your social woe to show? Do it the Post way.

JOHN LOVES MARY
ELMER LOVES PATTY
EVERYBODY LOVES
LIFE SAVERS

The candy with the hole still only 5¢

Co-Education

THIS SCENE is intended to be rich with the associations of childhood and national tradition, reaching into *Tom Sawyer* and the little red schoolhouse as well as the progressive school. But co-education and "symmetrical" or neutral child-rearing first had its roots in a set of circumstances different from those of the present. The one-room school was the result of frontier privation, with co-education merely incidental to the fact that a salary could be found for only one teacher for the school. There was no ideal of co-education at first.

Today there are both money and teachers, but co-education has become an ideal. Explanations and defense of this new ideal are scanty, and they all reduce to a single official argument, namely that being together "helps Johnny and Mary to understand each other." That very quaint and implausible suggestion conceals as mixed a batch of hopes, fears, and deceptions as the quaint old New England theory and practice of "bundling." The latter institution persists as "petting," and co-education can be viewed as only the classroom and campus version of bundling.

Mademoiselle (April, 1950) provides a bedtime story entitled "Solution for Two Unknowns" by Peggy Harding Love. It is all about Abbie "going to high school. . . for four ambivalent years" and the "vulgar horseplay in the corners," and about how Abbie "became increasingly conscious of the boy who sat beside her." This thrilling boy's name is Ray. For both Abbie and Ray, and for the great majority of school kids, the above few phrases provide a fairly complete account of the meaning and function of the classroom today. The authority of the subject, the thrill of entering on the acquisition of disciplines which have been learned by every civilized mind, these aspects of education are obliterated in the pink fog of becoming "conscious" of the boy or girl who sits beside her or him.

Co-education, therefore, enters the present book as one segment of the dreamlike world of industrial man. Education in a technological world of replaceable and expendable parts is neuter. Technology needs not people or minds but "hands." Unobservant of the automatic leveling process exercised by applied science, we have let it carry us along to the point where the same curriculum and the same room serve to prepare boys and girls alike for the neuter and impersonal routines of production and distribution.

Preoccupied with the problems and functions of sexual differentiation, Dr. Mead in *Male and Female* has no good to report of co-education. Sex competition among the very young she rightly sees to be a means of sterilizing sex. And after surveying the child-rearing patterns of several societies, she concludes that the greatest harmony and the "most specifically sexual" relation between adults is achieved in those societies where the "most conspicuous division is found between groups of small boys and girls." There is a good deal of uproarious comedy in a situation in which this exponent of anthropology and sociology warns the earnest students of the new science that for more fun in bed you've got to love that chaperone and avoid that co-educational classroom. When advanced science proclaims that "great-grandmother was so right," then the whirligig of time may be expected to bring in a great many more revenges. Broadway will soon be ripe for a Rodgers and Hammerstein musicale on the subject of *Male and Female*.

After fifty years of co-education, what about that sag in the heterosexuality quotient?

Why not? If modern jobs are neuter, don't they need a neuter sex to go with them ?

You think that any big ox is a masculine being?

A psychologically differentiated sex structure comes from coalescing boys and girls in the grades?

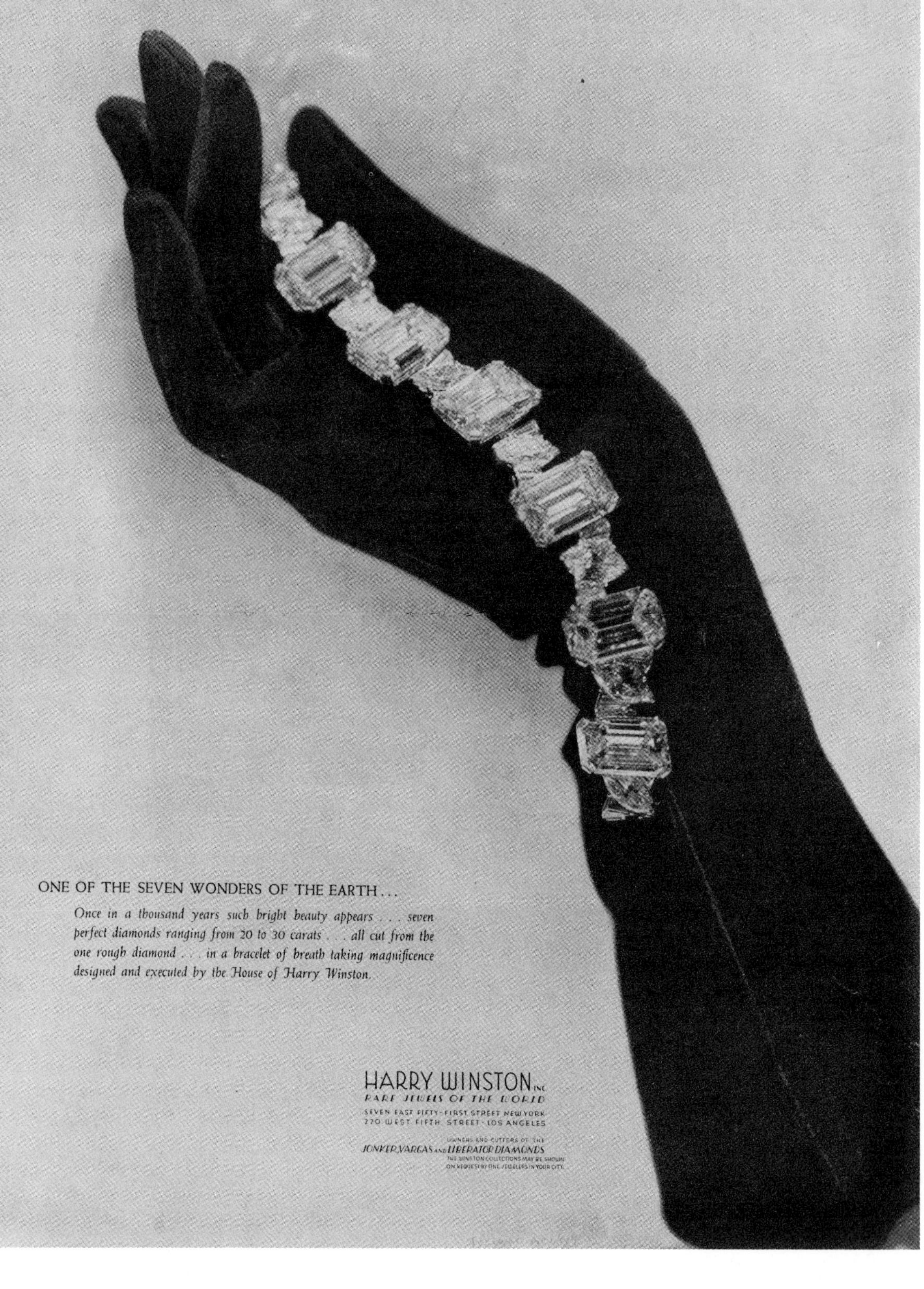
ONE OF THE SEVEN WONDERS OF THE EARTH...
Once in a thousand years such bright beauty appears . . . seven perfect diamonds ranging from 20 to 30 carats . . . all cut from the one rough diamond . . . in a bracelet of breath taking magnificence designed and executed by the House of Harry Winston.
HARRY WINSTON INC
RARE JEWELS OF THE WORLD
SEVEN EAST FIFTY-FIRST STREET NEW YORK
220 WEST FIFTH STREET - LOS ANGELES
OWNERS AND CUTTERS OF THE
JONKER, VARGAS AND LIBERATOR DIAMONDS
THE WINSTON COLLECTIONS MAY BE SHOWN
ON REQUEST BY FINE JEWELERS IN YOUR CITY.

The Poor Rich

In the past, the operation of great wealth has often been to free its possessors from ignoble pursuits and low company and to impose on them a sense of public responsibility. Today that tendency has been reversed.

All that glitters is jitters?

Why are the American rich such proletarians in mind and spirit?

Is there anything more tepid or timid or confused than a modern millionaire? Be careful, the answer may be "Yes."

Should we resent the Soviet aim to impose their flamboyant social caste system on our 'umble rich?

By far the majority of the rich are daily drudges in the same mills as the go-getters who are still on the make, and they work tirelessly at tasks which render the operation of their wealth and power as uncontrollable as that of any other marketeer. Thus, it may very well be that the effect of mass production and consumption is really to bring about a practical rather than a theoretic communism. When men and women have been transformed into replaceable parts by competitive success drives, and have become accustomed to the consumption of uniform products, it is hard to see where any individualism remains. Certainly the sense of personal or private property has become very weak in these circumstances. And the fanatic defenders of private enterprise are mainly those corporation bureaucrats who manipulate the savings of an anonymous crowd of invisible investors.

In practice, then, the very rich today are bureaucrats in their various monopolistic empires of soap, oil, steel, cars, movies, newspapers, magazines, and so on. And they have the minds of bureaucrats. They are timid, cautious conformists. Like anybody else, they accept the doctrine that economic success is rewarded by the power to conform.

Having the money for all the consumer goods, they have arrived. And at that point the success code plays them false. There are no more trees to climb. Having arrived at the top, they find no plateau on which to arrange a spacious and useful existence. As men at the top, they inherit a code of work and play no different from Tom's, Dick's, and Harry's down below them. The English or European businessman, once at the top, used to shift his mode of existence to the squirarchical in a generation or two. He could use his leisure in politics, scholarship, or in patronizing artists directly and personally. But not so today. For us it is the process of arriving that has meaning, not the positive content of possessing ourselves and of enriching our experience and that of others through our wealth and leisure.

This, then, is the dilemma of the behaviorist, the child of Calvinist forebears who saw not in wealth but in the process of acquiring wealth the surest means of defeating the devil's power over idle hands. (See R. H. Tawney's *Religion and the Rise of Capitalism.*) Having lost the Calvinist's motive, we are left only with his behavior patterns.

Consider the plight of the children of the rich. How can they go their parents one better and earn a good conscience for having come up the hard way? Life is dull for these children who cannot share the collective passion of those who hope to be rich. The speed, the struggle, the one-man fury are not for them.

Men of Distinction

In *Time and Free Will*, Henri Bergson puts this question: Suppose some mischievous genius could so manage things that all the motion in the universe were doubled in speed, and everything happened twice as fast as at present? How could we detect this fraud by which we would be deprived of half our lives? Easily, said Bergson. We could recognize the impoverishment of our conscious lives. The contents of our minds would be reduced.

Apply that criterion to those caught in the success trap, where speed is of the essence. What is the state of their minds? What is the content of their lives? Do they not rather despise anybody who pauses long enough to acquire a mental content from reflection or to win a wisdom which will only cut down his speed in making for the goal? And is it strange that those who travel so fast and so light should arrive in a nude and starving condition?

The very conditions of success render the rich suspicious of those failures whom they might be expected to assist. They have no training or taste which would enable them to select struggling artists or writers who might be worthy of aid. In these matters, therefore, they work through the dealers in old pictures or distribute many tiny gratuities through bureaucratic foundations which are run on the most finicky, academic lines. This, of course, overlooks these endowments for hospitals and libraries which are intended as family monuments. And it is not true to say that the rich are niggardly. The point here is simply that they are timid and unresourceful in a way which stands in stark contrast to the zip and push that has put them where they are.

The relative helplessness, social isolation, and irresponsibility of the rich highlights the same situation among those who are striving toward that goal. The circumstances of the struggle insure that the winners will arrive in no condition to enjoy their advantages.

Except in an economic sense, the rich do not even form a class, as, for example, the "film colony" does. So that when distinguished foreigners come to America they naturally seek the company of movie stars rather than of the wealthy. The stars have a personal symbolic relation to the currents of national life which the remote and anonymous figures of celestial finance do not. The stars are distinct individuals wearing human masks that represent some aspect of the collective dream. But the rich are dim and obscure, sharing the tastes and make-up of the very people above whom they have risen, and yet deprived of the satisfactions of mass solidarity in an egalitarian society.

Is it what's in the jigger that makes them bigger?

Why pick on the arts? Hasn't anyone in science or industry ever distinguished himself by drinking whiskey?

What about "Grow old along with me" for a whiskey ad, you snob sifters of the copy agencies?

Swank in every swig or the jig is up? Kilroy was here?

MR. VINTON FREEDLEY, THEATRICAL PRODUCER

MR. RUSSELL PATTERSON, DESIGNER AND ILLUSTRATOR

MR. ADOLPHE MENJOU, MOTION PICTURE ACTOR

SIR HUBERT WILKINS, EXPLORER

MR. HIRAM U. HELM, RANCHER

MR. ROBERT F. SIX, AIR LINES PRESIDENT

MR. ARTHUR LITTLE, JR., PUBLISHER

MR. DANTON WALKER, JOURNALIST

MR. PAUL LUKAS, STAGE AND SCREEN ACTOR

For Men of Distinction... LORD CALVERT

It is only natural that Lord Calvert is the whiskey preferred by so many of America's most distinguished men. For this "custom" blended whiskey... so *rare*... so *smooth*... so *mellow*... is produced expressly for those who appreciate the finest.

LORD CALVERT IS A "CUSTOM" BLENDED WHISKEY, 86.8 PROOF, 65% GRAIN NEUTRAL SPIRITS. CALVERT DISTILLERS CORP., NEW YORK CITY

Snob appeal might seem to be the most obvious feature of this type of ad, with its submerged syllogism that since all sorts of eminent men drink this whiskey they are eminent because they drink it. Or only this kind of whiskey is suited to the palate of distinguished men, therefore a taste for it confers, or at least displays an affinity for, distinction in those who have not yet achieved greatness. If greatness has not been thrust upon you, it is no fault of this ad, which generously thrusts the inexpensive means to greatness upon you. From that point of view there is nothing basically different here from the glamour ads, where *chic* models in posh surroundings prove their automatic mastery over any and every male by embalming themselves in some cream, deodorant, pancake mix, soap, hair wash, or other. Here, it is: "what's in the jigger that makes him bigger?" instead of "what's the trick that makes her click?"

What really emerges from this item is the notion of distinction and culture as being a matter of consumption rather than the possession of discriminating perception and judgment. That brings us to what some anthropologists call "cultural regularity," which is to say, a basic pattern lurking in a seemingly eccentric instance.

This whiskey ad bristles with techniques of persuasion. It is a blatant proclamation on culture as understood today. Consumers of expensive and refined clothes and whiskey, as pictured here, are cultured. They are distinct from the herd.

Recently there has been some panic about a tendency for culture to get out of hand. Russell Lynes, an editor of *Harper's* (*Harper's*, February, 1949), wrote an essay in which he claimed with some alarm that there was in America an emergent intellectual elite. These high-brows he distinguished from middle- and low-brows. Then *Life* (April 11, 1949) backed up the Lynes report with a loud bray that: "These are three basic categories of a new U.S. social structure, and the high-brows have the whip hand."

> To help the readers find their places Lynes, an upper middle-brow, has worked with *Life* to prepare a guidance chart. And for a spirited defense of the high-brow by *Life's* own high-brow, Winthrop Sargeant, turn to page 102.

That is the way the consumer's strait jacket gets tied on. That is the totalitarian technique of stratification by arbitrary cadres and ranks, just as it is the age-old dictator method of "divide and rule." Carve men up into middle-brow Midwestern dentist, or low-brow Eastern salesman, or high-brow Southern agrarian, and you can lead them around by the nose. Any fraction of a man can be sent to war against some other segment of himself; or any group can be panicked by a report about any other group. And, the more superficial the marks of difference, the more ferocious will be the hostility. The guidance chart by which *Life's* readers are to "find their places" is a pictorial one in accordance with consumer categories of clothes, furniture, useful objects, entertainment, salads, drinks, reading, sculpture, records, games, and social and political causes.

In accordance with that chart twenty million *Life* readers tied on their mental strait jackets with mingled feelings of disdain, envy, and shame. (But notice that the wealthy are not included anywhere on the chart.) In so doing they looked furtively at their friends, who, they hoped, were not observant enough to have noticed their partiality for some "lower middle-brow" salad.

This is much more insidious stuff than intelligence-rating or personality quotients. Of course, the fact is that everybody at some time "consumes" nearly everything on the entire guidance chart. The "high-brows" certainly do. But the items in the high-brow section, at once cheap and eccentric, mark these "high-brows" as "the enemies of democratic ways." Such real high-brows as Jefferson and Adams are deprived of their citizenship by this chart, which is an insult to any thoughtful person of any economic or consumer status. By proclaiming a set of social and intellectual distinctions in accordance with consumer goods, the chart ignores and conceals any real basis for such distinctions with a loud Bronx cheer. This is ever the way of *Time* and *Life*, and such is also the way of our cynical ad men.

It would be nonsense to pretend that culture ratings à la Emily Post are not often made in accordance with the consumer mentality. The present ad is only one of thousands which loudly insist on depriving men of their birthrights by rating them in accordance with their supposed preference for some purchased product. And to do so is perhaps a weakness inherent in any market economy. If success can be measured only by purchasing power, then the intellectually creative men with whom the future of mankind always rests will be regarded only as floperoos. Living as they do on $3,000 or so a year without respectful attention to current merchandise, they are easily felt to be unpatriotic: "Oh, our ways aren't good enough for you?" say the satisfied consumers of well-known brands.

The other side of that picture presents the phoney intellectual who takes unto himself the consumer features of the "high-brow"—the pictures, books, and music he hates. In England in the twenties it got so that all the studios of Bloomsbury and Chelsea were crowded with artist apes, millionaire bohemians who paid rentals so high that the real artists had to move out. Something like that happened in Greenwich Village about the same time. Real artists are never interested in arty surroundings.

One of the "high-brow" products of this century is James Joyce's *Ulysses.* In that work Joyce uses the symbolist techniques which Mallarmé, the great French poetic discoverer, had seen in the daily newspaper of 1890. The hero of *Ulysses* is a "middle-brow" Dubliner with a very "low-brow" wife. There is also the ironically presented Stephen Dedalus, the esthete-artist who corresponds to *Life's* resentfully romantic image of the high-brow. But Joyce was a real high-brow, a man of real distinction; that is to say, he was a man who took an intelligent interest in everybody and everything. He occupied simultaneously every corner of *Life's* big consumer chart for helping its readers to find their own isolated cultural category. He was very high-brow, very middle-brow, and especially very low-brow. To write his epic of the modern Ulysses he studied all his life the ads, the comics, the pulps, and popular speech. Nobody who had read Homer or Joyce could be taken in by the chart hoax.

In his admirable book *Music Ho!* Constant Lambert notes again and again that "the most striking feature of the art of our time is the way in which the popular, commercial and lowbrow arts have adopted the technical and spiritual sophistication of the highbrow arts." Jazz, he argues, was born from Debussy, and Debussy is to music what Mallarmé is to poetry. Further analysis would have revealed to Mr. Lambert that this process is not just a filtering down from high-brow to low-brow arts but equally a nourishing of the esoteric by the popular. The few must depend on the many as much as the many stand to gain from the few. That, it is to be hoped, is shown many times in this book.

With this in mind, let us note the trick in the chart hoax which Russell Lynes and *Life* cooked up for more than twenty million readers. By putting the "high-brow" at the top of the consumer list *in place of the rich,* the reader was discouraged from noting that all the other ratings were in terms of economic status. That is why the rich were not fitted into this chart at all. The mythical high-brow had alarmingly usurped the rightful role of the rich. And by representing the "high-brow" as "holding the whip hand" over all consumer categories, they immediately conferred on him the odium of an irresponsible upstart without any claim to the respect which goes to the tough boys who actually do hold the whip hand in business and who can afford to buy "the best."

In America, low, middle, high are consumer ratings, and nothing more. But woe to the indigent intellectual who accidentally acquires a "high" rating without the economic appendages. He is undermining the system. In England, low, middle, and high are caste ratings. So that a low-class English gent feels that for him to pretend to brains would be as absurd as for a poor man to pretend to shrewdness. But those who, like Mr. Lynes and *Life,* pretend to use low, middle, and high as real indications of levels of intellectual activity, are corrupters of the currency of speech and thought. The mind is, in varying degrees, dead or alive, and high and low may be used as an index of vitality. Naturally, the low-vitality mind tends toward the robot categories of Lynes and *Life,* regardless of economic or consumer status. And, just as naturally, the alert and detached mind ignores such categories.

How Not to Offend

A message for all thinking and/or stinking people?

Why all this camp-meeting hysteria about personal hygiene?

Everybody's lonesome because he's a polecat?

If even your best friends won't tell you, and four out of five have it, who is a dog's best friend?

Now we know why Little B.O. Peep lost her sheep?

CLOSELY related to the combination of moral fervor and know-how is the cult of hygiene. If it is a duty to buy those appliances which free the body from toil and thus enable housewives not to hate their husbands, equally urgent is the duty to "be dainty and fresh." Under the scream caption we are told in tones of Kaltenborn unction:

> Too late, when love has gone, for a wife to plead that no one warned her of danger. Because a wise, considerate wife makes it her business to *find out* how to safeguard her daintiness in order to protect precious married love and happiness.

It would take much space just to list the current words and phrases related to B.O. and to "leading the life of Life Buoy." Mouth washes, gargles, tooth pastes, hair removers, bubble baths, skin cleansers, and dirt chasers are backed by long-standing national advertising campaigns. "Even your best friends won't tell you." "Why be an Airedale?" and so on.

The present ad for Lysol, "a concentrated germ-killer," is typical of the shrill melodramatic warnings that accompany these products and should be thought of in connection with the agonies of the daytime soap serials. The colored comics in the Sunday supplements frequently carry six or eight frame spot-dramas of the terrible penalties and dazzling rewards that life hands out to those who are neglectful or careful, as the case may be. In one of these, entitled "Georgie's Black Eye," a twelve-year-old boy is bragging to his mother how he got a shiner for defending her honor at school. Some of the fellows were sneering that her husband was running out on her. She didn't have what it takes to keep a man. Mom, mortified, gets busy with the tooth paste. Soon Dad is waltzing her around the living room and Georgie calls in the fellows to see for themselves. "Gosh," they say, "looks like he's going to haul off and kiss her."

Most of these ads feature ravishing chicks left in sordid isolation because they "offend." Or a young couple on a bench sitting too far apart, the boy sulking. Overhead an old owl says, "Ooh, ooh, no woo." Or a handsome lad with dance card asks, "May I have the last waltz?" to an indignant girl who raps out, "You've *had* it!" Again, two girls are making up a party list and one says, with disgust on her face: "Invite *him*?—Over my dead body!" Of course, he was a swell kid, but: "Of late he had been pretty careless about a rather important thing, and the news got around fast. . . . While some cases of halitosis are of systemic origin, most cases, say a number of authorities . . ."

TOO LATE TO CRY OUT IN ANGUISH!

Beware of the one intimate neglect that can engulf you in marital grief

Too late, when love has gone, for a wife to plead that no one warned her of danger. Because a wise, considerate wife makes it her business to *find out* how to safeguard her daintiness in order to protect precious married love and happiness.

One of the soundest ways for a wife to keep married love in bloom is to achieve dainty allure by practicing *effective* feminine hygiene such as *regular* vaginal douches with reliable "Lysol."

Germs destroyed swiftly

"Lysol" has amazing, *proved* power to kill germ-life on contact . . . truly cleanses the vaginal canal even in the presence of mucous matter. Thus "Lysol" *acts* in a way that makeshifts like soap, salt or soda *never can.*

Appealing daintiness is assured, because the very source of objectionable odors is eliminated.

Use whenever needed!

Gentle, non-caustic "Lysol" will not harm delicate tissue. Easy directions give correct douching solution. Many doctors advise their patients to douche regularly with "Lysol" brand disinfectant, just to insure daintiness alone, and to use it as often as they need it. No greasy aftereffect.

For feminine hygiene, three times more women use "Lysol" than any other liquid preparation. No other is more reliable. You, too, can rely on "Lysol" to help protect your married happiness . . . keep you desirable!

For complete Feminine Hygiene rely on . . .

"Lysol" Brand Disinfectant
REG. U.S. PAT. OFF.

A Concentrated Germ-Killer

Product of Lehn & Fink

NEW! . . . FEMININE HYGIENE FACTS!

FREE! New booklet of information by leading gynecological authority. Mail coupon to Lehn & Fink, 192 Bloomfield Avenue, Bloomfield, N. J.

*Name*__________

*Street*__________

*City*__________ *State*__________

D.M.-4911

Another full-page spread shows a threesome in a panic: "Here comes Herb! For Pete's sake duck!" After Herb goes back to his big car, they go on to say, "There ought to be a law."

Nair, a "cosmetic lotion to remove hair safely" pictures the sun leering at a pair of legs: Have "Second Look" legs! . . . leaves legs smoother . . . more exciting.

For Legs that Delight
Use *Nair* Tonight

Pages could be filled with familiar items like "Kissing is fun when you use . . ." and "Keep daintier for dancing this way," and "Their lost harmony restored by . . ." and "Use *Fresh* and be lovelier to love."

It all adds up to this, that when the hideous specter of body odor looms, all human ties are canceled. The offender, whether parent, spouse, or friend, puts himself outside the law. And when lovely woman stoops to B.O., she is a Medusa freezing every male within sniff. On the other hand, when scrubbed, deloused, germ-free, and depilatorized, when doused with synthetic odors and chemicals, then she is lovely to love. The question remains as to what is being loved, that gal or that soap? There is an age-old notion that healthy body odor is not only an aphrodisiac but a principal means of establishing human affinities.

Implied in the cult of hygiene is a disgust with the human organism which is linked with our treating it as a chemical factory. D. H. Lawrence, rebelling against the puritan culture in which he was reared, insisted all his life that industrialization was linked to the puritan hatred of the body and detestation of bodily tasks. This, he claimed, not only was reflected in our hatred of housework and physical tasks but in our dislike of having servants smelling up our houses while helping with that work. So that the small, hygienic family unit of our cities and suburbs is, from this viewpoint, the realization of a Calvinist dream.

There is an old Huguenot hymn which goes: "Everybody stinks but Jesus." And Kenneth Burke, in his *Ideas in History*, argues that the very synonym for scrupulous cleanliness, "a Dutch kitchen," means a Calvinist kitchen, and that the puritan world has merely substituted soap for the confessional. In the same way, Lewis Mumford in his *Culture of Cities* notes that: "Today, the degradation of inner life is symbolized by the fact that the only place sacred from interruption is the private toilet." Yet in the seventeenth century, when personal privacy was much valued, the highest classes of society openly performed acts of excretion at their *bidets* beside crowded dining tables. But today privacy stinks. The privacy that was once the refreshment of the mind and spirit is now associated only with those "shameful" and strenuous tasks by which the body is made fit for contact with other bodies. The modern nose, like the modern eye, has developed a sort of microscopic, intercellular intensity which makes our human contacts painful and revolting: "We might have had a wonderful life, but now she puts out both the cat and me." This is the world of Jonathan Swift, who foresaw and foresmelt these horrors. His Gulliver in the land of the giants records his disgust with the huge pores and monstrous smells of the Brobdingnagian beauties exactly in the spirit of current ad-agency rhetoric.

Clifton Webb as Lynn Belvedere recently enacted for the movies the role of the impeccable gentleman. In creating this role he has at once embodied mechanical efficiency, moral disdain for ordinary humanity, and horror at human messiness and dirt. He masters people and problems by sheer contempt. This witty role provides genuine insight into the cult of hygiene and the puritan mechanisms of modern applied science. Mr. Webb, as it were, satirically unrolls an entire landscape of related activities and attitudes. In that landscape human reproduction would be effected, if at all, by artificial insemination. "Sex pleasure" would be entirely auto-erotic. The feeding of babies would dispense with the foulness of the human and animal secretion known as milk. The preparation and consumption of food would be conducted in a clinic by white-coated officials. And excretion from the cradle to the grave would be presided over by a special caste of robots, who would care for the victims of such necessities in germ- and odor-proof laboratories.

Fear of the human touch and hatred of the human smell are perfectly recorded by Mr. Webb in his role of Lynn Belvedere, the super baby trainer. They are also a principal theme of Dr. Mead's *Male and Female,* where the reader will discover her indignation that the child's earliest notions of virtue are associated with punctual urination and excretion:

> The clean white-tiled restaurant and the clean white-tiled bathroom are both parts of the ritual, with the mother's voice standing by, saying: "If every rule of health is complied with, then you can enjoy life."

The bathroom has been elevated to the very stratosphere of industrial folklore, it being the gleam, the larger hope, which we are appointed to follow. But in a world accustomed to the dominant imagery of mechanical production and consumption, what could be more natural than our coming to submit our bodies and fantasies to the same processes? The anal-erotic obsession of such a world is inevitable. And it is our cloacal obsession which produces the hysterical hygiene ads, the paradox here being much like our death and mayhem obsession in the pulps on one hand, and, on the other, our refusal to face death at all in the mortician parlor.

Li'l Abner

Will Capp be the first stripper to get a Nobel prize?

Must Capp, like William Faulkner, wait for the French to discover him?

Is there anybody in the audience who knows of anyone who has done more for sanity than Al Capp?

You like Capp? Then you'll like *Finnegans Wake.*

DISNEY went genteel almost as soon as color tempted him to accept the appetizing eye appeal of the food ads. He now offers largely a cotton-candy world, as far as the screen is concerned. Hollywood went genteel long ago, even before the rise of the book clubs. The genteel is a mighty catafalque of service-with-a-smile and flattering solicitude smothering every spontaneous movement of thought or feeling. But from under this catafalque peers the irreverent puss of Al Capp, offering the free of his hand to the fanatical ninnies and nannies of production and sales promotion. Capp is the only robust satirical force in American life.

A young art student in Greenwich Village, confronted with radio hill-billy stuff and feeling the full beat of the big phoney heart of a public which craved massive self-deception—that is the angle of Capp's vision. It is reminiscent of Ring Lardner. Chick Young, creator of "Blondie," hasn't a scrap of Capp's kind of ironic recognition. In comparison, Chick Young has only a formula like *The New Yorker.*

Dogpatch is not in the South. It is not in the country. Rather, it is the country of the ordinary mind insofar as that mind is bamboozled by chaotic imagery from the outside and drugged by sentiment from the inside.

At times Dogpatch is the big-city idea of the country, as when Capp has society swells returning to visit their Dogpatch relations. On such occasions the satire cuts both ways, because there is never a moment of sentimental preference displayed for town or country. When Li'l Abner visits his Boston or New York relatives, it is not to permit city readers to patronize the yokel. Capp wouldn't be seen dead with *The New Yorker* postulate that "our intellectual and social standards offer a real basis for measuring the inadequacies of other sections of the community." Arno, Nash, and Thurber are brittle, wistful little *précieux* beside Capp. Li'l Abner himself is a cluster of the swarming hero images from which Capp extracts now one sample, now another. One day his face resembles a Frankie Sinatra, the next it may have the somber cast of Gary Cooper or the determination of Dick Tracy. Huck Finn, the poor man's Thoreau, is to be read there, too. But, whereas Twain overvalued Huck for his daring indifference to the pressures of feminine social constraints, Capp has no such sentimental illusions. Mark Twain seemed to feel that the alternatives lay between Huck and respectability, between anarchy and a sort of perpetual tea presided over by Emily Post. But Capp is aware of at least the possibility of a world both adult and imaginative. Because of his vigor, he can dispense with the anonymous group sneer of *Time.* He can function as a critically conscious individual.

Li'l Abner, the hundred-per-cent, full-blooded American boy devoted to Salomé, Fearless Fosdick, and muscular narcissism, elicits raucous guffaws from Capp, not because there is anything wrong with girl-shy adolescence but because this figure is really not only the ideal of the adolescent but of so many of the chronologically adult. So Li'l Abner is not a picture of American youth but of the confirmed adolescents of mature years—the people who educate and glorify youth and activism.

It is obvious that Capp finds Mammy Yokum and Daisy Mae relatively satisfactory beings. Their motives are human and intact. It is Pappy and his son who live in a world of trashy delusions. The senile and querulous malice of the elder Yokum is precisely the old age reserved for the hensure types who squander their best energies in maintaining the sentimental illusions of commercially imposed social ideals.

The exuberant fancy which has produced a regiment of Any-Faces and Bet-a-Billion Bashbys is not unlike that of Charles Dickens. Capp creates and forgets in a month enough characters to make the success of half a dozen novels and strips. But such novels and strips will never be written, because only he could keep them in motion. His keen eye for political, commercial, and social humbug is the result of a critical intelligence which is notably lacking at the more respected levels of writing.

Capp looks at the disordered world around him not as a social reformer who imagines that much good would result from a few changes in external features of business and political administration; he sees these situations refracted through the deeply willed deceptions which every person practices upon himself. The criticism which is embedded in his highly parabolic entertainment, therefore, has a complexity which is the mark of a wisdom. He moves in a world of many dimensions, each of which includes and reflects upon the other.

From under the oppressive blanket of merchandising sentiment there hangs out the bare face of the irrepressible Capp, his vitality suggesting that perhaps the obsequies of our popular culture have been prematurely sung.

Orphan Annie

Nobody understands you or loves you? Then join the Daddy Warbucks-Sam Insull league.

The rock-ribbed individualist feels like an orphan in a hostile world?

Why not study the comic strips as moral landscapes expressing local impulse and motive?

The unexamined life isn't worth living? Yes, but who's living anyway?

HAROLD GRAY's strip finds a natural setting and sponsor in the Patterson-McCormick enterprise. From this strip alone it is possible to document the central thesis of Margaret Mead's excellent book, *And Keep Your Powder Dry.* As an anthropologist, Margaret Mead works on the postulate of the organic unity or "cultural regularity" of societies. Her own example of this postulate is that of the sudden fame of a movie star which must be explained to the public as the result not of luck but of know-how. Before being successful, the star had to have her teeth capped, her nose rebuilt, her dresses designed to hide a big tummy, and special music written to distract attention from her clumsy, shambling walk. Her publicity must suggest that any well-fed youngster would have *deserved* the same success.

Working on this postulate of "cultural regularity," the very strangeness of this version of the Cinderella story suggests to the anthropologist that the pressures behind the movie-star publicity are the same as those producing the normal patterns of the same society. And so Margaret Mead concludes that it is our Puritan view that work must be rewarded and that failure is the mark of moral deficiency which is behind the need to make luck appear to be the reward of virtue. For this Puritan view of work versus luck is socially constitutive. It confers cultural regularity. Seeming exceptions will therefore prove to be variations on this theme rather than contradictions of it.

Obviously speaking from her teaching experience, Dr. Mead says: "American girls of college age can be thrown into a near panic by the description of cultures in which parents do not love their children." In our Puritan culture, she insists, where even parental love is unconsciously awarded to the child who is meritorious in eating, in toilet habits, in dress, and in school grades, the majority of children feel insecure because they know they do not merit this parental love. So they fall back on the *instinct* of maternal love, which they feel will insure some small increment of affection even to their unworthiness. When they hear an anthropologist undermine this residual conviction, they become very upset. For, as a famous American educator has remarked, "No one can love unconditionally a child with an I.Q. over 90." The moron may gather in a bit of unearned love, but not the normal child. The ordinary child must be on its toes, brimful of "promise" and precocity in order to assure himself of human affection.

In addition to an anxiety engendered by a parental love awarded on a basis of competitive merit, Dr. Mead points out, the American child is typically limited to the affection of two parents. The very housing conditions nowadays forbid the regular presence of numerous relatives and the generalized presence of the whole community in the form of adopted "uncles" and "aunts":

> So the young American starts life with a tremendous impetus towards success. His family, his little slender family, just a couple of parents alone in the world, are the narrow platform on which he stands.

The plot begins to get exciting at this point in the success story, according to Dr. Mead. For success consists not only in winning the approval of parents but in surpassing them. On that premise rests the American way of life, she says. We must, in the most signal way, show our superiority to our parents in every department, or we have failed to give meaning to their efforts and to our own selves.

In a social and economic sense, success, it would appear, means the virtual rejection of the parents, so that in a symbolic way the child bitten with the success spirit is already an orphan. A Lincoln could stimulate himself with the belief that he was the illegitimate child of an aristocrat, but the child of today, says Dr. Mead, nurses the feeling of being only "adopted."

At this level Tom Sawyer and Huck Finn have a basic position among our folk myths. They are contrasted symbols that focus complex feelings and ideas. Huck is the shiftless, unambitious son of a disreputable father. Impossible for him to earn marks for progressive behavior. He cannot sink, he cannot rise. He simply exists, however gloriously, a horror to the parents but the envy of the boys: snoozing in an old hogshead; publicly and

openly smoking his corn-cob pipe; indifferent to truant officers; hunting, fishing, drifting on a raft. But Tom is a craft on other lines. He is marked out for success. And *he has no parents*. He is the *adopted* child of his Aunt Sally. That means he recognizes that he must make his way by his own wits and energy in an unfriendly world.

And such is the position of Orphan Annie today, in a strip and in a press dedicated to individual enterprise and success. Annie finds affection and security mainly in her dog Sandy, as she circumvents and triumphs over weasel-like crooks and chiselers. Always on the move, brimful of Eden-innocence and goodness, she embodies that self-image of a knight in shining armor nursed in the bosom of every tycoon as the picture of his true self. Girded only with her own goodness, but menaced on every hand by human malice and stupidity, she wins through by shrewdness, luck, and elusiveness.

Apart from Daddy Warbucks (a war profiteer of transcendant virtue), her allies are the little people, who, like Annie, have to contend with the frustrations brought about by bureaucratic bungling and interference. In a recent episode she discovered a fortune of many millions in an old cave, and at once formed a scheme to found orphanages and hospitals. But Washington locked up the cave pending the imposition of taxes, and then, in a forceful move to get at the treasure, blew up the mountain. Result, no orphanages or hospitals.

Daddy Warbucks, the benevolent war profiteer, is less a piece of folklore than of special pleading. His operations are on a world scale, and he maintains private "police" and an information bureau in every country in the world. His great enemy is "the Count," type and pattern of European ruthlessness and corruption. All of which is obvious enough as Republican journalism. But not so Orphan Annie herself. In her isolation and feminine "helplessness" Harold Gray has portrayed for millions of readers the central success drama of America—that of the young, committed to the rejection of parents, that they may justify both the parents and themselves.

Curiously, it is not a theme that "serious" writers have chosen to exploit since Mark Twain. We have here just one instance of popular entertainment keeping in play a major psychological tension in America to which the sophisticated writers are often blind.

Bringing Up Father

What to do with the rejected Father? The white woman's burden?

Why is Jiggs so slow to appreciate the importance of Emily Post?

Is Jiggs first generation?

Does the American immigrant have to reject his father?

THE COMIC STRIP by George McManus is in some ways less adequate to represent the transition between *Life With Father* and "Blondie" than, say, *My Life and Hard Times* by James Thurber. In that book "Father" and "Mother" have simply switched the roles they played in the world of Clarence Day.

Thurber's "Mother" is a flint-eyed, iron-willed, Republican matriarch. His "Father" is an unclassifiable fish. And the children of both Day and Thurber situations have retired to a philosophic knoll to do a little uneasy kibitzing. They constitute a sort of dramatic chorus, making Fanny Hurst noises about the fate which has settled on both their houses. Humor has never appeared more starkly as a device for evading painful realities than in these "funny" books. In fact, these books tell us a great deal that their authors never intended they should.

The situation on which George McManus fixed his eye was partly that of Day-Thurber and partly that of first-generation immigrants who quickly made good and were therefore forced to "understand," or at least to imitate, the domestic patterns of the successful middle class. As working man and woman, Maggie and Jiggs had a *rapport* in which their different roles were fairly well defined for them. But as would-be conspicuous consumers they have no present dignity or meaning for *themselves* at all. The meaning is all in the future. Assuming that a radically different future is the meaning of their lives, they use the present either to forget the past or to invent for themselves an imaginary past which will be worthy of the future they cannot yet grasp.

Another way of looking at the same situation presented in "Bringing Up Father" is provided by Margaret Mead in *And Keep Your Powder Dry*. According to her anthropological categories, we can say that the father of Clarence Day represented the vestiges of a nondynamic, patriarchal social order. The elder Day could think of the Founding Fathers of America as his own ancestors. So he does not think of going *them* one better. But he wishes to maintain his position. Not so Jiggs. Jiggs is first generation. He *has* gone his dad one better. He has made good in a land of opportunity. For Maggie, however, the past and the present are a discord, but she can dream of her grandchildren, at least, as inheriting harmoniously the American past of Washington and Jefferson from which she is excluded. To this end Jiggs is useless to her and to her daughter, partly because his first-generation success entitles him to flaunt the crudity and vulgarity which her daughter must shun. Jiggs has served his purpose. He is a has-been, isolated in his own family. He is an autumn sunset seen against the brewery and the gas works.

So Maggie becomes the aspirant to culture and refinement, urging competitive consumer habits on her daughter. Jiggs is portrayed stubby, crass, almost featureless, dethroned. Maggie is raucous and angular, living the thrills of conspicuous waste, socially aggressive but meeting only snubs and mortification. The appalling exuberance of her cheesecake is a masterpiece of "masculine protest," which hits off the suffragette era to which she belongs. But while a Jiggs had an intense motive toward success in that, having rejected his father and his past, he was obliged to succeed, the next generation will not feel the same pressure. It will want to "settle in" and enjoy the sense of belonging in America. In Thurber's *My Life and Hard Times* the father is just such a second-generation type. Spineless, bewildered, overawed by an aggressive wife who knows that the future belongs to her children, he is a figure of decline in a small prosperous town. He is the sort who bristles with "Americanism" and hostility to "foreigners" and "foreign entanglements." The sort who is ashamed of the un-American speech and habits of his parents.

But the third generation, which has taken over America since 1940, can forget this self-conscious Americanism and really get into the success groove which makes all the dads obsolete every twenty years or so.

Blondie

Putting up with Father?

Why is that shrill, frantic, seedy, saggy little guy so popular?

Why those piratical raids on the icebox?

Is Dagwood the American backbone?

Why is Blondie so crisp, cute, and bossily assured?

It is not without point that Chic Young's strip is now misnamed and that popular use has long since changed its title to "Dagwood." This is because Blondie herself is of no interest. She is a married woman. It is only the sufferings, the morose stupidities, and the indignities of her husband, Dagwood Bumstead, which matter. These make up the diary of a nobody.

Blondie is cute. She started out as a Tillie the Toiler, a frisky coke-ad girl, supposed to be universally desirable because twice-bathed, powdered, patted, deodorized, and depilatorized. But the moment this little love-goddess is married, she is of little interest to anybody but to the advertisers and to her children. And to them she is conscience, the urgent voice of striving and aspiration. To them she apportions affection as reward for meritorious effort. She has "poise and confidence," know-how, and drive. Dagwood is a supernumerary tooth with weak hams and a cuckold hair-do. Blondie is trim, pert, resourceful. Dagwood is seedy, saggy, bewildered, and weakly dependent. Blondie lives for her children, who are respectful toward her and contemptuous of Dagwood. Dagwood is "living and partly living" in hope of a little quiet, a little privacy, and a wee bit of mothering affection from Blondie and his son, Alexander. He is an apologetic intruder into a hygienic, and, save for himself, a well-ordered dormitory. His attempts to eke out some sort of existence in the bathroom or on the sofa (face to the wall) are always promptly challenged. He is a joke which his children thoroughly understand. He has failed, but Alexander will succeed.

Dagwood expresses the frustration of the suburban commuters of our time. His lack of self-respect is due partly to his ignoble tasks, partly to his failure to be hep to success doctrines. His detestation of his job is plain in the postponement of the morning departure till there comes the crescendo of despair and the turbulent take-off. Rising and departure are traumatic experiences for him, involving self-violence. His swashbuckling, midnight forays to the icebox, whence he returns covered with mayonnaise and the gore of catsup, is a wordless charade of self-pity and Mitty-Mouse rebellion. Promiscuous gormandizing as a basic dramatic symbol of the abused and the insecure has long been understood.

The number of suburban-marriage strips and radio programs is increasing. Each has the same theme—model mother saddled with a sad sack and a dope. We are confronted on a large scale with what Wyndham Lewis has described as mothering-wedlock. Each evening the male tends to assume the little-boy role, not only in the hope of reducing the frightening tensions which still attach to his vestigial father role but also to excuse himself from the burden of being a downtown quarterback by day.

It is part of the success of Chic Young's entertaining strip that he glorifies Dagwood quite as much as he glorifies Blondie, the industrial girl. And this, it would seem, is the measure of his inferiority to Al Capp, who refuses to glorify the inglorious. Capp is conscious of what standards he employs; Young is much less so. It was likewise part of Charlie Chaplin's career and fame that he dramatized with wit and genius the pathos of the little man of an industrial world. Chaplin saved himself from the worst effects of his syrupy sentiment by assimilating his little-man-what-now figure to that of the traditional clown. By that means he maintained a taproot reaching down to the deeper terrors and desires of the heart. And by the same taproot and by means of intelligent insight Kafka, Rouault, and Picasso have raised this combination of clown and citizen to levels of tragic intensity.

Chic Young's timidity appears simply in his exploiting, rather than exploring, a popular image of domesticity. In the same way, however, can be seen the failure of many serious American artists and writers to employ the rich materials of popular art. Serious American artists equally pursue not the serious but the genteel by working from the outside, with only the themes and manners of European art and literature. They appear to lack any conviction that the probing of native tradition can bring them into the main current of traditional human experience. When it comes to art, they have the immigrant humility. Perhaps it is part of our willingness to believe that we are "different" from the rest of mankind because we wish to believe that we are better. If that Pollyanna fixation is the root of the trouble, it can scarcely last much longer. Meantime it is the function of the critic to direct serious, controversial attention to the layers of human significance beneath the most banal and evasive features of native tradition and experience.

To put Young's amiable strip in terms of cold anthropological categories, Dagwood is second generation. His father (first generation) made good because he was compelled to do so to justify his rejection of his European father. (Blondie was originally introduced as the elder Bumstead's stenographer.) But Dagwood doesn't feel the same inner tensions. His very desire to belong passively and comfortably in a country in which his father was only a new arrival robs him of his success drive. But Blondie sees and admires the pattern of competitive striving which Dagwood neglects and, rigid with the social cocksureness of the schoolmarm, she points out the arduous path to her children, who are soon to leave the monotonous flats along which Dagwood is idling.

All of which is to say that we are still riding a psychological escalator which seems to raise us above the perennial human problems that will begin to confront the "fourth generation." The present, or "third," generation is once again success-ridden, like the first generation, but it has exhausted the obvious frontiers, leaving its children free to get out of the squirrel cage of success obsession. But has not that interim mechanism of immigrant adjustment served its function? If allowed to continue its operations, would it not prove an instrument of unnecessary mental torture and social perversion?

In short, the prospect of soon reaching, at least for a time, the end of success obsession may prove to be a serious crisis which for many will look like the end of "the American way of life." But Chic Young's strip seems to be assured of survival into a world which will be as alien to it as it already is to McManus's Jiggs. Those who grew up with Dagwood will, like those who grew up with Jiggs, insist on growing old with him. For many millions on this continent Jiggs and Dagwood are fixed points of geniality, beacons of orientation, amid flux and stress. They represent a new kind of entertainment, a sort of magically recurrent daily ritual which now exerts on the spontaneous popular feelings a rhythmic reassurance that does substitute service, as it were, for the old popular experience of the recurrence of the seasons.

Perhaps that is why "the strip must go on" even when authors die. It also suggests a reason for the strange indifference the public has always felt toward the authors of these strips. Even frequent mention of the name of the author does little to disturb his anonymity. Their creations have been caught up in the gentler ebb and flow of habitual existence, serving a very different function from equally popular art forms like the sports page and detective fiction.

The Bold Look

Are we in a new masculine era again?

The face that launched a thousand hips?

Does the Bold Look mean that the crooner and his tummyache are finished?

Are prosperity and male confidence the fruits of war?

Would the face pictured here seek its reflection in the eyes of a career woman?

As FEATURED in this exhibit from *Esquire* (April, 1948), the Bold Look comprises a variety of ingredients, including the sharp-witted reporter of Big Town, the adventuresome private detective, a football coach, and a department-store executive. Even in the comic strips this type has begun to appear with the Buz Sawyers, Rip Kirbys, and Steve Canyons, examples of aggressive, severe, and knowledgeable masculinity. Their adventures frequently include the breaking of feminine hearts, and they are also made to appear as equally capable of cracking a good book. A man who is neither girl-shy nor book-shy is a portent for America.

One effect of World War II in putting millions of men in military uniform was to restore to them a large degree of masculine confidence and certitude. So it was quite early in the forties that a rather ambiguous cry was heard in America: "All Men Are Wolves!" It was partly a cry of dismay, partly one of delicious excitement. About the same time, the vogue of Frank Sinatra began among the bobby-soxers. It may be fanciful to suggest that the rather unwolfish Frankie, a crooner whose professional style invited a high degree of maternal response, came at a time of emotional crisis, and that he was the answer to the maidenly prayers of many who were not prepared to make the sudden shift to fending for themselves among the new wolf pack.

Other barometer readings for such popular entertainers are certainly possible. And if in the preceding sections on Jiggs and Dagwood there has seemed to appear a thesis contradicted by the Bold Look, this is a good place at which to disclaim any interest in defending such a position as the thesis of this book. The social climate differs at various points of the compass, and the object of this survey is to use many kinds of positions and views in relation to the popular imagery of industrial society as a means to getting as clear an over-all sense of the situation as can be done. Using the shifting imagery of our society as a barometer requires range and agility rather than rigid adherence to a single position.

May it not be, therefore, that the Bold Look, vouched for and sponsored by *Esquire*, is a hangover from the masculine confidence developed by the war? It was easy to note during the war that just as Dagwood, as it were, changed into uniform, so Blondie switched into dresses and manners which were often a throwback to the "sweetly feminine" frills and flounces of a period which preceded that of the gristly and emancipated female. And that backward flip got dubbed "The New Look."

To anybody who keeps an eye on such shifts of fashion as signs of really significant social readjustment, a book like Margaret Mead's *Male and Female*

BOLD LOOK.....TH
.....THE BOLD LOOK.....THE

will have especial interest. It represents a radical shift in the social climate. Had Dr. Mead been discussing the same matters even twenty years earlier, she would have made a very different report. But, writing in 1949, she announces, in effect, the end of the sex war which was fought on so many fashion fronts and in so many schools, forums, homes, and offices. In the name of comparative social anthropology she reports that it was a desperate and misconceived affair fought in the face of facts and against the interests of all. Dr. Mead does not seem particularly interested in the causes of that emotionally disastrous struggle which was at a high pitch from 1900-1935. She seems to have given no attention to the powerful pressures of a machine economy to abolish sex differentiation along with the rest of human tradition and experience. But she does come out emphatically for change in a way which chimes exactly with the *Esquire* editorial on the Bold Look:

> Notice anything new about American men? Well-groomed American men, that is—the kind you always notice? They have a new look. We call it the Bold Look. . . . It's a self-confident look and it's as distinctive as it is distinguished. It's as virile as football—as masculine as the Marine Corps—as American as the Sunday comics. And new as it is, it's as mature as the country itself, because it's grown with the country. . . .
>
> The newest styles that are appearing . . . exemplify the Bold Look . . . they're designed with the accent on authority.

Another straw which suggests the wind is blowing steadily from the same quarter appears in *Mademoiselle* (April, 1950), where Bernice Peck writes under the heading of "The Groom's Grooming" across from a full-page photo of a bride who is beaming lyrically at her husband as he shaves before a mirror.

> See? There's really nothing too good for the lug once he's yours. Not if you want him to feel cared about, fussed over and pleased with both of you. Which you do. Just look at the 1950-model bride opposite. She's so new she's just discovering another of Laughing Boy's remarkable talents: he can shave himself. . . . So be darling to your guy and never make fun of his bathroom baritone—Every man is his own Ezio Pinza.

This attitude, it will be agreed, represents an almost comic reversal of familiar folkways. Only a decade ago it was the prim, self-possessed little glamour girl just extracted from the boss's office who expected to hold the center of the stage. And it was that pattern which made of Dagwood the supernumerary tooth.

In the radically different situation reflected in the feature quoted from *Mademoiselle* and also in *Esquire's* Bold Look it is natural for Dr. Mead to suggest once more the advantages of chaperonage for unmarried girls. The unchaperoned girl has to be so self-possessed that when she marries there is little for her husband to possess. She has to be so rigorously self-controlled during several years of dating that she loses her powers of spontaneity and surrender. Hence, says Dr. Mead, our great fantasy stress in song and story on images of utter abandon and wild surrender. These popular fantasies are compensation for the exactly opposite state of affairs brought about by the emancipated woman. A two-page ad for *Stromboli*, featuring an erupting volcano and a midnight storm, carried these captions:

> RAGING ISLAND . . . RAGING PASSIONS!
> THIS IS IT!
> the place:
> STROMBOLI
> the star:
> BERGMAN
> under the inspired direction of
> ROSSELLINI

It is interesting that the face in the *Esquire* feature is carefully selected to avoid the suggestion of anything much above the average. To have exaggerated its masculinity or its intelligence would have been to risk sales resistance. The thoughtful care and prolonged meditation that precedes the maneuvers of pictorial and verbal ad layout is proportioned, on one hand, to the great expense of the ads themselves, and, on the other, to the high stakes toward which they are slanted. And here, in the exact *gearing* between the appeal, the public, and the product, it is plain that the power-nexus and the cash-nexus are one.

The thoughtful observer will find some cause for dismay in the disproportion between the educational budget of the advertising industry and that for the education of the young in school and college. The classroom cannot compete with the glitter and the billion-dollar success and prestige of this commercial education. Least of all with a commercial education program which is disguised as entertainment and which by-passes the intelligence while operating directly on the will and the desires. The result, inevitably, is that the curriculum now wistfully tags along behind the ad industry, and is even becoming geared to that industry.

From Top to Toe

> Macy's Little Shop revives the cape of '68. It's a flutter of Victorian fancy to toss across a shoulder, float above an evening dress, act as buffer to a breeze. . . . From an actual 19th century cape.

THE WORLD of fashion hitched to industrial and market turnover has long been a kaleidoscopic affair. A headline of August 4, 1949, leered roguishly:

> Gable's War On Undies Carried On By De Carlo

After Clark Gable's appearance without an undershirt in *It Happened One Night*, the manufacturers' protests highlighted the close gearing between Hollywood production and the textile marketeers. Yvonne De Carlo got a little publicity by "wearing no undies at all" and thus threatening to wreck "the bra-and-pantie business."

The headlines of a single woman's page go like this:

> Still Attractive If Over 45?
>
> From Top to Toe
>
> Right In Line For Fall
>
> To Be Up To The Minute You Must Sparkle

Vogue (August 15, 1949) boasted of its activities in skimming the best college brains each year in its annual "Prix de Paris" contest. The "Prix" with "about 1300 starters" each year "now plays talent scout for all Condé Nast Publications. In addition, the Prix introduces the contestants to hundreds of other companies in the fashion, publishing, advertising, and merchandising world. . . ."

Quick (May 8, 1950) suggests that beards are back for romantic actors and says:

> Be Quick to watch for the new fashions which may emerge from Broadway's enchanting new hit-production of Barrie's beloved *Peter Pan*. . . . Peter Pan's laced suede jerkin may go off to college . . . Wendy's hooded jersey cape may return for evening.

Men may now put on beards, and women may borrow that little-girl look from *Peter Pan* for a few weeks, but *Quick*, May 29, 1950, warns women to reef in brassieres:

> Veteran showman Ken Murray . . . made a surprising announcement. "Overbustiness is on the way out

---

How often do you change your mind, your politics, your clothes?

Are you properly impressed by what people are saying, seeing, doing, discarding?

Are you in the groove? That is, are you moving in ever-diminishing circles?

Macy★s

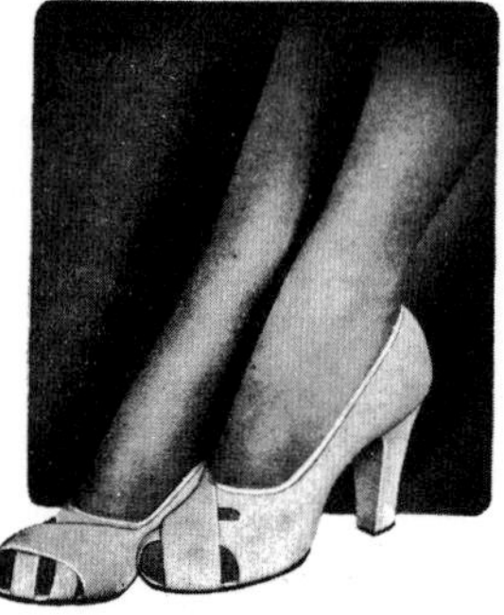

It's a Naturalizer—
famed as "the shoe
with the beautiful fit"

How lovely this white suede pump looks on your foot, too. Because it fits so well, the sides don't gap, the heel won't slip. It's closed in back, sandal-cool at the toe, pretty as can be with sheers and prints. Sizes 4 to 9. Sorry, no mail or phone. New Shoe Centre, Sixth Floor. **9.95**

Also at Macy's-Parkchester

Macy★s

Macy's Little Shop revives the cape of '68

for evening
—in soft
Summer fabrics

It's a flutter of Victorian fancy to toss across a shoulder, float above an evening dress, act as buffer to a breeze. Macy's stylist picked up the pure clinging line of the shoulder, the stole-like style from an actual 19th century cape. We had it copied faithfully for you in the (A.) swish of black rayon taffeta, 11.98, the piquancy of (B.) white Birdseye waffle pique, 9.98 or (C.) white eyelet pique, 8.98, the delicacy of (D.) black lace over net, 11.98. Sorry, no mail or phone orders. All ours alone in The Little Shop, Macy's 2nd Floor.

★**MACY'S PRICE POLICY:** *We endeavor to have the prices of our merchandise reflect at least a six per cent saving for cash, except on price-fixed merchandise.*

as a feminine ideal. What's killing it is television . . . women decided bustiness was the ideal because that's what movies and the stage gave them. But TV, remember, goes right into the living room where kids, their parents and the old folks all watch it together."

Suggestions like these make very explicit the reciprocal connections between *chic* and the entertainment industries. But usually the connections are concealed in dignified verbiage such as this Reuters dispatch from way, way back, on August 9, 1948:

> Paris designers all agree—skirts are going up again. . . . Most general new trend is the directoire. Both Jeanne Lafaurie and Carven claim inspiration with Napoleon's Return from Egypt.

Here the comment is given in the style of stockmarket operations or weather predictions, suggesting the functioning of cosmic laws. It is a very wise clothes designer, we are given to believe, who knows what century it will be tomorrow. It is as though a newsreel were to present a march-past of millions of uniformed people who were automatically, and *en masse,* given a different uniform every minute or so. As everyone can discover by a visit to a movie or actual newsreel of five, ten, or fifteen years ago, the bodily attitudes and the facial expressions of these marchers "abreast with fashion" change with equal suddenness. And the ideas people have of themselves are put on and put off with the same celerity as their clothes.

To assist the gearing of clothes and ideas there are the mechanisms of the book clubs and such big snob levers as *Vogue's* guide to "what people are reading and saying." So that there is really very little time-lag between putting on "the cape of '68" and getting hep to Victorian poetry or glassware for a few hours. The same process is unconsciously at work in the intellectual world, where recently many people complained of having caught "an everlasting cold" during the latest shift of mental costume.

Impersonal, irresponsible, and unconscious as most of this process is, there can be no question that it renders the individual and the mass alike helpless. The more acceleration, the more helpless. And those who call the changes are just as helpless as their victims, because all are equally sold on the joys of immersion in this destructive element.

It must be admitted that the process of fashion itself, as it operates today, is linked to industry in a way which calls for thought rather than drastic programs of direct action. For example, the speed with which people can be popped into the costumes of '68 or those of China, Egypt, or Peru is matched by the modern press, which brings all cultures and ages together in a daily *collage.* (See "Front Page.") So that, from one point of view, the fashion parade can be seen as a preview of a world society being born from the destruction of all existing cultures.

Thus André Malraux's *Psychology of Art* shows how the modern artist, deluged with the art styles of all times and places (thanks to archaeology and anthropology), was obliged for mere self-preservation to seek not *a* style but to penetrate to the essence of the art function and process itself. Exactly the same program is forced upon political and social thought today. Either we penetrate to the essential character of man and society and discover the outlines of a world order, or we continue as flotsam and jetsam on a flood of transient fads and ideas that will drown us with impartiality.

It is here suggested that the outlines of world order are already quite visible to the student of the swirling flood released by industrial technique. And they are to be discerned in the very way in which the flood operates. Poe's sailor in "The Maelstrom" saved himself by co-operating with the action of the "strom" itself.

In the same way we can learn from the art of such moderns as Mallarmé and Joyce analogical techniques not only of survival but of advance. Mallarmé and Joyce refused to be distracted by the fashion-conscious sirens of content and subject matter and proceeded straight to the utilization of the universal forms of the artistic process itself. The political analogue of that strategy is to ignore all the national and local time-trappings of comfort, fashion, prosperity, and utility in order to seize upon the master forms of human responsibility and community. In art this brought about the transformation of the artist from bohemian "victim" to culture "hero." In politics it calls for a proportionate extension of arduous vision.

Looking Up to My Son

THE AD AGENCIES, at least, are never likely to underestimate the power of a woman. Dip into the daytime serial world and you will find the dissatisfaction and anxiety experienced by millions of women who live isolated lives from 8:00 A.M. till 6:00 P.M. They look up to their sons or live for their children because they are unable to find any meaning or satisfaction in the present. In small towns a man often goes home to lunch and spends very little time getting to and from work. In rural society men are within shout of home most of the time, and mother and children are daily witnesses and even assistants of their labors. Even in big cities a few decades ago it was common for home and shop to be closely connected, while in the London of Charles Lamb not only work but the rural countryside could be reached on foot in a few minutes. Under these conditions not only were father, mother, and children often united during the day, but they were close to an intimately known community.

Why do the ad men hitch on to religious art with such unction?

Silver cord or umbilical cord?

And remember, kiddie, you already possess all the qualities of mind your world requires or tolerates.

In these circumstances most of our current marital problems and child-rearing headaches did not exist. And today Le Corbusier, Lewis Mumford, and Siegfried Giedion alike have shown how we may by a reasonable distribution of modern power and by town and country planning enjoy all these lost advantages without sacrifice of any new gains.

The present ad is already a bit old-fashioned because in the past five years mothers have been taught to ask themselves anxiously not "Did I give my baby the right capsules?" but "Did I give my baby an Oedipus complex?" Otherwise the pattern of maternal concentration on the child as a substitute for an absentee father and a defaulting community life remains unchanged.

If Dad is the downtown quarterback whose work is a remote abstraction to his family, and if that work requires endless pep and smiles and an outpouring of psychological energies in narrow and rigid patterns of cheerful confidence, he is likely to remain a little on the adolescent side of maturity. He will tend to be a bore to a woman who has another pattern of existence which includes much leisure to brood on the margin of the full flow of commercial life. Mom begins to "dream of looking up to my son," a son different from his father, a son who will be a much bigger and tougher quarterback. Our ad reads:

> I will help him grow in stature . . . by giving him care which will add inches to his height, help him form straight, sturdy limbs, build a back as erect as a great tree, and develop a mighty chest. This dream I will make come true!

The ad then goes into the familiar routine of treating the body as a factory for producing statistically ascertainable results which will justify the maternal dream.

The most disconcerting fact is the dream itself. It is a dream of aggression geared to an impersonal business community. And it is a dream which, as is shown in other exhibits, isolates business success from every other social quality.

Pictorially, the ad links the most lofty sentiments of motherly devotion and sacrifice to a dream that is unconsciously crude and base. This helps to explain how it occurs that refined and idealistic women in our world are so often the mothers of ruthless men who enslave themselves to the low drudgery of avarice or who live in thrice-heated furnaces of passion for dubious distinction. The objectives of a commercial society, when filtered through the medium of maternal idealism, acquire a lethal intensity. For women don't invent the goals of society. They interpret them to their children. In her

Male and Female, Dr. Mead explores the American paradox of "conditional love," showing from many points of view the emotional structuring which results, especially in boys and men, from affection that is tendered or withdrawn as a reward or penalty, at first for eating and toilet habits, later for assertiveness at school and in business. In this prevalent situation a child or adult merits love only when he is successful. The present ad is that entire drama in capsule form. But the drama is not of recent origin, as Dr. Mead is aware.

The mother pictured here, anxiously and expectantly poised over her child, has been taught to regard the child not as spiritually masculine but as a sexually neutral bundle of potential energy which vocational training will gear to high achievement. Her first job, however, is to pump the maximal number of vitamins and calories into this little chemical factory. And the child soon learns to regard itself as primed for success both by food and facts. The food will insure the big chest and athletic prowess; the facts will answer the sixty-four-dollar questions. Every child today is thus a potential genius, promise-crammed.

The ultimate absurdity of this attitude gets frequent expression in those dog-food ads which exhort us to "nourish every inch of him with old horse if you want to have more fun with him." The ad men for the canned-horse industry have found no better way to sell their product than to parody the ads of the kiddie-food industry.

If it were possible to define success in a great number of ways, a success drive might not be destructive. If there were as many recognized kinds of success as there are temperaments, tastes, skills, and degrees of knowledge, a society dedicated to success might yet develop very great harmony amid variety and richness of experience and insight. As Whitehead put it in *Adventures of Ideas:*

> The vigour of civilized societies is preserved by the widespread sense that high aims are worthwhile. . . . All strong interests easily become impersonal, the love of a good job well done. There is a sense of harmony about such an accomplishment, the Peace brought by something worthwhile. Such personal gratification arises from an aim beyond personality.

But in an industrial world, which measures success in terms of consumption goods, the result of a personal and private success obsession is to exclude most of the varieties of human temperament and talent from the overcrowded race to the narrow goal. Poverty, rather than richness, of experience and expression is the re-

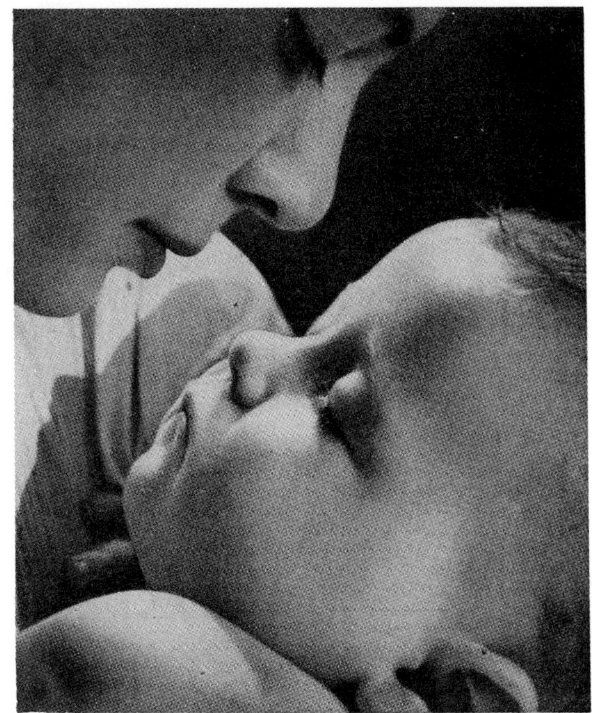

I dream of

LOOKING UP *to my son...*

I see him one day as a man of stature . . . a new-world man

towering free and confident in an untroubled generation.

I WILL HELP HIM GROW IN STATURE . . . by giving him care which

will add inches to his height, help him form straight, sturdy limbs,

build a back as erect as a great tree, and develop a mighty chest.

This dream I will make come true!

A SECRET TO GREATER HEIGHT. To be certain that *your* baby gets enough of a critical element needed for growing bones . . . and to make them hard and sound . . . give him Squibb Cod Liver Oil daily. Squibb's will supply the Vitamin D so essential to help your baby reach his full height, and to help build *a well-shaped head, a fine, full chest, straight legs, a strong back, and sound teeth.* It also provides Vitamin A. Get Squibb's for your baby!

One-half of his full stature attained at the age of two!

Because a baby attains over 50% of his height by the end of the second year, it's of greatest importance to supply enough Vitamin D—by giving Squibb Cod Liver Oil regularly *every day!*

sult. And bitterness rather than quiet self-possession is the state of mind of those not qualified for the narrow goals set up by technological and executive pursuits.

For the failures there is also the sense that they have forfeited the parental and wifely affection which was conditionally tendered during their period of "promise." But even for the successful there is often the sense of paying too much for a success which, after all, does little to satisfy their deeper human qualities or which easily palls on the daily domestic audience. Not to have lived according to the dictates of one's own reason but to have sought, even successfully, goals alien to oneself is no recipe for happiness.

The baby boy in the ad will grow up to say in a thousand different ways: "Look, Mom, I'm dancing! I owe it all to you, Mom!" Every act of his life will be directed to an audience from which he will expect sympathy and approval. Even the epileptic contortions of a Danny Kaye or a Betty Hutton are a popular dramatic expression of these social attitudes and expectations, which were even more vividly rendered by Al Jolson on his knees singing "Mammy." Less obviously, the same insatiable craving for audience approval appears in Clifton Webb's satiric portrayal of the virtuoso of unexpected accomplishments: "They laughed when I took up the vaulting pole," or "when I entered the delivery room," or "when I picked up the conductor's baton." Even if he should be a conqueror who has crushed many other lives, he will still expect sympathy and approval. Dale Carnegie based his *How To Win Friends and Influence People* on the premise that since the typical gangster regards himself as a misunderstood public benefactor, how much more does the respectable businessman require truckloads of adulation to keep him in good humor. Dale Carnegie's jackal strategy is to advise each of us to be an approving mom to the toughies of the world of action so that they will pay and pay to keep us near them. Just keep looking up to these tousled sons with wonder and admiration in your eyes. In all they do, let them know that "mother would approve."

Because the present ad, with its hook-up between mother love, vitamins, and personal ambition, is very centrally located in the dynamics of our culture, it would be possible to relate it legitimately to much more of our world. For it is of the nature of human life to have a consistency of some sort, conscious or unconscious, rational or irrational. It is here assumed that there is some point in bringing as much as possible of our lives within the harmonic scheme of a critically conscious and reasonable order.

Eye Appeal

Does this make you unhappy about your feminine acquaintances? You know the ballad of the long-legged bait?

Napoleon said an army marched on its stomach. Is the pin-up girl the modern substitute for calories—and gals?

Do the Vargas-girl pipe dreams leave a growing girl in doubt about which way to grow?

Has the age-old battle between art and nature entered its last phase?

NOTEWORTHY AS A basic principle for the understanding of the imagery spawned by the modern imagination is Baudelaire's observation that "Intoxication is a number." And numbers, in statistical science, appear as curves. The public is a number which is not only expressed in curves but which is bombarded with curves. When producers want to know what the public wants, they graph it as curves. When they want to tell the public what to get, they say it in curves. The relation between these facts and the present ad, therefore, is not so whimsical as a mere glance might lead one to suppose.

Professor Kinsey has charted the erotic life of the male animal in a series of curves, the co-ordinate axes of which are of the utmost value to producers and distributors of consumer goods. He has stressed the close connection between our highly cerebral sex life and the visual stimulants provided by ads and entertainment. In fact, from the point of view of a producer or distributor, there is much more thrill value in Professor Kinsey's abstract charts or the neural-itch graph of Audience Research, Inc. than in the contours of the lubricious chick who says she goes ga-ga when Big Barnsmell strolls by.

But, for all that, the thrills provided by both kinds of curves are calculated to ensnare and enslave, or to melt and waylay, the spectator. So far as the chick is concerned, there is nothing new in the eager dream of Circean servitude which she engenders. All question of morality aside, it is evident that exuberant feminine nudity does not constitute an environment in which the adolescent or the adult male is going to develop his powers of rational detachment and appraisal. There will be no intellectual flowering or emotional maturity in such a milieu. To see things steadily and to see them whole means something rather specialized to the patrons of a burlesque show, and likewise to the kids who grow up in an environment swarming with pictorial sirens and synthetic, seductive perfumes.

The average male educated in and by this environment tends to be not so much conscious of distinct physical and intellectual objects as he is of a variable volume of registered excitement within himself. Jazz provides an analogy. Its patterns, too, swell or contract as a volume of kinesthesia, or muscular excitement. Jazz selections are numbers; gals are numbers. Some are hot; some, not so hot. Some are sweet, some are sophisticated. Such is the content of the mental life of the Hemingway hero and the good guy in general. Every day he gets beaten into a servile pulp by his own mechanical reflexes, which are constantly busy registering

and reacting to the violent stimuli which his big, noisy, kinesthetic environment has provided for his unreflective reception.

Many an ad boasts of bringing about this state of affairs. For example, the one in *Printer's Ink* for *Better Homes and Gardens:*

It Takes Emotion To Move Merchandise.
[Our Magazine] Is Perpetual Emotion.

The ad even goes on to explain how the stories, articles, and layout of the magazine are "*geared* emotionally and editorially to sway 5,000,000 suburban readers who will buy your product."

Woman in a Mirror

Just another stallion and a sweet kid?

What was that sound of glass? A window gone in the subconscious? Or was it Nature's fire-alarm box?

The ad men break through the mind again?

The Senate sub-committee on mental hygiene reports that it wasn't loaded?

The Greeks manage these matters in myths?

THIS AD employs the same technique as Picasso in *The Mirror*. The differences, of course, are obvious enough. By setting a conventional day-self over against a tragic night-self, Picasso is able to provide a time capsule of an entire life. He reduces a full-length novel (or movie) like *Madame Bovary* to a single image of great intensity. By juxtaposition and contrast he is able to "say" a great deal and to provide much intelligibility for daily life. This artistic discovery for achieving rich implication by withholding the syntactical connection is stated as a principle of modern physics by A. N. Whitehead in *Science and the Modern World.*

> In being aware of the bodily experience, we must thereby be aware of aspects of the whole spatio-temporal world as mirrored within the bodily life . . . . my theory involves the entire abandonment of the notion that simple location is the primary way in which things are involved in space-time.

Which is to say, among other things, that there can be symbolic unity among the most diverse and externally unconnected facts or situations.

The layout men of the present ad debased this technique by making it a vehicle for "saying" a great deal about sex, stallions, and "ritzy dames" who are provided with custom-built allure.

Superficially, the ad shows a horse, which suggests classical sculpture, and a woman as serenely innocent as a coke-ad damsel. The opposition of the cool elements, phallic and ambrosial, provides a chain reaction. The girl in the ad is the familiar Hollywood Bergman type of "somnambule," or the dream walker. Stately, modest, and "classical," she is the "good girl," usually counterpointed against the "good-time girl," who is wideawake and peppy. The stately dream girl comes trailing clouds

Reprinted by permission of the Berkshire Knitting Mills

of culture as from some European castle. Effective advertising gains its ends partly by distracting the attention of the reader from its presuppositions and by its quiet fusion with other levels of experience. And in this respect it is the supreme form of cynical demagogic flattery.

The color in the original ad is described as "borrowed from the sun-soaked gold of a stallion's satin coat. . . the color that's pure sensation. . . for the loveliest legs in the world." The rearing horse completes the general idea. Many ads now follow this method of gentle, nudging "subtlety." Juxtaposition of items permits the advertiser to "say," by methods which *Time* has used to great effect, what could never pass the censor of consciousness. A most necessary contrast to "raging animality" is that a girl should appear gentle, refined, aloof, and innocent. It's her innocence, her obvious "class" that's terrific, because dramatically opposed to the suggestion of brutal violation. Describing his heroine in *The Great Gatsby*, Scott Fitzgerald notes:

> Her face was sad and lovely with bright things in it, bright eyes and a bright passionate mouth. . . a promise that she had done gay, exciting things just awhile since and that there were gay, exciting things hovering in the next hour.

She sits down at the table "as if she were getting into bed."

This sort of thing in Fitzgerald pretty well does what the present ad does. When Gatsby kisses this girl there is a kind of breathless round-up of the ad man's rhetoric.

> His heart beat faster and faster as Daisy's white face came up to his own. He knew that when he kissed this girl and forever wed his unutterable vision to her perishable breath, his mind would never romp again like the mind of God. So he waited, listening for a moment longer to the tuning-fork that had struck upon a star. Then he kissed her. At his lips' touch she blossomed for him like a flower, and the incarnation was complete.

It would seem to take a certain amount of theology to bring off these masterpieces of sentimental vulgarity. A kind of spectacular emptying out of established meanings and significances is necessary to the great thrills. Something important, a man or a thought, must be destroyed in order to deliver the supreme visceral wallop. In the present ad it is "refinement," "naturalness," and "girlish grace" which are offered up. In one movie ad the woman says: "I killed a man for this kiss, so you'd better make it good." Romantic formula for fission?

Husband's Choice

AN AD FOR Auto-Lite spark plugs following the "which twin has the Toni?" pattern asks: "Which Is Really Rosalind Russell? Spark Plugs Also Look Alike, But

---

Love at first flight?

Has the car taken up the burden of sex in an increasingly neuter world?

Have we been rushed into some sort of polygamy by the car?

"There's a helluva good universe next door. Let's go?"

White sidewall tires, as illustrated, available at extra cost.

YOUR KEY TO GREATER VALUE

Ready, Willing - and Waiting

ONLY one thing is needed to complete this picture.

For, the day is bright, as you can see.

The top's down on this tidy Buick Convertible, all ready to let in the wind and the soft, warm air.

Under its bonnet, 150 Fireball horsepower wait the touch of a toe that gives them smooth and quiet-voiced life.

Beneath the floor boards, a modern miracle in engineering called Dynaflow Drive is ready to take shifting off your mind—and put satiny smoothness in all your going.

The seats are wide, deep and restful. Handy controls run windows up or down, adjust the front seat to your comfort, swing the top up at command. A deep-seated frame, big billowy tires and gentle coil springing assure a ride that's like a dream.

In short, here are all the makings of a grand time—except for one thing.

That's you.

To step into this picture, why not step down now to your Buick dealer—see what a whale of a buy this Buick is—find out the happy news about deliveries—and get a firm order in?

BUICK *Division of* GENERAL MOTORS

Tune in HENRY J. TAYLOR, ABC Network, every Monday evening.

When better automobiles are built Buick will build them

. . . Only Wide-Gap Auto-Lite Resistor Spark Plugs Give You

SMOOTHER PERFORMANCE
DOUBLE LIFE

One of the two photographs in the ad is of Rosalind Russell, the other of "charming Florence Williams of Brooklyn, New York, who is often mistaken for Miss Russell." This fact is given in connection with the main verb, as it were: "Millions of car owners are switching from narrow-gap spark plugs to the sensational wide-gap . . . etc." After the "Woman in a Mirror" analysis, this kind of technique of symbolic suggestion will be sufficiently plain.

In the motorcar field this sort of symbolic situation, in which car is set beside girl, has been much followed ever since the "Bodies by Fisher" slogan cut its groove in the brain cortex. The present Buick ad goes far to insist on the car as a date with a dream, a dream with "Dynaflow Drive," "quiet-voiced life," "satiny smoothness," "big billowy tires," and "under its bonnet, 150 Fireball horsepower wait the touch of a toe. . . ."

A Pontiac ad features the face of Lisa Kirk, singing star in the Broadway hit *Kiss me, Kate,* in bridal costume, hovering like a dream over the car. The copy begins:

When You Make a Sweetheart Your Own!

Exactly according to this wedding of allure and engineering is a Kaiser-Frazer ad which features a Nettie Rosenstein model in apposition with the car. The copy plays up the blend of feminine and car bodies and concludes: "P.S. Husbands know that the Kaiser and Frazer are as advanced mechanically as in exterior and interior styling."

It is a common mistake to regard this brand of advertising as a mere "vulgar" effort to hitch sales curves to sex curves. The mistake is made by not observing how girdles and related equipment are sold on an engineering and technological basis: "an all-way stretch and resilient control. Girdle and garters act in harmony to give you a slim hip and thigh line. . . . It lives and breathes with you." The body as a living machine is now correlative with cars as vibrant and attractive organisms. An Ethyl ad reproves those who look on cars as mere vehicles and applauds the man or woman whose car is "as much alive as though it were housed in flesh and blood . . . responding to every mood . . ."

Some clues to this interfusion of sex and technology were given in "Know-How." A general trend to get inside some mechanical strait jacket was shown to be parallel to the situation in which "primitive" men once got collectively and psychologically inside the totem animal. The present ad merely reveals that process in a new setting. And Dr. Mead, while not viewing these matters from the same angle of vision, volunteers the independent observation that: "The beginning of an egoistic valuation of the male organ . . . sets the stage for the little girl's envy . . . that is like her envy of another child's bicycle or roller-skates, an active seeking envy for something you can do something with . . ." Dr. Mead is not considering the car as a "dream date" offered to men, but as it is valued by women. She adds that this envy of the male organ, which in the United States is not a deep psychic wound (as in Europe) but merely desire for an instrument of power, is "expressed most vividly in one form in women's insistence on driving their own motor cars, and in another form in the cult of high breasts and legs."

In both these respects it can be seen how the body gets linked with the desires, sexual and otherwise, for mechanical power. The cult of Superman and rocket ships has a phallic relationship which has frequently been pointed to by psychologists who have not succeeded in carrying the observation past this point of the symbolic reference. But the car ads make it plain that there is widespread acceptance of the car as a womb symbol and, paradoxically enough, as a phallic power symbol.

And the industrial designer, working today in conjunction with Galluputian and marketeer, and just as eager to interpret these public desires as any Hollywood producer, incongruously misapplies streamlining to every kind of mass-produced object. This tendency marks recent decades as much as the organic shell form overran every shape and function in the period of the late baroque. And the fact that streamlining tries to go in two directions explains why, paradoxically, so many examples of it "from automobile to vacuum cleaner become increasingly bloated." The attempt to represent speed and phallic power, so much in demand on the distaff side, is crossed up by the attempt to create a world of "floating power" and womblike comfort and ease. Exactly the same contradiction is expressed in the "sweetheart of a figure," which seems all bust and long boyish legs. The meaning of the twin desires for "comfort and power" could not be more directly stated in terms of sex and technology. The fact that these conflicting wishes are incorporated unconsciously in a wide range of popular objects testifies at once to their prevalence and to the character of the collective trance which prevents the recognition of the tensions.

Magic that Changes Mood

Do you see something that looks like a witch doctor? What you do to me is voodoo?

Want to rip a rug and live in tiger ragtime? We also have fairies at the bottom of our garden?

Do you crave to merge with the primitive terrors of the earliest ages? Let go with a platter.

It was a swell life thirty seconds ago?

THE VERY NAME "Wurlitzer," with its telescoping of "waltz" and "whirl," conveys the idea of vertigo. The face of the machine, with its garish cascade of lights, is like the phosphorescent mask of a tribal witch doctor. And the squat massive bulk of the box resembles those figures of African sculpture in which terror has retracted the limbs, leaving only a torso for contemplation. Also, there is real propriety in applying "magic" to the ensemble of emotions and activities evoked by this machine, whose voodoo spells are hooked mechanically to the nickel slug.

For tribal man space itself is the enemy because charged with voodoo menace. For such a man the beautiful is that which suggests the indestructible or the invulnerable, just as for the time-frayed the womblike security of the limousine is beautiful because a promise of pneumatic bliss. For tribal man space was the uncontrollable mystery. For technological man it is time that occupies the same role. Time is still loaded with a thousand decisions and indecisions which terrify a society that has yielded so much of its autonomy to merely automatic processes and routines. The problem, therefore, is to control panic by "killing time" or by shredding it into "ragtime." To reduce it to an imbecilic bebop point. We seek to hide in the tight bebop moment, as the tribesman hid in the squat spatial unit. As André Malraux says in *The Psychology of Art:* "The more the new demons appeared in Europe, so much the more did European art find its ancestors in cultures that had known the ancient demons."

A European such as Le Corbusier or Moholy-Nagy can get so excited about American jazz because he finds in it many of the most sophisticated techniques of Mallarmé, Debussy, and Picasso. Le Corbusier says in *When the Cathedrals Were White:*

> Negroes have virgin ears, a fresh curiosity. The sounds of life echo in them . . . the grinding of the street-cars, the unchained madness of the subway . . . From this new uproar around our lives they make music.

He sees Manhattan as "hot jazz in stone," offering a focus of attention like that which the Negroes have fixed in a music that is "the equivalent of a beautiful turbine running in the midst of human conversations."

In *Music Ho!* Constant Lambert argues that syncopation in modern music is the symbolist technique of getting cosmic coverage by omission of syntactical connections (see "Front Page"). That, of course, is the literal Greek sense of "symbol"—the putting together of two unconnected things. The abrupt apposition of

The Magic That Changes Moods!

WURLITZER
PHONOGRAPH
MUSIC

Musical Fun for Everyone

The old saying, "Two's company, three's a crowd," doesn't always hold. There are times when every couple longs for music, laughter and the companionship of a crowd.

Whenever you long for such diversion, you will find it wherever there is Wurlitzer Music. Before you hang up your hat, you will be having fun.

Like magic, you will find Wurlitzer Music will change your mood, brighten and lighten your outlook. You will go home refreshed and relaxed for having had a wonderful time. The Rudolph Wurlitzer Company, North Tonawanda, N. Y. ★★★ See Phonograph Section of Classified Telephone Directory for names of Wurlitzer Dealers.

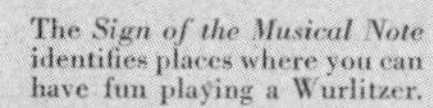

The *Sign of the Musical Note* identifies places where you can have fun playing a Wurlitzer.

THE NAME THAT MEANS *Music* TO MILLIONS

The music of Wurlitzer pianos, accordions and commercial phonographs is heard "'round the world." Wurlitzer, America's largest manufacturer of pianos all produced under one name...also America's largest, best-known manufacturer of juke boxes and accordions, now has in production a great new electronic organ.

images, sounds, rhythms, facts is omnipresent in the modern poem, symphony, dance, and newspaper. Jazz, Lambert suggests, derives from Debussy via New York, rather than from Africa. True or not, it is easy to see that the basic techniques of both high and popular arts are now the same. Eisenstein is certainly of this opinion in his *Film Sense*, when he quotes René Guilleré on the close relation between jazz and cubism. In jazz, says Guilleré:

> Rhythm is stated by angle—protruding edge, sharp profile . . . seeks volume of sound, volume of phrase. Classical music was based on planes . . . planes arranged in layers, planes erected on top of one another . . . all receding into a deep perspective. In jazz all elements are brought to the foreground. This is an important law which can be found in painting, in stage design, in films, and in the poetry of this period.

For the purposes of the present book it is also important to detect this "law" at work all around us because of the intelligibility it releases from such diverse situations. As the unity of the modern world becomes increasingly a technological rather than a social affair, the techniques of the arts provide the most valuable means of insight into the real direction of our own collective purposes. Conversely, the arts can become a primary means of social orientation and self-criticism. As Burckhardt saw, Machiavelli stands at the gate of the modern age, divorcing technique from social purpose. Thenceforth the state was free to develop in accordance with the laws of mechanics and "power politics." The "state as a work of art" becomes unified in accordance with the laws of power for the sake of power. Today we are in a position to criticize the state as a work of art, and the arts can often provide us with the tools of analysis for that job. The arts both as storehouse of achieved values and as the antennae of new awareness and discovery make possible both a unified and an inclusive human consciousness in which there is easy commerce between old and new, between assured success and tentative inquiry and experiment.

No longer is it possible for modern man, individually or collectively, to live in any exclusive segment of human experience or achieved social pattern. The modern mind, whether in its subconscious collective dream or in its intellectual citadel of vivid awareness, is a stage on which is contained and re-enacted the entire experience of the human race. There are no more remote and easy perspectives, either artistic or national. Everything is present in the foreground. That fact is stressed equally in current physics, jazz, newspapers, and psychoanalysis. And it is not a question of preference or taste. This flood has already immersed us. And whether it is to be a benign flood, cleansing the Augean stables of speech and experience, as envisaged in Joyce's *Finnegans Wake*, or a merely destructive element, may to some extent depend on the degree of exertion and direction which we elicit in ourselves.

The magic that changes moods is not in any mechanism. It is critical vision alone which can mitigate the unimpeded operation of the automatic.

The Drowned Man

No harm in a little soft soap or a little clean fun?

You dreamed you went shopping in your bubble bath?

Please, teacher, is this our secret weapon?

A preview of bacteriological warfare?

In a squib which links up with "Magic that changes moods," *Quick* (May 8, 1950) says "For Women Only":

> Be Quick to recapture the nostalgic player-piano music of the past by acquiring the new record album which transfers the peculiar quality of these old rolls to modern phonograph records.

That sort of thing may fairly be designated as a tiny but representative example of trickle from the psychological floodgates. The present ad merely represents symbolically another part of the flood. It appeared in the same issue of *Fortune* (November, 1947) as the editorial in which the flood was described as follows:

> The American citizen lives in a state of siege from dawn till bedtime. Nearly everything he sees, hears, tastes, touches, and smells is an attempt to sell him something. Luckily for his sanity he becomes calloused shortly after diaperhood; now, to break through his protective shell, the advertisers must continuously shock, tease, tickle, or irritate him, or wear him down by the drip-drip-drip or Chinese water-torture method of endless repetition. Advertising is the handwriting on the wall, the sign in the sky, the bush that burns regularly every night. No place on earth is geographically beyond the reach of the hawkers and hucksters; the only oases of peace . . . are the darkened sickrooms of the dying where the customer is not worth bothering. . . .

This flood or barrage is related by the editors to the statement in the Declaration of Independence that all men are created equal:

> Rich man, poor man, beggar man, and thief outlasted the feudal economy—and yet they all come to buy essentially the same wares in the same general markets, subject only to the pocketbook.

The pocketbook is the gland in the new body politic that permits the flood of goods and sensations not to be arrested by our protective shell but to sweep into our lives. This gland compensates for the calloused state that sets in "shortly after diaperhood" and propels us into the dream tunnel of equality and conformity.

It is helpful in getting our bearings in these circumstances to notice the reaction of certain Europeans to the same flood of goods and sensations created by applied science. In 1909, Marinetti, Italian millionaire manufacturer, released his Futurist Manifesto in the Parisian newspaper *Figaro* with Nietzschean *brio:* "We shall

Whether soap's your product—or cereal or shoes—it needs a touch of the dramatic to become the people's choice.

To fill this need—and fill it well—you'll find the most effective means in films. They bring real "theater" to a sales presentation . . . put any product in a bright dramatic light that can hardly fail to win favor.

For films and films alone enable you to tell your sales story within an absorbing plot—with the impact of pictures . . . color . . . action . . . sound. A story that has showmanship—that *sells.*

Real need for showmanship today. With more and more products competing for attention, you need a selling medium with dramatic impact—films. And films are ready. Production, projection, and distribution technics were never better . . . and a commercial film producer is ready to help. Call him in . . . soon.

Eastman Kodak Company, Rochester 4, N. Y.

Business Films

. . . another important function of photography

Kodak

sing the love of danger, the habit of energy and boldness." He had staked everything on the machine with its "vitality" and its "speed." His manifesto is a series of promises and commands, blended, as in an advertisement, in such a way as to release the unconscious pressures and desires of the mind. Nurtured in Schopenhauer's "pessimism" and Nietzsche's "energy," he seized the machine as the true agent of the superman and the only escape from anxiety and esthetic languors:

> We disengage ourselves today from the chaos of new sensitivities . . . to substitute . . . mechanical splendor. It has for its elements the sun relit by the will, healthful forgetfulness . . . controlled force, speed, light, will, order, discipline, method, the instinct of man multiplied by the motor, the feeling of the great town, aggressive optimism obtained by physical culture and sport, the intelligent woman (pleasure, fecundity, business), imagination with no strings attached . . . which characterize touring, big business and journalism, passion for success, the record, enthusiastic imitation of electricity and machine . . . the beneficial precision of cog wheels and lubricated thoughts, the competition of converging energies into one sense of action.

Whitman had already caught some of this monistic lyricism, with its heady intoxication with primal energies and the submerging of the self in the cosmic flood. Mussolini, the jazz addict, was all for this Marinetti extroversion of the self and fusion with the activity of the machine. Hitler preferred Wagner and the introverted megalomaniac dream which hitches the superhuman energies of the machine to the psyche itself. But whatever the nature of this intoxication and lyricism—be it physical or psychological—it fetches up at the same result—the drowned man and the blood bath.

Since we are not yet finally committed to either of these merging courses, we are happily permitted some degree of critical reflection on other alternatives.

The Voice of the Lab

The next voice you hear? The shape of things to come?

Watch out, lad; that thing may contain all of last year's singing commercials.

Isn't it wonderful how the ad agencies create symbols for a general state of mind?

You little culture vulture, you!

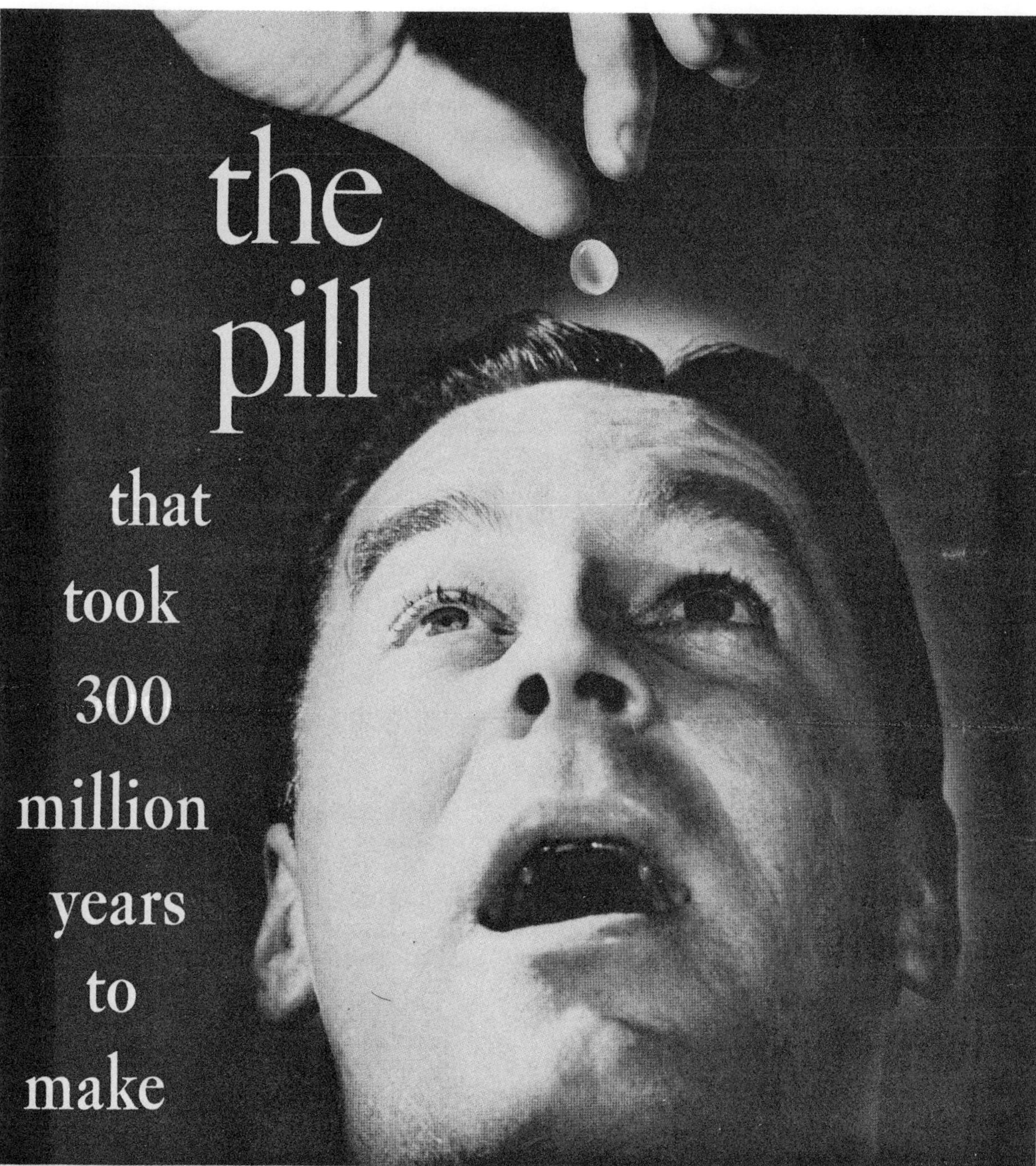

It began before there were men on earth. A mighty forest was crushed deep into the soil and turned into the substance we call coal.

Millions of years later, men learned to extract from coal a tar of many uses. From this tar they derived colorless liquids called quinoline and pyridine, and from these they make a pure white powder which now serves the nutritional needs of people the world over. It is nicotinamide, an important component in the familiar Vitamin B Complex pill.

Barrett's refined coal-tar bases are the source of scores of other medicines, including many of the famous sulfa drugs which have reduced the deadliness of dread diseases. We at Barrett are key suppliers of basic coal-tar chemicals which help you achieve better health and better all-around living.

COAL-TAR CHEMICALS—Benzol, toluol, naphthalene, tar acids, tar bases, solvents, Cumar* resins, products for rubber, etc. BUILDING MATERIALS—Barrett Specification* Roofs, Shingles, Sidings, Roll Roofings, Waterproofing, Rock Wool Insulation, Bituminous Paints. WOOD PRESERVATIVES—Creosote Oil and Carbosota*. PAVING MATERIALS—Tarvia* and Tarvia-lithic*. PROTECTIVE COATINGS—Pipeline Enamel and Waterworks Enamel. NITROGEN PRODUCTS—Anhydrous Ammonia, Sulphate of Ammonia and Arcadian*, the *American* Nitrate of Soda.

ONE OF AMERICA'S GREAT BASIC BUSINESSES

Barrett

THE BARRETT DIVISION
ALLIED CHEMICAL & DYE CORPORATION
40 Rector Street, New York 6, N.Y.

*Reg. U.S. Pat. Off.

A Bell Telephone ad features the Greek god Mercury standing on a tiny globe and chants the praises of its research laboratories under the head:

> The Search That Never Ends

Insofar as science is under consideration in this book, it is not science considered as the passion for truth but applied science, the science geared to the laws of the market. The marketing agents reciprocate by using still more applied science to bring the consumer under exact observation and control.

In *The Art of Being Ruled,* Wyndham Lewis explored this subject, pointing to the unfortunate social effects of the vulgarization of scientific thought. Superficially, this vulgarization of science flatters, consoles, and makes promises exactly in the spirit of the present ad. Popularized science encourages people to avoid many unpleasant truths only to confront them suddenly in practical life with Professor Wiener's type of prospect that the electronic brain will certainly eliminate the ordinary man from the human scene. Or it promises trips to the moon by means of discoveries which, already geared to the war machines, will first reduce the number of available passengers to the vanishing point.

Mr. Lewis locates such paradoxes in the center of an even more complex situation:

> It is plainly the popularization of science that is responsible for the fever and instability apparent on all sides. To withhold knowledge from people, or to place unassimilable knowledge in their hands, are both equally effective, if you wish to render them helpless.

Fever, unrest, instability, liquidation, these are the conditions most favorable to the current market conditions and the ever-pressing need for quick turnover if expenses are to be met. Naturally, therefore, they are the conditions of planned obsolescence, which are fostered, consciously and unconsciously, by every commercial agency of production, publicity, and entertainment. For example, if old movies were as available as old books, the movie industry would collapse into a modest affair.

The Bell Telephone ad points up the relation between science and industry as follows:

> Improvements in industry *can* be left to chance. . . . the other way is to organize so that new knowledge shall always be coming from the researches in the fundamental sciences and engineering arts on which business is based. From that steady stream will arise inventions and new methods.

Yet Professor Wiener assures us that the new electronic brains dwarf the human performance in all utility operations. In the immediate prospect, as he sees it, the only function left for the human mind are pure speculation, on one hand, or the manufacture of ever greater mechanical brains, on the other. Those who are not fitted for either of these arduous pursuits—the great majority of men—will inevitably sink into a serfdom for which they have already been very well conditioned. The life of the great majority will be exactly as pictured in the present ad, except that it will not be just medicine in the pill. All experience, thought, and feeling will be administered in that way. And it is a mistake to think that we have not already come very close to this condition.

It is only necessary to check the comic books and *Reader's Digest* to see the extent of the influence of applied science on the popular imagination. How much it is used to provide an atmosphere of endless thrill and excitement, quite apart from its accidental menace or utility, one can decide from such typical daily headlines as these:

> *London, March 10, 1947, Reuters:*
> ROCKET TO MOON SEEN POSSIBLE
> BUT THOUSANDS TO DIE IN ATTEMPT
>
> *Cleveland, January 5, 1948.*
> LIFE SPAN OF 100
> BE YOUNG AT 80
> ATOM PREDICTION
>
> *Washington, June 11, 1947.*
> SCIENTISTS AWAIT COW'S DEATH
> TO SOLVE MATHEMATICS PROBLEM
>
> *Needham Market, Suffolk, England. (U.P.)*
> VICAR PROPOSES BABIES FOR YEARNING SPINSTERS
> TEST-TUBE BABIES WILL PRODUCE ROBOTS
>
> *Washington, D.C., January 3, 1948.*
> U.S. FLYER PASSING SONIC BARRIER OPENS NEW VISTAS OF DESTRUCTION
> ONE OF BRAVEST ACTS IN HISTORY

Those headlines represent "human interest" attempts to gear science to the human nervous system. It is also the voice of the lab hitched to politics, which is heard in the words of Rear Admiral Oscar C. Badger, as reported in the *Journal-American,* July 21, 1947:

> You have heard people claim that one atomic weapon cannot be resisted. That kind of talk isn't American. Atomic weapons should be a challenge to the people of the United States.

Perhaps time-masks, instead of gas-masks, are to be issued to us in the next war? The time-mask will enable us, in Buck Rogers style, to scoot into the year 24,076 B.C. or 15,425 A.D. by a flick of a wrist-dial. Instead of creeping into the bowels of the earth, science will enable us to hide out in some inaccessible time pocket until the atomic clouds have cleared and biological warfare has quieted down.

The misleading effect of books like George Orwell's *1984* is to project into the future a state of affairs that already exists. Such books distract attention from the present actuality. In the same way spoof books like *Science Is a Sacred Cow* by Anthony Standen provide entertainment rather than insight into the processes by which science gets onto the liability side of the social ledger. That's why *Life* saw fit to give it a big spread.

Genuine science, of course, is neutral. But its practical effects, when harnessed to the appetites of the market, are something less than neutral. Heartbeats are human, but when harnessed to a public-address system, they can be terrifying. Ordinary human appetites for comfort, prestige, or power have in history been troublesome enough, but when they are given exaggerated expression by means of applied science they promise swift destruction.

Love-Goddess Assembly Line

The voice of the lab or the voice of the turtle decides our rapid changes of erotic styles?

Did you notice the Model-T bodies of the women in that revived 1930 movie last night?

Can the feminine body keep pace with the demands of the textile industry?

Are women's legs getting longer? Is the sun cooling off?

It isn't often feasible to arrange exhibits side by side without diminishing their visibility. The risk has been taken in the present instance. The Ivory Flakes ad, "What makes a gal a good number?" and "Nature's Rival" featuring "Four-in-one proportioned girdles," taken together, practically engirdle the globe of the interests of industrial man. When Bergson first introduced his philosophy of flux and *élan vital* to Paris, a wit is reported to have said that "Bergson has put a corset around the Absolute." We expect rather less of philosophy today, since we are content to regard as the Absolute whatever corsets and bras embrace.

These ads are presented here because of their insistence on technique and also because of the special technique they employ. The "good number" item is presented in an X-ray method familiar in motorcar engine displays of "working models." For a while the same ad carried the caption: "What's the trick that makes her click?" "Nature's Rival," by its shadow technique, evokes the aura of science and intercellular photography. The "good number" copy lisps coyly:

> The Girls who get the calls . . . the girls who get the rings . . . are the girls who are in the know. . . . So we show you the inside story of one who has *a way* with her clothes . . .

"Nature's Rival" begins:

> Four Figures—all different, but with one common factor . . . the waist line!

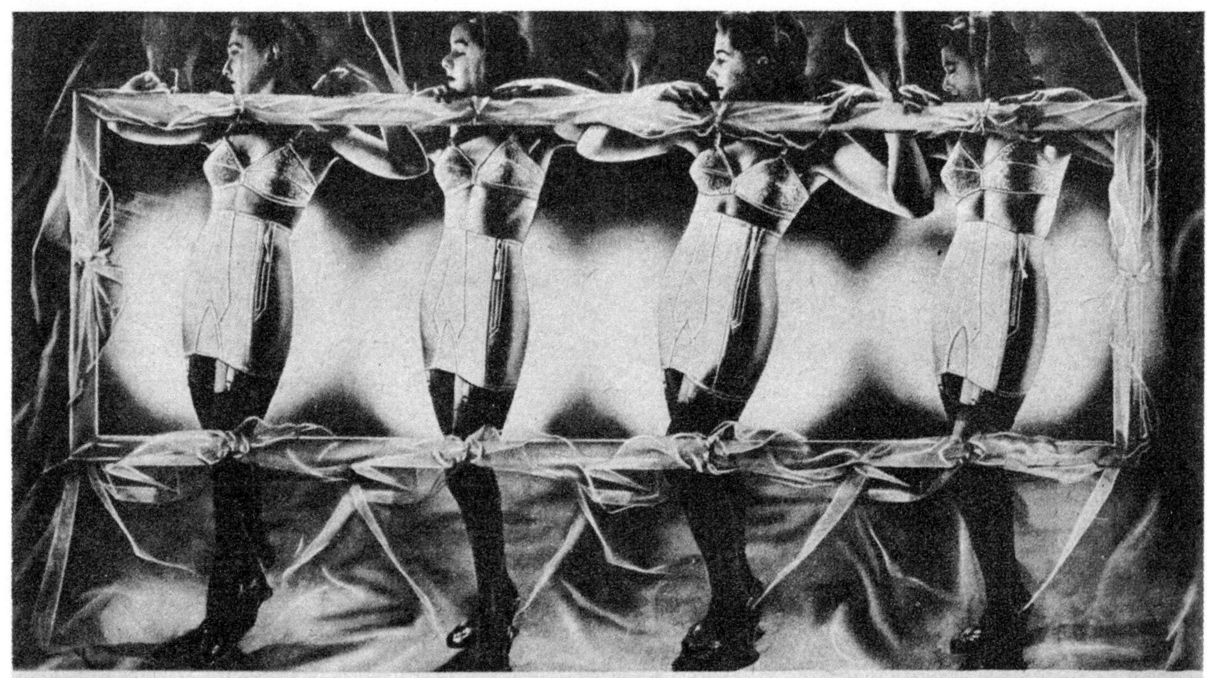

Held within a single filmy frame, these figures are a dream, secure in its irresistibility. The resemblance to "the line" of a beauty chorus is a factor of some interest. The trade motto "Bodies by Fisher" is relevant to the present discussion because it insists on the close relation of motorcar glamour to sex, just as the feminine glamour ads and the modern beauty chorus insist on their relation to the machine.

These two ads help us to see one of the most peculiar features of our world—the interfusion of sex and technology. It is not a feature created by the ad men, but it seems rather to be born of a hungry curiosity to explore and enlarge the domain of sex by mechanical technique, on one hand, and, on the other, to *possess* machines in a sexually gratifying way. For the moment, it will be useful to note some of the more superficial aspects of this strange marriage.

The method of "glorifying the American girl," associated with Ziegfeld, was to assemble them in a line that was then regularly broken up into a dynamic floral vortex. The basic reason for breaking the line was, and is, to form a giant flower, which is choreographed to open and close in a seductive way. But the "line" itself, with its smooth, clicking routines, is even more basic than the sex symbol of the flower. There is nothing very human about twenty painted dolls rehearsing a series of clockwork taps, kicks, and swings. When this very frigid aspect of the beauty chorus was being discussed, Ring Lardner is reported to have made the famous remark: "Some like 'em cold." But there is some sort of

What makes a gal a good number?

THE GIRLS who get the calls . . . the girls who get the rings . . . are the girls who are in the know when it comes to caring for their clothes. So we show you the inside story of one who has *a way* with all her clothes . . . both those that show and those that don't.

Daisy-Fresh:

Her undies are bright and right, of course! Ivory Flakes—gentle care—keep the colors radiant longer . . . guard against fraying straps . . . help keep undies *so* nice and dainty. There's *your* cue: Shun strong soaps, rough handling. Wash your undies in Ivory Flakes—the fast flake form of baby's pure, mild Ivory.

Smooth, Smooth Figure:

And so simple! Frequent washings in Ivory Flakes help her girdle keep its fit longer, wear longer. So her lines stay trim and slim. If that's for you, remember this: Pure, mild Ivory Flakes is one soap fashion designers and fabric experts recommend to pamper the style and fit of your clothes.

Head-turning legs:

Because gentle Ivory Flakes care helps safeguard sheerest nylons from embarrassing, eye-catching runs. Strain tests prove nightly rinsings with Ivory Flakes slow down stocking runs up to 50%!

The full impression:

Color, yes! Colors perk up—brighten up—when you suds your washables in Ivory Flakes. Take this dress of Foreman's Tubrite fabric. Ivory Flakes care helps *preserve* both its fit and color. There's no finer soap than Ivory Flakes—'cause Ivory Flakes are mild and pure—99⁴⁴/₁₀₀% pure!

If it's lovely to wear
it's worth Ivory Flakes care

relation between the dynamo of abstract power which imparts motion to "the line" and the dynamo of abstract finance and engineering which moves the passions of the tired businessmen idolatrously seated in front of that line. "The line" is not carnal or sexy in the way in which the hoofers of burlesque aim to be.

"The revue," wrote Gilbert Seldes in *The Seven Lively Arts*, "corresponds to those de luxe railway trains which are always exactly on time, to the millions of spare parts that always fit, to the ease of commerce when there is a fixed price; jazz or symphony may sound from the orchestra pit, but underneath is the real tone of the review, the steady incorruptible purr of the dynamo." Mr. Seldes finds this wedding of the painted dolls to the "Super Chief" by the priestly dynamo most satisfactory. In the same way, austere Henry Adams, nostalgic for the twelfth-century Virgin of Chartres, unexpectedly found her at the St. Louis World's Fair in 1904. There, faced with a huge electric dynamo, he removed his hat and pronounced the dynamo the twentieth-century equivalent of the twelfth-century "cult of the Virgin."

There may be no point whatever in trying to understand these matters. But for those who suppose that there is something intelligible in such things, the present ads, "the line," as well as the testimony of Mr. Seldes and Henry Adams, are data of importance. They form a pattern which recurs in our world with regularity. Thus, one answer to the ad's query: "What makes a gal a good number?" is simply "looking like a number of other gals"; to the query, "What's the trick that makes her click?" the answer is "being a replaceable part." Just as success and personality know-how consist of recipes and formulas for reducing everybody to the same pattern, we seem to demand, in harmony with this principle, that love goddesses be all alike. Perhaps the impulse behind this self-defeating process is the craving for a power thrill that comes from identity with a huge, anonymous crowd. The craving for intense individuality and attention merges with the opposite extreme of security through uniformity.

There is intoxication in numbers and also release from personal responsibility. Crowds are intoxicating. Statistics and production charts are part of the dithyrambic poetry of industrial man. Telephone numbers of girls who are good numbers, smooth numbers, hot numbers, slick numbers, Maxfactorized, streamlined, synthetic blondes—these are at once abstract and exciting. Girls become intoxicating "dates" when they are recognizable parts of a vast machine. To be seen in public with these numbers is a sure sign that you are clicking on all cylinders. Any interest that they have in themselves is incidental.

The tendency of a minority to react against this situation merely underlines its prevalence. Frederic Wakeman's hero in *The Hucksters* gets a thrill from falling off the "good number" band wagon:

> Her innocence was wonderful. In his world of hep, glamorous dames, he'd forgotten about the jeune fille, thought she had disappeared from life and certainly from the upper east side of New York. And here she was, reincarnated at the age of thirty-two.

Of course, he gets a big bang out of her resemblance to Ingrid Bergman, which puts him back on the consumer band wagon with the well-known brands. Bust 36″, waist 19″, hips 34″, ankle 7″. The poetry of numbers, human curves plotted as an abstract curve.

It is ironic but significant to have a comment on this situation from Cecil B. DeMille. In Hollywood, naturally, the love-goddess assembly line is hooked to the statistical mechanism of box office and fan mail. It was as far back as March 27, 1943, that DeMille was annoyed:

> Trouble is, remarked C.B., they all look alike, "just as though they were stamped out of a mint like silver dollars. . . . They've been coming in one door and going out the other . . . and could keep right on coming in and going out in a continuous circle and I wouldn't know one from the other.
>
> "The girls themselves have nothing to do with this. Many of them are distinctive-looking and different-looking when they arrive. But they don't come out that way. The eyes, the lips, the mouth, the hair, all are done in a certain typed way. Their faces look like slabs of concrete.
>
> "Maybe the average Hollywood glamour girl should be numbered instead of named."

The meaning of this is very different for the student of popular culture, who develops the same sort of eye for morphological conformities as the folklorist and anthropologist do for the migration of symbols and situations. When the same patterns recur, these observers are alerted to the possibilities of similar underlying dynamics. No culture will give popular nourishment and support to images or patterns which are alien to its dominant impulses and aspirations. And among the multifarious forms and images sustained by any society it is reasonable to expect to find some sort of melodic curve. There will be many variations, but they will tend to be variations on certain recognizable themes. And these themes will be the "laws" of that society, laws which will mould its songs and art and social expression.

A. N. Whitehead states the procedures of modern

physics somewhat in the same way in *Science and the Modern World.* In place of a single mechanical unity in all phenomena, "some theory of discontinuous existence is required." But discontinuity, whether in cultures or physics, unavoidably invokes the ancient notion of harmony. And it is out of the extreme discontinuity of modern existence, with its mingling of many cultures and periods, that there is being born today the vision of a rich and complex harmony. We do not have a single, coherent present to live in, and so we need a multiple vision in order to see at all.

At first it is only natural that this way of seeing should be put to the service of discovering the proportions and cleavages within one's immediate time and society, even though that soon proves to be a very provincial affair. And it is here that the ad agencies are so very useful. They express for the collective society that which dreams and uncensored behavior do in individuals. They give spatial form to hidden impulse and, when analyzed, make possible bringing into reasonable order a great deal that could not otherwise be observed or discussed. Gouging away at the surface of public sales resistance, the ad men are constantly breaking through into the *Alice in Wonderland* territory behind the looking glass which is the world of subrational impulse and appetites. Moreover, the ad agencies are so set on the business of administering major wallops to the buyer's unconscious, and have their attention so concentrated on the sensational effect of their activities, that they unconsciously reveal the primary motivations of large areas of our contemporary existence.

In this respect the ad agencies function in relation to the commercial world much as Hollywood does in respect to the world of entertainment. In his cogent study, *The Hollywood Hallucination,* Parker Tyler summed it up in a sentence: "The movie theater is the psychoanalytic clinic of the average worker's daylight dream." That is, the spectator dreams in the darkened theater. He dreams the dreams that money can buy but which he can neither afford nor earn in the daylight world. In the dark theater he dreams the dreams which tend to keep even his frustrations within a dream world.

So Hollywood is like the ad agencies in constantly striving to enter and control the unconscious minds of a vast public, not in order to understand or to present these minds, as the serious novelist does, but in order to exploit them for profit. The novelist tries to get inside his characters in order to tell you what is happening on the invisible stage of their minds. The ad agencies and Hollywood, in their different ways, are always trying to get inside the public mind in order to impose their collective dreams on that inner stage. And in the pursuit of this goal both Hollywood and the advertising agencies themselves give major exhibitions of unconscious behavior. One dream opens into another until reality and fantasy are made interchangeable. The ad agencies flood the daytime world of conscious purpose and control with erotic imagery from the night world in order to drown, by suggestion, all sales resistance. Hollywood floods the night world with daytime imagery in which synthetic gods and goddesses (stars) appear to assume the roles of our wakeaday existence in order to flatter and console us for the failures of our daily lives. The ad agencies hold out for each of us the dream of a spot on Olympus where we can quaff and loll forever amid well-known brands. The movies reverse this procedure by showing us the stars—who, we are assured, dwell on "beds of amaranth and moly"—descending to our level. Thorne Smith seems to have grasped this trick mechanism in his well-known story of the *Night Life of the Gods.*

Yet, had the Hollywood tycoons better understood the function of their own star system, they would not have undermined the system by overcrowding. Floods of new stars and starlets coming off the assembly lines have unconsciously sabotaged the illusion of their being gods and goddesses. Attention is too widely dispersed. The magic is weakening, and many of the dreamers are stirring discontentedly.

Striving constantly, however, to watch, anticipate, and control events on the inner, invisible stage of the collective dream, the ad agencies and Hollywood turn themselves unwittingly into a sort of collective novelist, whose characters, imagery, and situations are an intimate revelation of the passions of the age. But this huge collective novel can be read only by someone trained to use his eyes and ears, and in detachment from the visceral riot that this sensational fare tends to produce. The reader has to be a second Ulysses in order to withstand the siren onslaught. Or, to vary the image, the uncritical reader of this collective novel is like the person who looked directly at the face of Medusa without the mirror of conscious reflection. He stands in danger of being frozen into a helpless robot. Without the mirror of the mind, nobody can live a human life in the face of our present mechanized dream.

The Mechanical Bride

Noticed any very spare parts lately?

Have you got what it takes to hook a date? See us for the highest bid on your old model.

"The walk," "the legs," "the body," "the hips," "the look," "the lips." Did she fall off a wall? Call all the king's horses and men.

Anybody who takes time to study the techniques of pictorial reportage in the popular press and magazines will easily find a dominant pattern composed of sex and technology. Hovering around this pair will usually be found images of hectic speed, mayhem, violence, and sudden death. *Look* and *Life* are only the most obvious places in which to study this cluster of interests. Amid what otherwise may appear as a mere hodgepodge of isolated events, this very consistent pattern stands out. I do not pretend to understand all of it, but it is there for everyone to study, and it is certainly linked to the patterns noted in "Love-Goddess Assembly Line." Many a time have the legs in this exhibit stood on their pedestal by the tall column of *Life's* staff, emblemizing the trick that keeps the big team clicking. They are the slick and visible sign of the dynamo purring contentedly in the Time and Life building, but not only there. And they need to be seen in association with those window displays of car engines on a revolving pedestal, with pistons sliding smoothly while a loudspeaker conveys Strauss waltzes to those on the sidewalk.

To the mind of the modern girl, legs, like busts, are power points which she has been taught to tailor, but as parts of the success kit rather than erotically or sensuously. She swings her legs from the hip with masculine drive and confidence. She knows that "a long-legged gal can go places." As such, her legs are not intimately associated with her taste or with her unique self but are merely display objects like the grill work on a car. They are date-baited power levers for the management of the male audience.

Thus, for example, the legs "on a Pedestal" presented by the Gotham Hosiery company are one facet of our "replaceable parts" cultural dynamics. In a specialist world it is natural that we should select some single part of the body for attention. Al Capp expressed this ironically when he had Li'l Abner fall desperately in love with the pictorial scrap of a woman's knee, saying (January 21, 1950), "Why *not*? Some boys fall in love with the expression on a gal's *face*. Ah is a knee man!" Four months and many lethal and romantic adventures later, Li'l Abner was closing in on the owner of the knee.

The "Phantom Pencil Seam Nylons" ad presents another set of spare parts against a romantic landscape. Some people have heard of "Ideas with legs," but everybody today has been brought up on pictures like these, which would rather appear to be "legs with ideas." Legs today have been indoctrinated. They are self-conscious. They speak. They have huge audiences. They are taken on dates. And in varying degrees the ad agencies have extended this specialist treatment to every other segment of the feminine anatomy. A car plus a well-filled pair of nylons is a recognized formula for both feminine and male success and happiness. Ads like these not only express but also encourage that strange dissociation of sex not only from the human person but even from the unity of the body. This visual and not particularly voluptuous character of commercially sponsored glamour is perhaps what gives it so heavy a narcissistic quality. The brittle, self-conscious pose of the mannequin suggests the activities of competitive display rather than spontaneous sensuality. And the smartly turned-out girl walks and behaves like a being who *sees* herself as a slick object rather than is aware of herself as a person. "Ever see a dream walking?" asks a glamour ad. The Hiroshima bomb was named "Gilda" in honor of Rita Hayworth.

Current sociological study of the precocious dating habits of middle-class children reveals that neither sex nor personal interest in other persons is responsible so much as an eagerness to be "in there pitching." This may be reassuring to the parents of the young, but it may create insoluble problems for the same youngsters later on. When sex later becomes a personal actuality, the established feminine pattern of sex as an instrument of power, in an industrial and consumer contest, is a liability. The switch-over from competitive display to personal affection is not easy for the girl. Her mannequin past is in the way. On the male, this display of power to which he is expected to respond with cars and dates has various effects. The display of current feminine sex power seems to many males to demand an impossible virility of assertion.

Fair tresses man's imperial race ensnare,
And beauty draws us with a single hair.

Men are readily captured by such gentleness and guile, but, surrounded by legs on pedestals, they feel not won but slugged. To this current exaggeration of date-bait some people reply that the glamour business, like the entertainment world, is crammed with both women-haters and men-haters of dubious sex polarity. Hence the malicious insistence on a sort of abstract sex. But whatever truth there may be in this, there is more obvious truth in the way in which sex has been exaggerated by getting hooked to the mechanisms of the market and the impersonal techniques of industrial production.

As early as 1872, Samuel Butler's *Erewhon* explored the curious ways in which machines were coming to resemble organisms not only in the way they obtained power by digestion of fuel but in their capacity to evolve ever new types of themselves with the help of the machine tenders. This organic character of the machines, he saw, was more than matched by the speed with which people who minded them were taking on the rigidity and thoughtless behaviorism of the machine. In a pre-industrial world a great swordsman, horseman, or animal-breeder was expected to take on some of the character of his interests. But how much more is this the case with great crowds of people who spend their waking energies on using and improving machines with powers so very much greater than theirs.

It would be a mistake, therefore, to equate the intensity of the current glamour campaigns and techniques with any corresponding new heights of a man-woman madness. Sex weariness and sex sluggishness are, in measure at least, both the cause and increasingly the outcome of these campaigns. No sensitivity of response could long survive such a barrage. What does survive is the view of the human body as a sort of love-machine capable merely of specific thrills. This extremely behavioristic view of sex, which reduces sex experience to a problem in mechanics and hygiene, is exactly what is implied and expressed on all sides. It makes inevitable both the divorce between physical pleasure and reproduction and also the case for homosexuality. In the era of thinking machines, it would be surprising, indeed, if the love-machine were not thought of as well.

Woman appears as a disagreeable but challenging sex machine in Edmund Wilson's *Memoirs of Hecate County*. But the hero, as an expert sex mechanic, does a skillful job on a variety of these coldly intricate and maxfactorized products of the assembly line. There may be some relation between the fact that England, the first country to develop know-how and industrial technique, was also the first to develop the *ideal* of the frigid woman.

In Budd Schulberg's *What Makes Sammy Run?*, Kit, the heroine, is fascinated by the ferocious little robot that is Sammy. She hates him but is curious to know what it would be like to have this dynamo of pep and drive roaring inside her. With situations of this sort we move over into territory somehow allied to sex and technology but also very closely related to destruction and death. There are some signs that sex weariness may be a factor in the cult of violence, although Wilhelm Reich, the psychologist, argues that it is a mere substitute for sex in those who have acquired the rigidities of a mechanized environment. This view is ably sponsored in G. Legman's *Love and Death*, a study of violence in comic books and literature. And his book certainly doesn't contradict anything said here. But there is surely much to be said also for the view that sadistic violence, real or fictional, in some situations is an at-

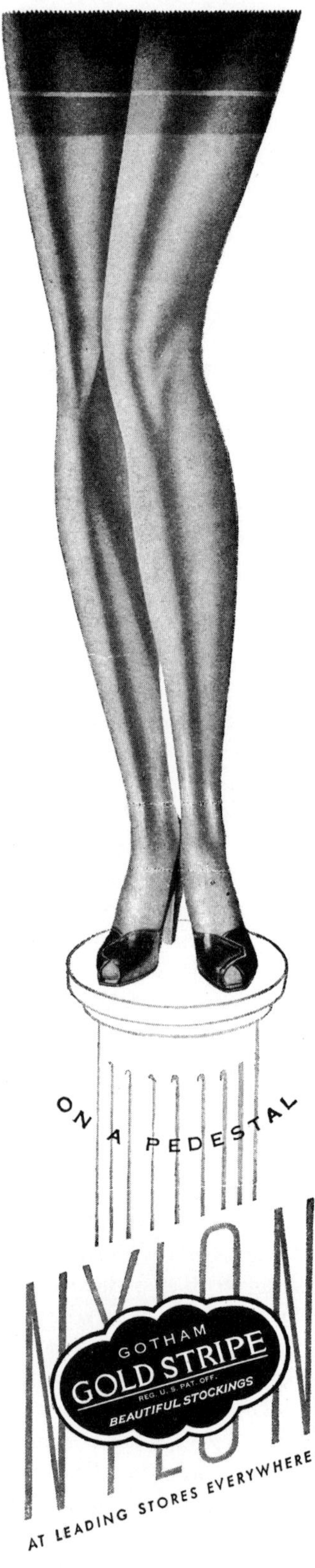

tempt to invade persons not only sexually but metaphysically. It is an effort to pass the frontiers of sex, to achieve a more intense thrill than sex affords. There was certainly a good deal of destruction intermixed with the pleasure ideals of the Marquis de Sade.

A news item of March 2, 1950, reported the five-hour flight of a jet Vampire from coast to coast. When the pilot climbed out, he said only that "It was rather boring." For the satiated, both sex and speed are pretty boring until the element of danger and even death is introduced. Sensation and sadism are near twins. And for those for whom the sex act has come to seem mechanical and merely the meeting and manipulation of body parts, there often remains a hunger which can be called metaphysical but which is not recognized as such, and which seeks satisfaction in physical danger, or sometimes in torture, suicide, or murder. Many of the Frankenstein fantasies depend on the horror of a synthetic robot running amok in revenge for its lack of a "soul." Is this not merely a symbolic way of expressing the actual fact that many people have become so mechanized that they feel a dim resentment at being deprived of full human status?

This is a different way of phrasing what is for Wilhelm Reich only a behavioristic fact. Too simply, he thinks of our machine landscape as an environment which makes people incapable of genital satisfaction. Therefore, he says, they break out in fascist violence. Complete and frequent genital satisfaction from the cradle to the grave is the only way, he suggests, to avoid the recurrence of the age-old vicious circle of patriarchal authority and mechanical servitude. Reflecting on *Moby Dick* in his *Studies in Classic American Literature*, D. H. Lawrence saw deeper:

> So you see, the sinking of the *Pequod* was only a metaphysical tragedy, after all. The world goes on just the same. The ship of the soul is sunk. But the machine-manipulating body works just the same: digests, chews gum, admires Botticelli, and aches with amorous love.

Was it not the mistake of D. H. Lawrence to overlook the comedy in a situation of this type? The human person who thinks, works, or dreams himself into the role of a machine is as funny an object as the world provides. And, in fact, he can only be freed from this trap by the detaching power of wild laughter. The famous portrait of a "Nude Descending a Staircase," with its resemblance to an artichoke doing a strip tease, is a cleansing bit of fun intended to free the human robot from his dreamlike fetters. And so with Wyndham Lewis's *The Apes of God*, Picasso's *Doll Women*, and *Finnegans Wake* by James Joyce—the latter especially being a great intellectual effort aimed at rinsing the Augean stables of speech and society with geysers of laughter. It is not a laughter or comedy to be compared with the whimsy-whamsy article of James Thurber or Ogden Nash. For the latter kind is merely a narcotic which confirms the victim in a condition he has neither the energy not appetite to change.

In a story called "The Girl with the Hungry Eyes," by Fritz Leiber, an ad photographer gives a job to a not too promising model. Soon, however, she is "plastered all over the country" because she has the hungriest eyes in the world. "Nothing vulgar, but just the same they're looking at you with a hunger that's all sex and something more than sex." Something similar may be said of the legs on a pedestal. Abstracted from the body that gives them their ordinary meaning, they become "something more than sex," a metaphysical enticement, a cerebral itch, an abstract torment. Mr. Leiber's girl hypnotizes the country with her hungry eyes and finally accepts the attentions of the photographer who barely escapes with his life. In this vampire, not of the blood but of spirit, he finds "the horror behind the bright billboard. . . . She's the eyes that lead you on and on and then show you death." She says to him: "I want you. I want your high spots. I want everything that's made you happy and everything that's hurt you bad. I want your first girl. . . . I want that licking. . . . I want Betty's legs. . . . I want your mother's death. . . . I want your wanting me. I want your life. Feed me, baby, feed me."

As an instance of how the curious fusion of sex, technology and death persists amid the most unlikely circumstances, the reader may be interested in a display of "Ten Years of *Look*" (October 29, 1946), in which the central picture was a wounded man coming home "to face it all another day down another death-swept road." Flanking him was a sprawling pin-up: "Half a million servicemen wrote in for this one." And underneath him in exactly the same posture of surrender as the pin-up girl was a nude female corpse with a rope around the neck: "Enraged Nazis hanged this Russian guerrilla." If only "for increased reading pleasure" readers should study these editorial ghoul techniques—conscious or not as they may be—and their poetic associations of linked and contrasting imagery.

Perhaps that is what the public wants when it reaches out for the *inside* story smoking hot from the entrails of vice or innocence. That may well be what draws people to the death shows of the speedways and fills the press and magazines with close-ups of executions, suicides, and smashed bodies. A metaphysical hunger to experience everything sexually, to pluck out the heart of the mystery for a super-thrill.

Life, on January 5, 1948, ran a big picture captioned "Ten Seconds Before Death." A Chicago woman called the press and told them she was going to commit suicide. A photographer rushed to her apartment and snapped her. "Just as he took this anguished portrait, she brushed by him, leaped out the third-story window to her death."

This is merely an extreme instance of what is literally ghoulishness. The ghoul tears and devours human flesh in search of he knows not what. His hunger is not earthly. And a very large section of the "human interest" and "true story" activity of our time wears the face of the ghoul and the vampire. That is probably the meaning of the popular phrases "the inside dirt," the "real inside dope." There is very little stress on understanding as compared with the immediate bang of "history in the making." Get the *feel* of it. Put that sidewalk microphone right up against the heart of that school kid who is looking at the Empire State Building for the first time. "Shirley Temple gets her first screen kiss in a picture you'll never forget," and so on.

In all such situations the role of modern technology in providing ever intenser thrills is evident. Mr. Leiber has thus written a very witty parable which shows an intuitive grasp of the mysterious links between sex, technology, and death. Many people were disagreeably surprised by the similar parable of Charlie Chaplin's *Monsieur Verdoux*. The wistful, self-pitying, chivalrous little figure had gone. Here instead was a lady killer in every sense. As Parker Tyler pointed out in his book *Chaplin: Last of the Clowns*, the early Charlie was a man-child seeking the security of the womb in a harsh world. In *Monsieur Verdoux* he in a sense exchanges womb for tomb. In order to have material comfort and security, he is ready to kill. But womb, tomb, and comfort have always been interchangeable symbols in his world. He was the giant killer in his first pictures, the lady killer in his last. The same mechanism of sentimentality dominates both. In other words, his is a popular dream art which works trance-like inside a situation that is never grasped or seen. And this trance seems to be what perpetuates the widely occurring cluster image of sex, technology, and death which constitutes the mystery of the mechanical bride.

Superman

"Superman" was dreamed up by two high-school boys in about 1935. That in itself is indicative of the "science fiction" mentality to which the strip appeals. But this strip works at two levels. It provides fantasies of the usual *Super Science Stories* variety, in which the reader plays hopscotch and leapfrog with the centuries and with solar systems alike, in such stories as "The Voyage that Lasted 600 Years." But "Superman" is not only a narrative of the conquests, actual or imagined, of a technological age; it is also a drama of the psychological defeat of technological man. In ordinary life Superman is Clark Kent, a nobody. As a third-rate reporter whose incompetence wins him the pity and contempt of the virile Lois Lane, his hidden superself is an adolescent dream of imaginary triumphs. While Clark Kent can't win even the admiration of Lois Lane, Superman is besieged by clamorous viragos. Superman accepts a self-imposed celibacy with the resignation of a stamping forge, while Kent is merely resigned.

It was this character and situation which Danny Kaye portrayed in the movie version of *The Secret Life of Walter Mitty*. The Thurber fans protested that the movie was a travesty of Thurber's original Walter Mitty. And it is true that Thurber denies any fantasy triumphs to his character. Thurber prefers to keep Mitty in a state of bitter humiliation, permitting him an occasional frantic revenge.

The attitudes of Superman to current social problems likewise reflect the strong-arm totalitarian methods of the immature and barbaric mind. Like Daddy Warbucks in "Orphan Annie," Superman is ruthlessly efficient in carrying on a one-man crusade against crooks and anti-social forces. In neither case is there any appeal to process of law. Justice is represented as an affair of personal strength alone. Any appraisal of the political tendencies of "Superman" (and also its many relatives in the comic-book world of violent adventure known as the "Squinky" division of entertainment) would have to include an admission that today the dreams of youths and adults alike seem to embody a mounting impatience with the laborious processes of civilized life and a restless eagerness to embrace violent solutions. For the reading public of this type of entertainment cuts across all boundaries of age and experience quite as much as the pressures of the technological world are felt alike by child and adult, by sad sack and sage. Unconsciously, it must be assumed, the anonymous oppression by our impersonal and mechanized ways has piled up a bitterness that seeks fantasy outlets in the flood of fictional violence which is now being gulped in such a variety of forms.

Some readers may be interested in the way in which

Superman or subman?

Fantasy outlet for helpless incompetence?

The man's answer to a machine world is to become a machine?

Do you think the dreams of the modern laboratory expert or corporation head are very different from the feats of superman?

The top brass produces the low dream? Or is it the other way around?

Superman corresponds to the medieval speculations about the nature of angels. The economist Werner Sombart argued that modern abstract finance and mathematical science was a realization at the material level of the elaborate speculations of medieval philosophy. In the same way it could be argued that Superman is the comic-strip brother of the medieval angels. For the angels, as explained by Thomas Aquinas, are quite superior to time or space, yet can exert a local and material energy of superhuman kind. Like Superman, they require neither education nor experience, but they possess, without effort, flawless intelligence about all things. Men have dreamed of becoming like these beings for quite a while. However, fallen angels are known as devils. And imperfect men, possessing superhuman material power, are not a reassuring prospect.

Tarzan

Just as the important fact about Superman is that he is the daydream of the feeble Clark Kent, so the principal feature of Tarzan is that, in civilized life, he is the genteel Lord Greystoke. In fact, pedigrees of the contemporary sleuths, cowboys, toughs, and tycoons intersect at several points. Once the basic postulate of mind-body mechanism went to work in society, curious

To what collective prayer is this amalgam of noble savage and the aristocratic sleuth an answer?

Is it just an accident that Tarzan, the nature force, is unclogged by family life? Just another cowboy?

The Boy Scout to end Nature Lore?

Is Superman's jungle of criminals nearer to us than Tarzan's jungle of beasts?

dualities were bound to spring up in education and popular entertainment. First, the body politic fell apart into the incompatible spheres of business and government. Rousseau popularized the idea of the noble savage and opposed nature to civilization. Then the poet and artist identified himself with nature, and society began to glare at him with distrust. As the world of business encased itself in mechanical routines it envisaged as hitched to the cosmic laws of the universe, the individual was compelled to make endless "adjustments" to the procrustean force. Scorning such soft compliance, however, was the residual aristocrat—the unreconstructed survivor of the wreck of feudalism. Byron became the ultimate archetype of this resistance:

> High mountains are a feeling, and to me the hum
> Of human cities torture.

For the ethics and mealy-mouthed slogans of the new commercial society he felt the same contempt as did Sherlock Holmes or Joyce's Stephen Dedalus.

By 1914, when Edgar Rice Burroughs's *Tarzan of the Apes* was published, the Byronic pose had been thoroughly mixed up with Cooper's noble red men, and Lord Greystoke had inherited Deerslayer's discarded loincloth. Henceforth the jungle rather than the salon became the habitat of the English nobleman. In 1929 the public proclaimed its joyful acceptance of this solution for the social problems of the vanishing blue blood. It was then that Harold Foster began the Tarzan strip based on Burroughs's stories.

Like the sleuth, Tarzan is invincible. Like St. Francis, he talks to the birds and the beasts; like Androcles and Elijah, he is helped by them. Queens lust for him, their Inca-like savagery melting into soft feminine grace at his approach. He picks scores of beautiful maidens from the limbs of trees, the jaws of beasts, or the embraces of apes, and restores them to home and mother, safety and fortune, or bed and board, from which they insist on mass exodus toward his haunts. A nude beauty is as safe in the jungle with Tarzan for a month or two as she would be if she were a wax model in a store window.

Like a disinterested archaeologist, Tarzan lives amid the fragmentary splendors of lost civilizations and forgotten tribes. The rubies and pearls of whole empires stand in neglected piles around him. His values are elsewhere. He stands forth as a secular saint, a monolith of muscular integrity, becoming, like Caesar's wife, as the wit said, all things to all men. The spirit of the Y.M.C.A. and of Kipling and of Baden-Powell—all meet in Tarzan.

The Corpse as Still Life

How high-brow is a corpse? Is this a frame-up?

Would the thriller fan be abashed to learn that the whodunit anticipated the techniques of modern science and art?

Cinema, cubism, symbolism, and thriller use the same method of simultaneous vision by reconstruction?

In the beginning was montage?

730

730

The Case of the Murdered Mistress

The BODY *in the* BED

BILL S. BALLINGER

THE BODY IN THE BED Bill S. Ballinger

WITH GOLDEN HEAD, red lips, blue eyes wide open, the corpse in the picture was, according to the blurb, "strangled in her bed as she waited for her businessman lover to come out of the shower." Barr Breed is the sleuth on the job, and he has "to fight off an assortment of trigger- and sap-happy thugs." Critic Edward Dermot Doyle of the *San Francisco Chronicle* summed up Bill Ballinger's first mystery saying, ". . . the brethren who like their crimes to be rough, tough and nasty will look upon this item as the . . . season's tastiest dish."

As the title of this section suggests, there is a relation between the technique of "seeing" in modern painting and the technique by which the popular modern sleuth "reconstructs the crime." Conan Doyle was not unaware of this when he wrote in *A Study in Scarlet:*

> A study in scarlet, eh? Why shouldn't we use a little art jargon. There's the scarlet thread of murder running through the colorless skein of life, and our duty is to unravel it. . . . Leaning back in the cab, this amateur bloodhound carolled away like a lark while I meditated upon the manysidedness of the human mind.

That is a very frank statement of the theme of detective fiction, namely, its obsession with violent death and human gore, which contrasts with the colorless lives of its readers. This theme makes Holmes carol like a lark, filling him with lyrical excitement. Later in the story Holmes remarks: "In solving a problem of this sort, the grand thing is to be able to reason backwards."

A generation earlier Edgar Allan Poe hit upon this principle of "reconstruction," or reasoning backwards, and made of it the basic technique of crime fiction and symbolist poetry alike. Instead of developing a narrative straight forward, inventing scenes, characters, and description as he proceeded, in the Sir Walter Scott manner, Poe said: "I prefer commencing with the consideration of an *effect.*" Having in mind the precise effect *first,* the author has then to find the situations, the persons, and images, and the order which will produce that effect and no other.

That, for example, is the way T. S. Eliot composes his poems. Each is slanted to a different effect. So that it is not something his poems *say* but something they *do* that is essential about them. And the same is true of most significant painting and poetry since Poe and Baudelaire. Yet the baffled sections of the audience still seem to expect such work to deliver some message, some idea or other, and then they kick the cigarette machine, as it were, when it won't deliver the peanuts.

As for the detective story, which embodies the popular form of this new technique, what is necessary before writing one is not just the awareness of the *effect* but of the solution to the crime. The detective-story writer has to invent a murder and a solution for it, just as the jigsaw-puzzle maker has to have a complete picture before he carves it up into bits. Once the time sequence for the murder has been laid out in order of the occurrence of events leading to it, the author then begins backwards. That is, he introduces the reader to the corpse. The reader is convinced that he can reconstruct the crime by noticing the exact arrangement of details at the scene of the crime. He gets this notion from the procedure of the sleuth, who studies the corpse in its exact layout as a great critic would examine a masterpiece of painting. Murder, indeed, as De Quincey noted, has been united to the fine arts.

In order to keep the reader fooled, the writer has only to syncopate one or two items in the time sequence of events or to narrate occasionally by flashback. Meantime, while the reader's excitement mounts, the sleuth is made to seem busy reconstructing the crime. Narration by flashback is now used by almost all novelists, since it provides an oblique light, a richly varied view of character and action. In addition, the method of the sleuth *does* have some relation to contemporary science as well as to art. One of the procedures in modern chemical research, for example, is to take a compound or a chemical reaction and then to work backwards from that to the *formula* which will produce that compound or reaction.

The sleuth pursues his clues backwards to the cause which produced them. He investigates the possible motives of each suspect. Then he assembles all these different perspectives as though he were piecing together a movie that had been shot in separate sections. When all is assembled, he then projects, as it were, the continuous film before the assembled house guests at the scene of the murder. He relates the events in their true time sequence, thus *automatically* revealing the murderer.

It was Poe who discovered the technique of this intellectual cinematograph half a century before the movie camera was invented. And just as movie "stills" when projected in sequence can reconstruct human actions, so the mental movie of the sleuth reanimates the corpse in order that the reader may see exactly how and why he was killed.

From DaVinci to Holmes

Why are both scientist and artist crackpots and pariahs in the popular imagination?

Holmes, Renaissance titan or Last of the Mohicans?

Watson, wife or mother of the virtuoso of crime?

The sleuth cult foreshadows the arrival of the police state?

JOYCE'S FAMOUS REMARK that, "though he might have been more humble, there's no police like Holmes," contains a world of insight. It includes the modern world and elucidates it at the same instant. Joyce explored popular phraseology and heroes with a precision which this book cannot emulate. In the above phrase which refers to "no place like home," Joyce diagnoses the collapse of family life and the rise of the police state amidst a welter of sentiment which is partly rosy and partly lethal. Homes are now a part of a police system. Holmes, the home-hater and woman-hater, is the hero of the "home-loving" and feminized middle class. The arrogant, sterile Holmes and the happy prolific homes of the late Victorian world are fused in a single image which arrests the mind for contemplation and insight. The passion for Holmes and man-hunting literature (which gives the modern world a major point of correspondence with the symbolic figure of Nimrod and the tower of Babel) goes along with the commercial passion for exploiting the values of childhood, femininity, and domesticity. On paper there has never been such a cult of the home. In entertainment there has never been such a cult of the sleuth.

To provide in a few words a pedigree for the figure of the sleuth who dominates thriller fiction may not be very convincing. The quickest way to get a view of the matter is via Holmes, Kipling, and Darwin. However, Kipling's Mowgli and Edgar Queeny's "granitic believer in the law of the jungle," when taken together, open up interrelations between familiar vistas.

In the opening paragraph of Doyle's *A Scandal in Bohemia,* Holmes is described as follows:

> He was, I take it, the most perfect reasoning and observing machine that the world has seen; but, as a lover, he would have placed himself in a false position. He never spoke of the softer passions save with a gibe and a sneer . . . Grit in a sensitive instrument, or a crack in one of his own high-power lenses, would not be more disturbing than a strong emotion in a nature such as his.

Here is the split man of the head-versus-heart, thought-versus-feeling type who appeared in the early seventeenth century. But it was not until Darwin that the head (science) became definitely and consciously antisocial. Mr. Queeny derives his "law of the jungle" versus "crusading idealist" from this later nineteenth-century phase of the older split.

Could anything exceed the sentimentality or the lavish emotion with which Doyle (and all other writers of crime stories) embellish the figure of the detective? It is through the eyes of some doting Watson, dim of brain, or the dewy eyes of the female secretary, wistfully adoring, that the superman is seen and felt by the reader. This Nietzschean figure achieves his self-dramatization not directly, like the nihilistic malcontents of the Elizabethan stage, but on the inner stage of a mass dream. The sleuth is a recognizable descendant of the heroes who died in the odor of Seneca, but here he lives on, indestructibly, to report his own cause to the unsatisfied. Like the malcontent, the sleuth embodies an attitude, a personal strategy for meeting an opaque and bewildering situation. Both reject the attitude of submission and adjustment to obvious social pressures, affirming themselves as vividly as they can. But where have we met Doyle's description before? Writing in 1868, Thomas Henry Huxley said:

> That man, I think, has had a liberal education who has been so trained in his youth that his body is the ready servant of his will, and does with ease and pleasure all the work, that as a mechanism, it is capable of; whose intellect is a clear, cold, logic engine, with all the parts of equal strength, and in smooth working order; ready like a steam engine to be turned to any kind of work. . . .

To many people in 1868 this sentimental robotism didn't seem especially laughable as a "human" ideal. Perhaps not everybody even today would be prepared to recognize it for the lethal formula that it is. The connections between "the law of the jungle," "the spirit of enterprise," and "ringside seat" for the diesel-engine show become evident. Between "The Sparrow versus the Hawk" spirit in education and society, and the Holmes-Huxley-Kipling circuit, the relationship appears in Doyle's views of education in his inventory of Holmes's intellectual tools:

1. Knowledge of Literature—Nil
2. Knowledge of Philosophy—Nil
3. Knowledge of Astronomy—Nil
4. Knowledge of Politics—Feeble
5. Knowledge of Botany—Variable, well up in belladonna, opium and poisons generally
6. Knowledge of Geology—Practical but limited
7. Knowledge of Chemistry—Profound
8. Knowledge of Anatomy—Accurate
9. Knowledge of Sensational Literature—Immense. He appears to know every detail of every horror perpetrated in the century.

In addition, Holmes is a violinist, an all-round athlete, and a lawyer. That is what Doyle considered the ideal mental kit for the man-hunter. Note the slavering chop-smacking stress on Holmes's "immense" erudition in mayhem and murder. That is seemingly the price our world has paid for developing a mind that it sentimentally regards as a cold logic engine. And the curious reader will find it profitable to consult Wyndham Lewis's *Art of Being Ruled* on the nature of the modern scientist's obsession with the romance of destruction.

Let us get the habit of looking very closely at the detached scientific mind, to see whether its boasted detachment amounts to very much besides not choosing to link the significance of one part of its actions to other parts. In short, is its "detachment" just irresponsibility? Sherlock Holmes had about as much detachment as Buck Rogers or those who worked on the first atomic project and later dramatized the business for *The March of Time*, ardently playing themselves in this great melodrama of destruction.

Doyle, in common with his age and ours, was obsessed with the psychic stench that rose from his own splintered ego. This stench was not something that he understood or studied, like a Kirkegaard or a Baudelaire. But in it he lived and wallowed with strictly sensational satisfaction, like that passionate fondler of little girls, Lewis Carroll. A better test case for investigation than the sleuth himself would be hard to find, because by every test he is the superman of our dreams.

Even a Hemingway or a Steinbeck has a firmer grasp of realities and is much less emotionally involved in a merely tiny aspect of human affairs than a Doyle or the typical scientist. And it is worth noting the obvious contrast between the Hemingway hero and the sleuth. The sleuth acts, while the Hemingway hero suffers. The one dishes it out, the other has things done to him. The humanitarian victim type would seem to stem from the period of Don Quixote. His ineffectual benevolence becomes the typical mode of Fielding's *Tom Jones* as also of the romantic heroes of Scott, Thackeray, and Dickens. Nothing could be less like the aggressive and resourceful sleuth than these familiar figures from romantic fiction past and present. They suffer violence. The modern detective evokes it. So that there is a good deal of point in the claim that detective fiction is scientific. For the popular notion of the scientist as the center of a world of fantastic violence and malignity not only coincides with the world of violence portrayed in detective fiction but with the quality of much scientific vision and speculation.

The superman of thriller fiction, then, is a representative of an attitude for which all classes and conditions in our society have either an open or secret admiration. His pedigree, therefore, must be viewed with some curiosity. Among the common features of all sleuths is, first, their individualism and lonely pride; next, their man-of-the-worldishness; third, their multifarious but specialized learning; and, fourth, their passion for action and excitement. All four of these notes are also features of the Renaissance virtuoso. Since then they have become the marks of "the aristocratic type," especially as embodied in the English public-school boy; but there is no space here to trace the stages by which the intense individualism of this Renaissance scholar-courtier-soldier combination (mainly known to us by Hamlet) became in the Lovelace of Samuel Richardson's *Clarissa* and for the middle classes of the eighteenth century the representative of feudalism and the Devil. Yet the connection for the commercial or trading mind between the haughty aristocrat and the Devil is perfectly plain for the age of the Marquis de Sade, Lord Byron, Poe, and Baudelaire. It would be impossible to exaggerate the fascination which Byron held for the soul of the Watsonian shopkeeper and his family. Byron was the embodiment of the masochistic middle-class dream. The mixture of fear, awe, admiration, and revulsion which he inspired was such that henceforth all rebellion against the spirit of hawking and huckstering takes in large measure the Byronic form. That is how, for example, the image of the disdainful aesthete was achieved—a mold into which the shopkeeper's son could easily pour himself, since it embodies not only disgust with trade but devotion to beauty.

Dupin, the first detective, is thus an aesthete and a dandy. He was created by Poe, himself the aesthete and the dandy. Holmes arrived some decades later. The Byronic markings are strong on Holmes. Also the quarterings of the aesthete in his capricious interest in music, in "murder as a fine art," and his contempt for domesticity. That the preoccupation with crime is, equally in Poe and De Quincey, an expression of sadistic revolt against a sordid world devoted to money and the police protection of "ill-gotten gains," needs very little investigation. That the lonely aesthete-detective is at once a rebel against the crude middle-class conformity and also a type of extreme initiative and individualism helps however to explain the ambiguity of his appeal for the same middle class. He is at once a type of disinterested aristocratic superiority and of middle-class failure to create new social values. It is easy to note in this the same ambiguity that presides over commercial ads which feature simultaneously quality and cheapness, refinement and availability.

However, a major feature of the modern sleuth notably absent from Poe's Dupin is the quality of the man-hunter. The superman features don't change from Da Vinci to Byron and Heathcliff, but the man-hunting

proclivities, the endless sniffing out along the road to the supreme metaphysical thrill of murder, are not evident until Holmes. Byron and Poe were content with the aura of incest as a mark and gesture of antisocial thrill and also of emotional avarice. Baudelaire, Rimbaud, and Wilde explored other sexual variants of the antisocial. But murder, the cerebral itch to hunt down the inmost guilt and secret essence of man, that is the thrill sought by the man-hunter and shared by the thriller fans. Of course, it is vaguely present in all confessional literature of the romantic period, but usually in connection with other interests. Whereas in the literature of crime detection the concentration of specialized thrill is crudely focused on the hunt and the kill.

During the fifty years between Poe's Dupin and the appearance of Holmes, the European cult of Fenimore Cooper's redskins provides the necessary explanation of the rise of that hybrid of aesthete and man-hunter which dominates the popular mind today. The noble savage, utterly above society and commerce, with his unspoiled faculties of a superhuman perfection and keenness, his nose for danger, his eye for clues, and his stomach for scalps— here is the complex image built up sentimentally by Rousseau, digested by Darwin, and expressed by Doyle as the type at once of the sleuth and of the scientific mind.

A better instance of the network of the varied roots of popular culture would be hard to find. Important for present purposes is the fact that the complexities of such popular images as that of the sleuth are subterranean. So with the current image of the "businessman" or the "scientist." The indiscriminate cluster of items included in these images becomes in turn a means of "popular thinking" about society and politics. But real thinking or discrimination can't begin until the cluster has been considered genetically and analytically.

The scientist, the businessman, the artist, the extrovert, and the expert are only especially obvious examples of deep confusion to themselves and the popular mind alike. And the work of James Joyce, tightly linked as it is to popular imagery, is also deeply purgative of its confusion. Thus in *Ulysses* Stephen Dedalus is the ironic type of the aristocratic-aesthete-rebel and Leopold Bloom is obviously enough the type of the middle-class Watsonian worshiper of the artist as Lucifer, as Faustus, as Superman. As a mature artist Joyce had fully explored the entire genealogy of the "popular" images of the "artist" and the "middle class," in the course of which he included both of them in a wider action. For both are sentimentally muddled reflexes of each other. Just as Mr. Queeny's dual personality of crusader for human ideals and cold granitic believer in the law of the jungle ("The Spirit of Enterprise") represents not two things but one thing, or one thing and a dozen unexamined postulates and motivations. Mr. Queeny is as much a sentimentalist about "business" as the newspaperman about "human interest" or the aesthete is about "art."

The popular sleuth thus offers a window onto a complex psychological landscape. This landscape includes the figure of the superman as he has taken his stand on all the moral, political, and scientific issues of the West from Da Vinci to Holmes. It also includes the platform at Elsinore and the ghost-stricken figure of Hamlet. Hamlet the Dane saw one ghost. The modern Hamlet stares at a whole assembly. And not least among these is Philip Marlowe, Chandler's echo of Christopher Marlowe's supermen Tamburlaine and Dr. Faustus, that Nietzschean politician and scientist.

First Breakfast at Home

This time for keeps? Farewell to the typewriter?

Do many people accept scenes like this as commodity commands?

Home was always like this?

If she has the right brands of goods, life can be beautiful for a lonely suburban housewife?

First Breakfast at Home

You'll never forget the half-shy wonder of it.

Oh, it has to be special. Your prettiest trousseau housecoat. A man-size breakfast for this man who is suddenly, wonderfully your husband.

And on your best breakfast cloth . . . your most-precious International Sterling, the solid silver with beauty that lives forever. "Family silver," that you can hand down to your grandchildren.

Among all the superb artist-designed International patterns, there's one to fit into your dreams.

Choose a pattern of exquisite simplicity . . . a delicate floral . . . or a masterpiece of rich carving. You'll find one that seems dream-meant for you.

News for your purse! Prices on famous International Sterling have not been raised! Service for 8, as little as $148.25. A single place setting for as little as $19.65. Ask your dealer about his easy purchase plan . . . set a table of shining beauty this very night.

International Sterling

Note Your New Laugh Time

It's a new day and a new time for *The Adventures of Ozzie and Harriet.*

Now, instead of Sundays, tune in this hilarious show *every Friday Night* at 9:30 p.m., E.S.T. over the Dominion Network.

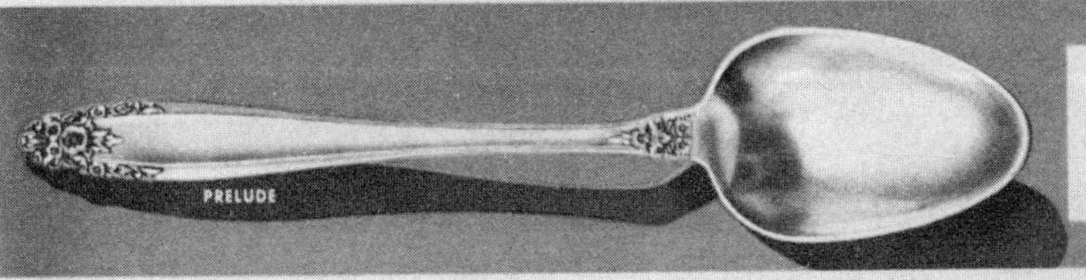

"PATTERN OF THE MONTH" is PRELUDE, one of International's more lavish Sterling patterns, ornamented by a rich, but dainty floral motif. See PRELUDE featured at your Silverware Dealer's all during April.

THIS AD BELONGS, perhaps, with another group of ads like "This Time for Keeps," which flash open a set of multiple perspectives on complex family problems and which call for a whole book to provide adequate comment.

The ad offers a view of "One Man's Family." Its object is to present a radiant image of upper-class comfort and commodities suggesting an aristocratic level of leisure and style within the range of a very average pocket. That is the standard come-on, and we are just beginning to appraise its cumulative effect in human terms. It would seem to be a formula inherent in an industrial economy. To create the widest possible market it is not only necessary to produce cheaply, but it is even more necessary to stimulate a constant readiness to discard habits and possessions alike. Market turnover calls for human turnover.

Thus, by endless stress on exclusiveness and fashion, the consumer can be made extremely conscious of the shabby character of the article he bought last year or five years ago. To go on using it in opposition to the new models becomes not just eccentricity but a complex challenge to the consumer community. To be without at least some of the new models marks a man as an economic failure. Or he is niggardly, or he is lacking a decent respect for the opinions of his neighbors.

These consumer pressures in turn affect the entire character of a society. The eye is anxiously turned on the neighbor or friend with a "How do I measure up?" "Do I rate?" This, in turn, brings about a tendency to live not only in terms of present commodities but of future ones. Unrest is present no matter what may be the present house, car, job. Living is done in terms of a future which cannot be seen rather than in terms of present human or material possibilities. And it is not so much that the future is thought of as better but as different. It is not a human future but only the shadow of next year's models.

The present ad pictures a corner of a home as typically presented in the numerous *American Home* or *Better Homes and Gardens* productions. These magazines, carefully geared to both the purse and heartstrings of their respective reader groups, feature houses and rooms in which almost nobody ever lives—certainly not the readers. These magazines would be useless commercially if they portrayed any scenes or homes that were already possessed by the income group to which they appeal.

And Hollywood and the star system are more or less consciously geared to the same calculated exaggeration. If the scene is from the village past of the leading character, it must be such a past as never was, but it must be one suited to the present eminence of the star. Excepted from this endless faking of the future and of pasts to fit the unreal present are gangsters and dead-end kids. They are off the consumer track.

An ad like this, then, is a machine for taking spectators for a ride. Our job here is to keep an eye out for the many views which that ride is not intended to reveal to the straphanger.

Understanding America

Don't run but look again, Reader. Find the Mechanical Bride.

In the second picture-story the car has been substituted for the sultan? Or for the harem?

Moral: You, too, can be a harem cutie in a gas-station?

THE THEME of the present ad is one which recurs in a series of appeals sponsored by the Oil Industry Information Committee: "Understand rivalry and you understand America." It might appear from this ad that the big men in oil suspect that the public regards them as oily sultans surrounded by sleek and slippery blisses. The point which they wish to get across to the public is that they are really a huge democratic crowd of eager beavers dedicated to the business of making life beautiful for your car. The picture story, however, releases a number of unintentional effects which constitute a more profund argument than "understand rivalry and you understand America." In fact, the picture story really says: "Understand our kind of rivalry and you understand why your car is somebody and you are nobody."

Another ad from the same industry featured a Mark Twainish scene in which three lads were performing feats on a board fence to dazzle a girl. The opening sentence of the copy read: "There's a lot more to this picture than three little boys competing for a maiden's favor." That is quite true, just as in the present ad more appears than is intended to appear. The technique of the three-boys-and-a-maiden item is to provide a whiff of *Tom Sawyer* or *Mother's Album* as an anesthetic for any brain cells that persist in keeping active in spite of a big kinesthetic extrovert way of life. Let the people have freedom, and let others have the power. Especially the power to tell them they are free and that they are consumed with the spirit of rivalry and success.

The *Tom Sawyer* world of "the days of real sport" featured in the above-mentioned ad makes a direct appeal to the emotions which are generally felt to give power to the drives of practical life. By comparison, the sultan and his harem dwindling into the citizen and his car is a weaker ad. The sex-drive as the success-drive gets lost in the gas station. But both ads illustrate the kind of inspirational art that is exhortation to a way of living. From this point of view ads can be seen as a kind of social ritual or magic that flatter and enhance us in our own eyes. What Kipling was to the aggressive British imperialists, these ads are to our domestic economy. They act as a sort of firing spark in the internal combusition engine.

Traditional folklore consists of the arts of song and dance of agricultural and nomadic peoples. But an industrial world cannot produce the same folk forms as can a society in a state of harmonious equilibrium with the soil and the seasons. Yet much of the industrial world's entertainment and public expression is just as unconsciously expressive of its inner life. Our hit-parade tunes and our jazz are quite as representative of our inner lives as any old ballad is of a past way of life.

Take one person... who has everything to himself... and you have a monopoly.

Take thousands of firms... that strive to out-do rivals... and you have the oil business.

NOWADAYS, well-informed people smile when the word "monopoly" is used to describe the oil business. They know the facts prove the exact opposite.

The truth is there are thousands of individual firms of all sizes in the oil business. Each competes in its field—producing, refining, transporting or marketing—with rivals to win *your* favor.

That's why more and more oil is discovered. That's why more than 1200 different oil products have been developed. That's why ways are always being found to make your fuels and lubricants better and better. That's why you pay the *lowest* oil prices in the world for the *finest* oil products in the world.

Competition is just as much a part of the oil industry as wells or refineries or service stations. It's standard equipment.

Thousands of oil companies mean competition...
competition means progress...
progress means better living for everyone

Oil Industry Information Committee, 50 West 50th St., New York

Reprinted by permission of the Petroleum Institute of America

As such, these popular expressions, even though produced by skillful technicians, are a valuable means of taking stock of our success or failure in developing a balanced existence.

There is a full-page ad of the Sun Oil Company (*New York Sun,* January 5, 1948) which starts off:

> There is only one freedom
> Freedom of choice

That is what we mean, the ad goes on further, when we say that, "The American Way" and freedom of choice are indivisible, like Peace. It is not from any doubt concerning the value or primacy of freedom that these outbursts of spontaneous joy in the recognition of freedom are here put under scrutiny, but one senses some incongruities which call for closer inspection. For example, there is something surprising about a passion for hymns to freedom arising in the rock-ribbed bosoms of those "regular guys" who profess indifference to "the finer things." If the National Association of Manufacturers suddenly printed millions of copies of Shelley and distributed them in factories and offices, and hired movie stars, Powers models, prize fighters, and baseball teams to stump up and down the land to promote a deeper understanding of that poet, it would arouse some comments and queries. Even smiles. Why not smiles, too, when, for example, any big bureaucratic monopoly sings hymns to Freedom?

The spirit of rivalry: Why are your teeth so much harder, bigger, stronger, thicker, and longer than mine? Why are your undies so much softer, comfier, slinkier, and whiter than mine? What's he got that I haven't got? Why is she the center of the party when I eat all the box-top specials myself?

The spirit of rivalry is a cinch, a ringer for the specially endowed in the matter of egotism and stark insensibility to the values of a common life; for the big, dynamic extrovert who heartily tramples all over the weaker limbs of his fellows. For the forty-two-inch chest puffing and stretching in the presence of a class of puny children. For the big firm which buys up or crushes its competitors.

The wild intensity of this spirit appears as a mere reflection in the Hollywood "star" system, in the exhibitionism and contortions of a Danny Kaye; but, most of all, in the psychological misery of millions whose budgets can never compass a fraction of the items considered indispensable if a family is to hold up its head in the competitive presence of those exactly like itself. Since conformity is the sign and reward of success, then go out and get the means to be a facsimile.

Striking studies of individuals obsessed with this spirit are Jerome Weidman's *I Can Get It for You Wholesale* and Budd Schulberg's *What Makes Sammy Run?* As successors to Sinclair Lewis's *Babbitt,* they illustrate how very far this corrosive spirit has penetrated the popular mind. In fact, the reader is left with the question whether there is anything left for this corrosive to destroy.

Freedom . . . American Style

IT'S the feeling you have when you get up in the morning and stand at an open window—the way you breathe in God's sunlight and fresh air. It's whistling before breakfast, disagreeing with the bank over your monthly statement, leaving a tip for the waitress if you feel like it.

It's working hard now with the idea of quitting someday. It's living where you like. It's looking forward with confidence —even while you willingly put up with gas rationing — to packing a lunch again and piling the family in the car for an outing.

It's keeping your car in condition against *that day*. It's realizing this is a nation on wheels that must be kept rolling—and that *your* wheels are part of all the wheels.

It's an oil company spending more money to make a better motor oil. It's giving that oil a brand name like Quaker State and being able to call it to your attention at a time like this, when your car needs extra care.

It's stating facts—that Quaker State is refined from Pennsylvania Grade Crude Oil; that it has won for itself, by its performance over the years, a reputation second to none in the field.

It's asking you to *try* Quaker State—in order to care for your car for your country in the best way possible. And, of course, it's your right to disregard this friendly advice if you feel so inclined. That's freedom—American style! Quaker State Oil Refining Corporation, Oil City, Pa.

QUAKER STATE
MOTOR OIL
CERTIFIED — GUARANTEED
Retail price 35¢ per quart

OIL IS AMMUNITION—USE IT WISELY

Freedom—American Style

The Utopia of the picnic inherited from the aristocratic pastoral convention?

Did Whitman give America the poetry of the open road?

What happens when the ad makers take over all the popular myths and poetry?

Are ads themselves the main form of industrial culture?

LET'S set this one up for an adult discussion group:

Study the items in this scene. What is intended as the general effect? Gaiety amid a fruitful and prosperous countryside?

What would you say was the income level of this family group? Estimate this from the car, the Scottie, the portable radio, and the appearance of the family. If this is "freedom . . . American Style," then is it not freedom and not American to have less money and fewer possessions? Was Henry Thoreau un-American?

What proportion of Americans enjoy this style of freedom?

Is there anything about the family group which is different from the Bumstead family?

Is there any basic connection between freedom and prosperity? Would Dagwood be free if he had the same job and the same thoughts, and earned a million a year?

Why take a radio into the countryside? Fear of boredom? Silence?

Looking at the standardized equipment of this family and their standardized pattern of living, discuss how far they can be said to be free as human beings. Consider whether a uniform educational system can be said to make for freedom. Does "freedom" mean the right to be and do exactly as everybody else? How much does this kind of uniformity depend on obeying the "orders" of commercial suggestion? If it takes a lot of money to conform in this way, does conformity become an ideal to strive for?

Discuss the habit of isolation of the American family. Consider the "Henry Aldrich" program or "One Man's Family." Why is there no sense of community in our festivities and relations? Whence this trait of "keeping it in the family?"

The copy under this scene announces that freedom is

> the feeling you have when you get up in the morning. . . . It's whistling before breakfast, disagreeing with the bank over your monthly statement, leaving a tip for the waitress when you feel like it. . . . It's working hard now with the idea of quitting someday. It's living where you like.
>
> It's an oil company spending more money to make a better motor oil. . . .
>
> It's asking you to *try* Quaker State—in order to care for your car for your country in the best way possible.

The big hefty heartiness of this is very familiar in the radio commercials. The loud, confident self-congratulation that we are as we are and that only a cheap sneak would ask any questions. The style of the old patent-medicine man has certainly been getting slicked up by those college men in the ad agencies. And the star-spangled scene of the free man cussing the bank or gypping the tired waitress who didn't sparkle and zip around is a curious way of getting at the essence of freedom.

As for working hard with the idea of quitting some day, that would not seem to be the idea of a man who loves his work. As for living where you like, there would seem to be relatively few people in this category, since nobody can do much about changing the noisy and unsalubrious character of the big cities in which most of us live and work.

The writer of the ad, in short, takes a dim view of the capacities of his readers, especially when he makes his final gesture of including, as it were, a can of motor oil in every picnic hamper.

Cokes and Cheesecake

Lead, kindly coke?

Love that bottle because of your baby training?

How about a shot of Abe Lincoln looking starry-eyed at a coke?

Is coke culture feminine? Is Coca Cola best because mother knows best?

In *God Is My Co-pilot,* the G.I.'s agreed that what they were fighting for was, after all, the American girl. To us, they said, she meant cokes, hamburgers, and clean places to sleep. Now, the American girl as portrayed by the coke ads has always been an archetype. No matter how much thigh she may be demurely sporting, she is sweet, nonsexual, and immatürely innocent. Her flesh is firm and full, but she is as pure as a soap bubble. She is clean *and* fun-loving.

In short, she is a cluster-symbol which embraces at one extreme Abe Lincoln's "All that I am and all that I hope to be I owe to my darling mother," and, at the other, Ziegfeld's dream of the glorified American girl as a group of tall, cold, glittering, mechanical dolls. The gyrations and patterns assumed by these dolls in a revue is intended to convey, if not the Beatific Vision, at least a Jacob's ladder of angelic hierarchies linking earth and heaven. We are pictorially encouraged to meet and mingle with these divine creatures in a sort of waking sleep, in which the male is not emotionally committed and in which the innocence of the doll is as renewable as a subscription to *The American Home.*

Coke ads concentrate on the "good girl" image as opposed to the dominant "bad girl" of popular entertainment—though there has been some recent tendency in Hollywood to blend the two types. The "good girl" is the nineteenth-century stock model which has long been merged with the mother image. So Margaret Mead's observations in *Male and Female* are especially relevant to understanding the success of coke ads. It is, she suggests, a result of our child-feeding habits that "Mouths are not a way of being with someone, but rather a way of meeting an impersonal environment. Mother is there to put things—bottles, spoons, crackers, teethers—into your mouth."[2] And so, she adds, the

DRINK
Coca-Cola
Refreshment...real refreshment
Ice-cold Coca-Cola—the real thing—never leaves you in any doubt...
or unrefreshed. It tingles with a delicious taste all its own and smacks
of continuous quality in every drop. Ice-cold Coca-Cola
gives you *the pause that refreshes.*
Coca-Cola
"Coke"
5¢
Ask for it either way... both trade-marks mean the same thing.
Have a Coke
DRINK
Coca-Cola
ICE COLD

American G.I. abroad puzzled foreigners by endless insistence on having something in his mouth most of the time. Gum, candy, cokes.

Apparently this has proved to be good advertising for Coca Cola. The coke has become a kind of rabbit's foot, as it were, for the foreigner. And *Time's* cover (May 15, 1950) pictures the globe sucking a coke. Love that coke, love that American way of life. Robert Winship Woodruff, coke executive, says, "We're playing the world long." That would seem to be a very small gamble, with the globe itself becoming a coke sucker.

It is easy to find the romantically immature Shelley conjuring up the same kind of infantile vision in "I rise from dreams of thee." It was new then. Further, it had a different sort of spice for Regency rakes. The Byronic dandy was a disillusioned worldling, who, hating the smell of adult flesh, got a special bang out of innocent girlhood as a vivid foil to his much-slaked lust. It was Byron who first promoted that image of the girl-wife later exploited by Thackeray and Dickens; and the Victorian male gratefully accepted these suggestions as the pattern of moral hygiene for his home life. "Real life" often appears, at least, to be an imitation of art. Today, of poster art.

The divorce, then, between the cloistered purity of the home and the cynicism and lust of the great battle raging in the world without is perhaps the most expressive dramatic feature of the nineteenth century. Without an understanding of the bearing of that drama, even such things as coke ads and Powers models are undecipherable hieroglyphics.

Here is how Frank Norris's tycoon Jadwin, in *The Pit,* saw it when inviting Laura to teach in his Sunday School:

> It's the indirect influence I'm thinking of—the indirect influence that a beautiful pure-hearted noble-minded woman spreads around her wherever she goes. . . . Men need good women, Miss Dearborn—men who are doing the work of the world. I believe in women as I believe in Christ. But I don't believe they were made, any more than Christ was, to cultivate—beyond a certain point—their own souls. . . . The men have all the get-up-and-get they want, but they need the women to point them straight and to show them how to lead that other kind of life that isn't all grind.

The willful self-deception, the obtuseness, and the ad-agency hamminess of these words are all to be found in the feminine images of our ads and magazine covers. Only, with us, there has been a shift from religion to soap as the guarantee of pure-hearted womanhood. For the rest, we are Jadwins.

The present coke ad features a Laura Dearborn, an old-fashioned mother-cum-sweetheart type, a dream drinking. This is the type portrayed by Ingrid Bergman. Recently, the furore over her Rossellini affair was an interesting example of what happens when two dreams get crossed up. She wantonly stepped out of her Hollywood stereotype, endangering a large investment. Rita Hayworth's stereotype, on the other hand, was not shattered by her affair. In presenting *Stromboli* to the American public, however, everything was done to cash in on the lurid possibilities of "good-girl-on-the-rampage."

Cokes as a soft drink naturally started out to appeal to the soft emotions. The wholesome harmlessness of the drink is insisted upon most successfully by the wholesome girls and situations which envelop the drink. These, in turn, have become linked to the entire range of home-mother-hygiene patterns which embrace a wide range of basic thoughts and feelings. So that it would be hard to suggest a more central item of current folklore, or one more subtly geared to evoke and release the emotions of practical life today.

Whether the drink was always as wholesome as the ads has been a matter of dispute among food analysts.

Love Novice

Mother Goose is on the loose? Tell the Marines she'll be coming round the mountain.

Who dreamed up that goose-stepping combination of military mechanism and jackbooted eroticism?

Are you there, Sacher-Masoch? Venus recurs not in furs but in uniform?

Say it with footballs and touchdowns?

NOT A LOVE GODDESS off the slick-chick assembly lines, but a love novice, the drum majorette is a newcomer to the crowded scenes where mass worship is paid to team spirit. The advantage in observing this widely popular item of spontaneous folklore is partly due to its recency. Perhaps drum majorettes appeared no earlier than 1920. Some people seem to remember them at Legion and Shriner parades as early as that. But their true vogue is much more recent. It is the high-school and college kids who have really taken over this strangely accoutered female. Why the rigid but flamboyant guardsman's helmet and the shining jack boots adorning a chorus girl? Mr. G. Legman, in *Love and Death,* mentions the drum majorette in connection with Wonder Woman of the comic books: "Wonder Woman's 'allure' is, of course, sexless, synthetic—the drum-majorette patriotism of star-spangled panties and spread-eagled breasts . . . Blondie with a bull-whip, an Amazon with mannish coat and tie. . . ." Wonder Woman lynches criminal males, and the drum majorette would seem to mow down her quota of male spectators in her own way. But the majorette is no man beater. She is cute and adolescent, whereas Wonder Woman and Blondie are ladies of decided maturity. Not even a Hollywood trouper of twenty-five to forty would do as a majorette, who at most must appear to be fourteen to seventeen.

A large crowd always craves some strong emotion to provide a sense of cohesive meaning and to start moving the undershaft of collective dynamism. The means dreamed up in the case of the majorette are curious. An adolescent love novice, a junior chorus girl in cavalry-officer attire, is instructed in the art of symbolic flagellation. She comes flailing along, head back, toes pointed, thighs flashing, while a brass band lends its throbbing emphasis to the occasion.

From the point of view of the young (her peers), the majorette is a glorification of youth and sport. Their lives are caught up into perspectives of adult grandeur and military display. For the old boys it is probably something else. Perhaps a willing surrender to the juggernaut of youth and irresistible femininity which may delightfully tempt them to rush out and hurl themselves under the remorseless, goose-stepping of the glamorous female warrior? Perhaps memories of former disciplines and austerity now deliciously mingled with images and occasions of license and relaxation?

These speculations are merely attempts to relate the majorette with some of the interests which have called her into synthetic being from out of the collective dream. For, like any social object, she is not an invention or a gadget so much as a cluster image that is both nourished by, and touches the life of, industrial man at several points. To say that she has neither dignity nor consistency but represents a crude, garish, and ludicrous hotchpotch of irreconcilable desires and imbecile motives is to make a responsible artistic and social judgment. But such a view merely draws attention to another fact: namely, that our supposedly wide-awake technological world is full of such childish bric-a-brac and sets much value on the same. The majorette offers one point at which to seek its origins and effects.

The Law of the Jungle

Have we submitted hypnotically to the hopper of mechanical processes?

Is our psychological world as much an internal-combustion engine as ads like this insist?

Is jet propulsion the humanistic answer to the mechanical jungle of Superman?

You find in science fiction the stirrings of a more humane state of mind?

THIS AD presents a drama which touches many themes of industrial society. Basically, it sets up a mechanical situation which is symbolic of the spirit of enterprise in human affairs.

RINGSIDE SEAT FOR A BATTLE ROYAL!

> Correct Lubrication Fights For You Inside Your Diesel and Throughout Your Plant!
> You're in the front row, looking at a terrific battle inside a big Diesel engine . . .
> This battle royal is typical of similar battles going on constantly inside all the machines in your plant.

The man who wrote the above copy had a natural feeling for the relations between the prize fight and heavy industry. The century of spectacular prize fighting which lies behind us coincides with the era of the maulers and bruisers of industry. A more subtle age of bureaucratic and monopolistic business enterprise calls for the more complex sport of "push-button football." Modern football would have bored to death the tycoons of yesteryear, because they would have found in it none of the dramatization of their own lives. Sport is a kind of magic or ritual, varying with the changing character of the dominant classes. And it embodies in a symbolic way the drives and tensions of a society.

Through sports a large spectator public is initiated into the psychological patterns of the few. As spectators, they participate, in various degrees, in the satisfactions of those who, in effect, control the spectators. But between fox hunting and college football there is a wide difference in the kind of participation and the kind of satisfaction. These two sports reflect widely differing conditions of men.

The present Socony-Vacuum ad cashes in on the popular rating of the prize fight. But it also brings the prize fight and the drama of heavy industry into a close relationship.

In 1943, Edgar M. Queeny, chairman of Monsanto Chemicals in St. Louis, published a book called *The Spirit of Enterprise* and announced therein: "I recognized my two selves: a crusading idealist and a cold, granitic believer in the law of the jungle." There have been some strange dual personalities abroad in fiction since Renaissance man split up into Don Quixote and Sancho Panza, Tom Jones and Blifil, Pickwick and Weller, Jekyll and Hyde, Holmes and Watson, heroes and valets. The split in question is always resolvable into a supposed opposition between "the head and the heart." For some reason the head or intelligence is supposed to be the seat of all inhumanity. But the heart

Ringside Seat for a *Battle Royal!*

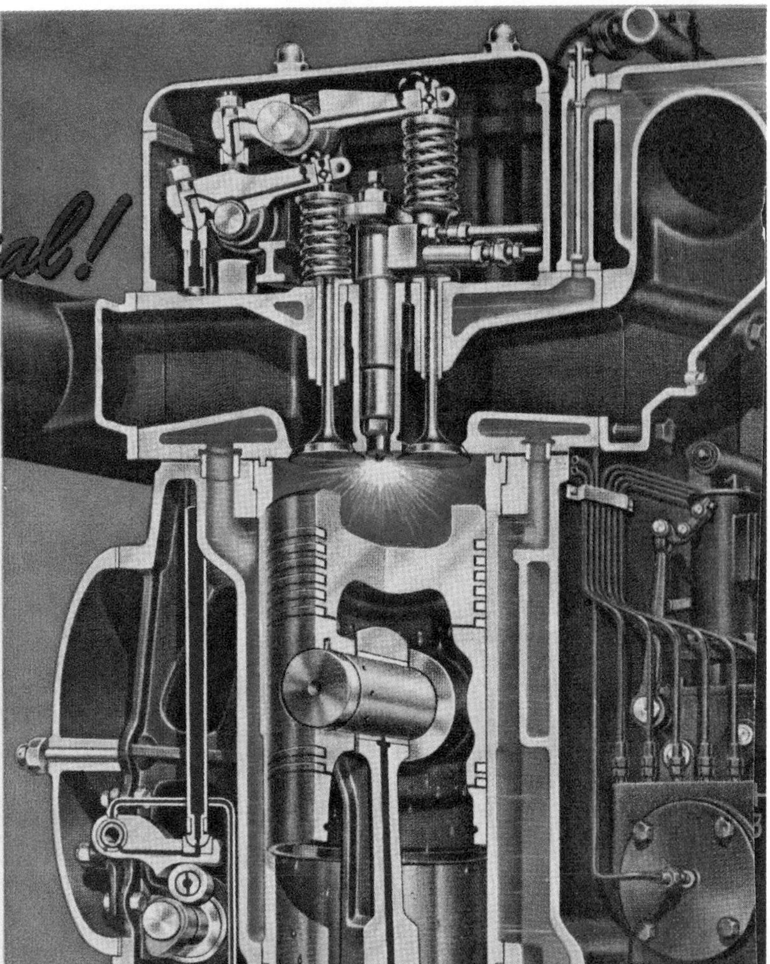

Correct Lubrication Fights For You Inside Your Diesel and Throughout Your Plant!

YOU'RE in the front row, looking at a terrific battle inside a big Diesel engine. Here, heat and oxygen gang together to attack the lubricating oil, shown in red.

This battle royal is typical of similar battles going on constantly inside all the machines in your plant. It points up the tremendous importance of Correct Lubrication to more continuous production, lower maintenance cost, greater over-all efficiency.

Increased net profit for your plant is the goal of the Socony-Vacuum representative who works with your staff.

He brings you our 78 years of lubrication experience, *greatest* in the world. He offers complete analysis of all your lubrication requirements and a sound practical Lubrication Plan to assure the application of the *right* oil in the *right* place, in the *right* way. You'll find it pays to have him supply all of your lubrication needs.

SOCONY-VACUUM OIL CO., INC.—Standard Oil of N. Y. Div. • White Star Div. • Lubrite Div. • Chicago Div. • White Eagle Div. • Wadhams Div. • Magnolia Petroleum Co. • General Petroleum Corp. of Calif.

TO HELP MAINTAIN CAPACITY PRODUCTION, CALL IN

SOCONY-VACUUM

for Correct Lubrication

and emotions are supposed to be on the side of mankind.

So far as Mr. Queeny is concerned, "the law of the jungle" means the "cold granitic" logic-engine which appears in the Socony-Vacuum ad as staging a battle royal. It is the law of the jungle that created this masterpiece of explosive force and power. No panty-waist humanitarianism here. No mollycoddling and encouragement of milksops. It took guts to make and market that engine. A cold granitic brain and an iron will went into it.

The granitic Kipling wrote in his *Jungle Book* for kiddies how Mowgli, the man's cub, had been initiated into the wolf pack, and how:

> . . . Father Wolf taught him his business, and the meaning of things in the jungle, till every rustle in the grass, every breath of warm night air, every note of the owls above his head . . . meant as much to him as the work of his office means to a businessman. . . . And he grew strong as a boy must grow who does not know that he is learning any lessons.

In those few words Kipling has stated not only the doctrines of nineteenth-century business enterprise but the formula of much of our education. These are the postulates with which Mr. Queeny works unquestioningly. They are his philosophic and scientific data. They mean touchdowns and sales promotions.

On March 18, 1946, *Time* ran an educational item that illustrates the pervasiveness of the Queeny-Kipling ethos:

THE SPARROW VS. THE HAWK.

> The veteran-on-campus was beginning to rustle the ivy. Last week the *Daily Bruin*, student newspaper of the University of California at Los Angeles, devoted a four-column spread to the educational opinions of 22-year-old Jay Douglas Haley, late of the A.A.F. Excerpts:
>
> The educational system of America is failing the youth of America! . . . It is fashioning sparrows and pushing them out to compete with hawks. . . . Why on earth should we be taught . . . this foolishness about honesty, truth and fair play? . . .
>
> If a student is majoring in law, he should be taught not only the laws but the most approved methods . . . of finding the loopholes. . . . If he is to be a doctor, he should not only learn medicine but how to milk the largest fees. . . . If an engineer, how to construct with the cheapest of materials. . . . If a journalist, how to slant, alter, lie. . . . In the securities field . . . the different methods of watering stocks and duping the suckers. . . .
>
> Let us get up petitions to remove these namby-pamby professors stumbling on their White Horse Truth, and get some good hardheaded businessmen in our colleges to teach us what we have to know to become a success.

It is exactly in this spirit that Professor Hooton of Harvard marshals anthropology on the side of the four-fisted he-men who see democracy threatened by current social consciousness. He rallies the ape to the side of the N.A.M. and views the combination as scientific. As reported in the *New York Sun* of February 13, 1948, he said:

> The idea that poverty-stricken, inefficient people have some innate right to be fed, clothed, housed, and supported in idleness from the public purse is a menace to democracy. . . .

In business, the same mind is, as we know, recorded in Norris's *The Pit.* Jadwin, the big bull of the Chicago wheat pit, is on one hand a crusading idealist and a Sunday school superintendent. The other side of his split personality is dedicated to the fury, the smash, and the grab.

But the twentieth-century version of the Darwinian creed is less personal and less dramatic. It appears in "Push-Button Football" (*Life*, December 1, 1947), in which "an executive like Michigan's H. O. ('Fritz') Crisler could sit on a bench in his chalk-striped suit . . . calling important plays through messenger-boy substitutes." As in business, the game is no less lethal, but the human features have been cut down to messenger-boy dimensions. In the same way, it would seem, the "big" stars of the movies or the "big" executives of business and the "big" statesmen of international politics are now puppets only vaguely aware of the strings controlling their movements.

The present Socony-Vacuum ad opens up a great many other social and personal vistas. An ad of this sort is a kind of clash of cymbals which sets vibrating a whole range of other objects and related situations. That is its intention. It sets up a sort of wild symphony in which we can see performers like Kipling, Andrew Carnegie, Darwin, Edgar M. Queeny, Professor Hooton, campus editors and football coaches all playing variations on the Socony-Vacuum theme. Like the performers in a symphony orchestra, they are unable to hear the music as it finally reaches the audience.

Education

Dare you ignore the Indian love call of vocational training? Your I.Q. is beckoning.

Let's all get adjusted to the process of getting adjusted to what isn't here any longer?

School must be glamorous in order to compete with agency models, hit parades, and television? The war is winning?

You'll never hit the jack pot unless you first become a slug for a machine?

MORE THAN WEALTH, more than birth or any other fact, education in America is by far the best means of improving one's social status today. It is also the best way of improving one's earning power. Such is the carefully considered view of competent students. On the other hand, less and less do men rise in industry and business by gradually acquired experience. More and more are the top jobs filled by specialists with technical-school training. And in this way, too, fathers are able to hand the reins directly to their sons instead of to those who have worked up from inside the enterprise.

In view of the wide availability of all types of education, the fact that it is also the largest social escalator is a most heartening fact. But the largest group coming off that escalator is still drawn from the top fifth of the economic brackets.

The teacher in America is admittedly in a peculiar position. Educationally qualified to advance himself economically, he or she appears to take a vow of poverty instead. The judgment of the community on the teacher has long been: "He can't take it." Assuming a voluntary noncompetitive poverty, the teacher stands as a reproach to the rest of the community engaged in the scramble for monetary reward. He asserts his "nerve of failure." The community retaliates with a certain degree of distrust and contempt. Distrust of his motives, contempt for his lowly status and lack of gumption.

But there is an even deeper cause for the distrust and resentment. The teacher in America is the appointed instrument of democratic opportunity and enlightenment. Parents entrust children to the teacher so that the children may be changed. The teacher is to make them "better than the parents." As such, the teacher alienates children from parents. But the teacher has to be "better than the parents" even in their eyes if he is to do his job. So that there is in the parent-teacher relationship a basic violation of the idea of equality even when the parent is much better off economically.

Of much greater import is the fact that education as a status escalator or mobility agent is also a very crude device for insuring that its products will often be mentally narrow to the point of helplessness. Those who submit to training only because it will link them more effectively to a great economic and bureaucratic mechanism are using their best years and faculties as a means of enslaving themselves. They are seizing opportunities in order to have the economic means to be exactly like everybody else.

Modern warfare is another point of vantage which enables the observer to note how the mere logistics of the war machine cause the spread of technological and specialist education. Really in the same order of cause

25 Subjects Simplified in One Time-Saving Volume . . . the Basic Knowledge You Need for Success in Business and Social Life!

THIS amazing new volume brings to your fingertips every subject contained within the scope of a High School education—presented with crystal clarity in fascinating *readable* form. If you never had a chance to finish school, or if your knowledge is hazy, rusty, in need of a brush-up, this up-to-date book is for YOU. Not only does it contain the 25 subjects taught in High School, but it also includes a complete *Study Outline and Self-Testing Examinations.* No easier, quicker, or more interesting method of self-instruction has ever been devised! All at a cost of less than 16 cents per subject—an astonishingly low-cost investment in education.

Latest edition of the famous book that has sold more than 500,000 copies!

Less Than 16¢ per subject

Truly a Bargain in Education!

New from Cover to Cover! 1,280 Pages! 300 New Illustrations! Many New Maps!

THIS new and enlarged edition of HIGH SCHOOL SUBJECTS SELF TAUGHT is a more useful book than ever before. New subjects, new illustrations, new full-page maps have been added. Every department has been rechecked, revised and brought up-to-date by experts. Here is the basis of a broad cultural background—the knowledge expected of you in business, professional and social life—which you can now absorb easily and pleasurably, without a schoolroom—without a teacher! How unnecessary, now, that feeling of inferiority because of the education you may have missed or simply *forgotten!* How unnecessary those embarrassing slips in English; those mistaken ideas of geography; those blunders in history; those blank moments when others talk of science, literature, art, government. You can start with any subjects you want first. You can use the *Study Outline* for systematic study in any or all 25 subjects. Just fifteen or twenty interesting minutes a day spent with this remarkable volume will help make you the well-informed person you want to be!

Makes Profitable Study a Delightful Pastime!

French and *Spanish*, for instance, are here in *conversational* form, so that you can begin to speak these languages from the first lesson! The essentials of good *English*, correct grammar, the right use of words are presented so you can absorb them quickly. *Mathematics* is so simply explained that you can apply many of its principles almost immediately. *History*, ancient and modern, comes alive with the color and sweep of a great story—not as a dusty collection of names and dates. *Literature* and *Art*, the masterpieces of all times and all nations, are presented in a guide which opens the door to new pleasures. *Physics, Chemistry, Biology*—the science of life—are so clearly explained that you will absorb the essentials of these subjects without effort. The guide to *Government* tells how our national system works; explains your rights and obligations as a citizen.

Nor is this all. A glance at the full list of 25 subjects given in the adjoining column will give you a better idea of the wealth of knowledge offered in this one volume.

A Virtual Encyclopedia of Knowledge—with Ready Reference Index of 7,500 Entries

HIGH SCHOOL SUBJECTS SELF TAUGHT is a work of complete authority, prepared by teachers with many years of practical experience. They have been assisted by a staff of editors, skilled in presenting educational subjects in the clearest, most concise, and most readable style. Whether you use the book for systematic self-instruction, for "brush-up," or for general reference, one thing is certain; the practical help, the cultural improvement, the daily usefulness you derive from it will prove to be worth many, many times its astonishing low price.

At Your Bookseller's, or Mail This Coupon Now

Garden City Publishing Co., Inc., Dept. 1 N. Y. T.,
9 Rockefeller Plaza, New York 20, N. Y.

Please send me for FREE TRIAL a copy of HIGH SCHOOL SUBJECTS SELF TAUGHT, new and enlarged edition. Within 5 days, if not completely satisfied, I may return the book without further obligation. If I keep it, I will send you a first payment of only 95 cents, plus postage, and $1.00 a month thereafter until the total price of only $3.95 is paid.

Mr.
Mrs. ....
Miss

Address ....

City and Zone .... State ....

Occupation .... Age if under 21 ....

☐ SAVE POSTAGE. Check here if enclosing with coupon remittance of $3.95, in which case, WE will pay postage. Same return privilege; refund guaranteed.

TRY IT AT HOME FOR 5 DAYS Free!

Send No Money Now - Pay Nothing to Postman - Judge It At Our Risk and Expense-No Obligation to You!

Fill out the coupon attached and mail it at once. HIGH SCHOOL SUBJECTS SELF TAUGHT will be sent to you by return mail. Examine the beautiful binding, the clear, easy-to-read type, the splendid illustrations and maps. Take your first few high school lessons with our compliments. Keep and read the book five days. Then, and only then, decide if you wish to own it at the extraordinary low price of only $3.95, plus a few cents postage. Easy monthly payments! Garden City Publishing Co., Inc., 9 Rockefeller Plaza, New York 20, N. Y.

Increase Your Earning Power—
Fill In the Gaps in Your Education!

25 SUBJECTS OF PRACTICAL AND CULTURAL VALUE—ALL IN ONE BOOK!

Study First What You Need First

Outline of Ancient History
The story of man's earliest civilizations up to the fall of the Roman Empire.

Outline of Medieval History
The "Dark Ages" to the beginnings of modern Europe. The crusades; the discovery of America.

Outline of Modern History
From the Reformation, through the French Revolution, the Industrial Revolution, the two World Wars, to our day.

Short History of the United States
Birth of Colonial America and struggle for freedom. Expansion and industrial development. Events of our times.

Civics and Government
Our rights and duties as American citizens. How government operates—city, state and national.

Geography for Everybody
A brief tour of the states of our country and countries of the world; physical, political and economic information.

Economics for Everybody
How wealth is created; money, inflation; laws of supply and demand; capitalism, socialism, communism, etc.

Sociology Simplified
The social relations of people; family life, health, culture and religion.

Good English Self Taught
How to avoid common errors. How to improve your vocabulary.

Effective Speaking
A practical outline of how to speak in public and improve everyday speech.

A Guide to Literature
A guided tour of English and world literature from the ancient classics to modern masterworks.

A Guide to the Arts
The art in the museums and in life about us. Painting, sculpture, architecture and music.

French Self Taught
An introduction to the most widely spoken foreign tongue. Easy conversational exercises.

Spanish Self Taught
An outline of this practical language with words and phrases in daily use.

Introduction to Latin
The age-old language of science, medicine and the Church, foremost of the classical tongues.

Mathematics Made Easy
Basic operations and short-cut in arithmetic for everyday use in the home and business.

Elementary Algebra
How algebra provides a shorter, faster way to solve mathematical problems.

Plane Geometry
The famous theorems of the ancient Greeks, and how they are in use today.

Biology for Beginners
The story of life itself. How the living organism grows, reproduces and repairs itself.

Physiology Simplified
The nervous system, the organs of the body; the vital processes of digestion, reproduction, etc.

Psychology for Beginners
Human behavior—emotions, sensations, thinking; intelligence tests, psychoanalysis.

Chemistry Self Taught
Elements and their combinations. Chemistry in its practical applications.

Physics Self Taught
Heat, sound, light, magnetism, electricity, mechanics, radar, photoelectric energy, radio, etc.

Astronomy for Everybody
The science of the universe—the sun, planets, stars, comets, meteors, etc.

Geology for Beginners
How the earth was formed and shaped. The basic mineral resources; weather and climate.

plus Study Guide, Self-Testing Quizzes, and a Comprehensive Index for Quick Reference and effect, mechanized or total war fosters prosperity and an economic well-being which is itself an immediate exposure of a situation in which we tend to have lost control and view of our own purposes. As the creator of wealth and opportunity for all, war has put peace to shame in our time. War has provided higher education and higher consumer standards for more people than peace ever did. So it is surprising that a war party has not supplanted present political parties.

This is merely a way of pointing once more to the central reality of our world. Accelerated change and planned obsolescence constitute the basic principle of an industrial power-economy built on applied science. Production for use? Yes. But for the briefest possible use consistent with the rigging of the market for the pyramiding of profits. Whether it's new books or light bulbs, they must not clutter up the scene for too long. A few weeks is enough for either. And education in this world? Is it education for use? Of course. But whose use? And for how long?

That man counts himself happy today whose school training wins him the privilege of getting at once into the technological meat grinder. That is what he went to school for. And what if he does have the consistency of hamburger after a few years? Isn't everybody else in the same shape? Hamburger is also more manageable than beef cuts. And the logic of a power economy is rigorous but crude. It laughs at political shadings, at Marxist and Fascist, but it frowns at heavy-boned characters who knock the teeth out of the meat grinder. Our educational process is necessarily geared to eliminate all bone. The supple, well-adjusted man is the one who has learned to hop into the meat grinder while humming a hit-parade tune. Individual resistance to that process is labeled *destructive* and *unco-operative.*

Far from teaching detachment or developing the power of gauging human goals, our higher education is servile and unrealistic. For to develop individuals with powerful minds and independent characters is to create a supply for which there is no demand. Why train men if there is only a market for robots? Most university presidents and deans understand the logic of their world. They are on the band wagon. Why train individuals, if the only available life is the collective dream of uniform tasks and mass entertainment? Why make life difficult? Why be different? Why use your brains to ensure poverty?

To put the whole thing briefly, a power economy cannot tolerate power that cannot be centrally controlled. It will not tolerate the unpredictable actions and thoughts of individual men. That is plain from every gesture and intonation of current social and market research as well as from the curricula of our schools.

But how is all this possible? How does it come about? Is there a conscious conspiracy to produce the results we see? Of course not. It comes about very simply. Great physical and industrial power rests on a multitude of powerless individuals, many of whom are deeply resentful of their condition. The smaller and meaner the man, the more he craves to possess not limited human powers, with all the effort of cultivation and all the responsibility that implies, but superhuman power. (That is the meaning of the Squinky comic books, and of "Superman.") The sadistic craving for enormous physical powers to revenge or compensate for human futility will always drive such people to link themselves to vast impersonal enterprises. They will follow automatically any road which promises to bring them to that goal. So that to be a switch thrower in a *big* plant looks better to them than any lonely task, however human. Such is also the attraction of bureaucratic jobs, whether in great corporations or in government. It is by a fantasy identification with the very big power unit that the very small man obtains his self-realization as a superman. The key to Superman is Clark Kent the useless. Therefore the more we create and centralize physical power, the more we suppress our human nature; and then that human nature queues up all the more to support the big physical power that crushes it. Far from being a conscious conspiracy, this is a nightmare dream from which we would do well to awaken at once. Return again, Finnegan.

There is actually emerging a large number of independent critical minds today. As the nightmare moves to its unwelcome dramatic peak, the sleeper stirs and writhes. It is nice to be enfolded in a collective dream as long as the comfort is greater than the pain. But we have nearly passed that critical point. Consciousness will come as a relief.

I'm Tough

Can you see through his adnoise?

Is that guy's slip showing?

Would this character look better in a horse opera of the gaslight era?

THIS OLD-FASHIONED gent trying to look as Neanderthal as possible is still common and influential. It would be convenient if the entire clan could be corralled and permitted to work on one another, or given a separate planet on which to play with the H-bomb. As it is, they have to be reckoned with here and now:

> Panty-waist stuff burns me. Work ten hours a day. Been at it since I was a kid. Gang at the plant call me "Chief." Own the place, now. . . .
>
> Give me cold facts—straight from the shoulder. I know that any outfit which makes its own stuff and takes it straight to the consumer plays fast ball.

Yet if there's anything this type of quick-turnover gent can't see with his overheated bloodshot gaze, it's cold facts. If we slide back a few decades, we can observe this type of person being glorified in popular fiction.

The hero of *The Pit* by Frank Norris is described as musing about Chicago before he decides to become the great bellowing bull operator:

> Often Jadwin had noted the scene, and, unimaginative though he was, had long since conceived the notion of some great, some resistless force within the Board of Trade Building that held the tide of the streets within its grip . . . sucking in the life-tides of the city . . . then vomiting them forth again . . . the chaotic spasm of a world-force, a primeval energy, blood-brother of the earthquake and the glacier, raging and wrathful that its power should be braved by some pinch of human spawn . . .

This is the megalomania of the Marquis de Sade, of Nietzsche, and of Hitler, full of aggressive contempt for man and civilization but ready to melt momentarily into self-pitying Wagnerian sentiment as a bracer-relaxer before a big putsch. It is the savage dream of Mistah Kurtz of Conrad's *Heart of Darkness*, the raper and rifler of nations and continents. And it would be a mistake to overlook the several points of resemblance in this ideal to the sentimental anarchism of Whitman and Carl Sandburg. The romantic afflatus of these popular writers blends very easily with the cult of dynamic action, affording insufficient protection for such human values as are still to be found in them.

Norris fairly drools over such characters, because he senses that they are in the groove of the *Zeitgeist*. Describing a firm of Chicago bears with which Jadwin had been associated, he trumpets:

I'M TOUGH
Panty-waist stuff burns me. Work ten hours a day. Been at it since I was a kid. Gang at the plant call me "Chief". Own the place, now.
Sure I've made money. Not a million—but enough to buy steak when I can get it. And good clothes.
Been getting my duds at Bond's—ever since I shed knee pants. Like the way they do business. No fancy fol-de-rol. No big promises. No arty labels dangling high-hat prices. Just good clothes with plenty of guts.
Give me cold facts—straight from the shoulder. I know that any outfit which makes its own stuff and takes it straight to the consumer plays fast ball. That's why Bond's story clicks. Show me topnotch woolens, honest tailoring, and I'll look. Quality like that stands up. Kick out wasteful, in-between costs the way Bond does it, and old Tough Tom signs on the dotted line. Horse sense, that's all.
Looks like I've plenty of company. They say more men wear Bond clothes than any other clothes in America. Always knew the Yanks were smart traders.
One thing I want to tell the boss at Bond's. Those clothes wear like iron. Durned fools to make 'em so good.
Spring Suits—100% pure wool
28.00 to 40.75
Rochester-Tailored Topcoats
28.50 to 39.75
BOND CLOTHES
Corner 8th and Washington
Open Every Monday, Noon till 9 P. M.

It was immensely wealthy and immensely important. It discouraged the growth of a clientele of country customers, of small adventurers. . . . The large, powerful Bears were its friends, the Bears strong of grip, tenacious of jaw, capable of pulling down the strongest Bull. Thus the firm had no consideration for the "outsiders," the "public"—the Lambs. The Lambs! Such a herd, timid, innocent, feeble, as much out of place in La Salle Street as a puppy in a cage of panthers . . . whom, in their mutual struggle of horn and claw, they crushed to death by the mere rolling of their bodies.

There is something quaintly pre-industrial about all this. It is so porous, so biological, so self-consciously self-congratulatory. Like the face in the present ad, it is theatrical and phoney in the same way as sports-page ferocity. The real toughness today has shifted from the personal Darwinian melodrama to the abstractions of logistics, Cybernetics, and consumer research. Thanks to the refinements and perversions of statistical measurement and International Business Machine logistics, it is now easy for little esthetish gents to be much more formidable than the Jadwins ever were. Goebbels was much more dangerously corrupt and destructive than Goering. James Aldridge, writing in the *New York Times* for June 24, 1942, gives a popular, Raymond Chandler sort of view of the post-Darwinian brand of abstract toughness. Darwinism got rid of the human quality in killing. Our time has gone a step farther and got rid of its animal character:

BRITISH IN AFRICA LACK KILLER URGE

The German Afrika Corps defeated the Eighth Army because it had speed, anger, virility and toughness. As soldiers in the traditional sense, the Germans are punk, absolutely punk. But Marshal Erwin Rommel and his gang are angry men, they are tough to the point of stupidity. They are virile and fast, they are thugs with little or no imagination. They are practical men, taken from a most practical and hard life to fight practically: Nazis are trained to kill. The German commanders are scientists, who are continually experimenting with and improving the hard, mathematical formula of killing. They are trained as mathematicians, engineers and chemists facing complicated problems. There is no art in it, there is no imagination. War is pure physics to them. The German soldier is trained with a psychology of the daredevil track rider. He is a professional killer, with no distractions. He believes he is so tough, and can be beaten soundly and quickly by a foe using the same ruthless speedy methods he uses . . . The British soldier is the most heroic on earth, but do not confuse that with military toughness. He has the toughness of determination but he has not the toughness which makes him scientifically kill his enemy.

As we suggest "The Mechanical Bride," sex is not enough in a technological world, and here is James Aldridge plainly giving the reasons why today brutality is not enough, and he advocates scientific killing in place of a mere brutality. Killing is now to be regarded as equivalent to the pre-scientific attempts to find and kill individual fleas or lice which are now handled *en masse*. Simply by unconsciously spouting the language of modern applied science, Aldridge arrives at the same concepts as those which inspired the methods of the Nazi death camps. Both sex and death have been subtly neutralized by the popularization of laboratory procedures.

What It Takes to Stay In

It takes what the public's got?

Did you ever meet a payroll in a dark alley?

I'm just a poor cowboy and don't like government interference?

Now you know why there's so little profit in running a business?

A TYPICAL N.A.M. ad is headed: "What do you need to go into business and *stay* in?" It then lists and pictures the steps in this process, the first being "an idea, or a service, or a product—*something to sell.*" The men pictured on the pole in the present Forbes Lithograph Company ad are scrambling for a new "facts line" which "delivers new merchandising impact." They have a big juicy bone to sell and are looking for a Pavlov technique that will make every jowl drool automatically when their product is mentioned. That hefty steel pole is a veritable beanstalk suggesting the towering profits to be snatched speedily by the lucky possessor of a "facts file." "What a lift for a sagging sales curve!"

The blurb for *The Underwriter's 1950 Commission Builder* offers it as "a brand new gateway to 8 particular types of prospect . . . their current need for coverage and how to gear your sales talk to it." Behind these now commonly assumed relations between producer, salesman, and buyer there are some interesting assumptions that reach back more than two centuries. Mere attacks on salesmanship are confusing and frustrating when these now-forgotten assumptions are missed. For example, there is the assumption that business is a game played between players whose interests are clearly inspected by each before any move is made. This game assumes not only a set of clearly seen interests but equally intelligent and equally motivated players. The possibility that many people have very vague ideas about their wants and interests or that they vary greatly in their power to make moves to satisfy these wants would, of course, cancel this assumption of the business game. It can then be seen as the effort of the seller to guide as many mice as possible to his particular outlet in a maze. To make just those signals and sounds which will attract the average mouse to his special outlet is the object of "the selling game."

In "classical economics" of the late eighteenth and early nineteenth centuries it was assumed that the "laws of the market" were psychologically geared to those of a mathematical universe. Each private person was a little world on the model of the physical universe. Driven by self-interest, he could at all times inspect his private wants and preferences, and, through the mechanism of the market, he could express these wants and preferences in production and consumption. From that point of view salesmanship was conceived as merely a service performed for a sluggish mechanism. It can only cause the whole interlocking system to move a bit faster. The system remains intact. The salesman is thus a godsend, a *deus ex machina,* a public benefactor. Quite apart from the fog of both idealism and accusation that surrounds the salesman today, is it not true that he is, in prac-

What do you need to go into business —and stay in?

1. The first thing you need when you go into business for yourself is an idea, or a service, or a product—*something to sell*, in other words. The better that "something" is, the better your chances of getting enough customers—and of keeping them satisfied.

2. Next you need money enough to get started and to keep going until income catches up with outgo. Maybe you use your own savings—or maybe you borrow from a bank—or from other people who have enough confidence in your proposition to *risk their savings.*

3. Then, of course, you need loyal employees who know their jobs, and a place in which to do business. And this will have to be equipped with supplies, or materials, or machinery—the "tools" with which to work.

4. Now comes good management. Maybe yours is the kind of business you can run all by yourself. If not, you'll have to hire a capable manager. If you fail here, competition will soon force you out of business. Then you and your backers will lose their money and you and your employees will be out of jobs.

5. And almost from the day you start, you'll need to do *enough* business to meet your payroll, your rent, your taxes and all your other expenses. And these charges must be paid before there'll be anything left for you or your backers.

6. Finally you need to make a fair profit—not just because you *want* one, but because that's the only way you can *stay* in business. Profits are the very *mainspring* of American industry. And they pay for the expansion and improvements that bring more products, more jobs, lower prices and greater security for all.

NATIONAL ASSOCIATION OF MANUFACTURERS

For a Better Tomorrow for Everybody

Write for your free copy of "Who Profits from Profits?" Address: NAM, 14 West 49th St., New York 20, N. Y.

Most Americans say they think 10 to 15 cents out of each dollar of sales would be a fair profit for business to make. As a matter of fact, industry averages less than half that much!

tice, an evangelist, and much given to thinking of himself as a do-gooder? And if anybody wants to see why a salesman can take up this attitude or wants to change the situation, he will have to look more carefully than can be done here into that Newtonian world which dazzled the Western mind at the end of the seventeenth century.

The idea of a self-regulating economic system, free from rational controls and powered simply by human appetites and passions, occurred very easily to the traders of 1690, who were goggling at the mathematical clockwork cosmology held up to their eyes by the speculations of Descartes, Leibnitz, and Newton. God, the great geometer, was outside the machine of the universe, to which he had merely given an initial push. The number of mechanical inventions which sprang into existence at this time, including clockwork robots that could walk and write (see Giedion's *Space, Time and Architecture*), is striking evidence of the power of philosophy in everyday concerns. Both the human body and the body politic soon came to be thought of as machines geared to the mathematical laws of the universe. The system of constitutional checks and balances hitched to the voting machine was the eighteenth-century contribution to political thought. For America it was decisive, since it coincided with her political origins.

On one hand there was the Jeffersonian idea of a self-regulating democracy based on a farmer-craftsman economy. As long as concentrations of men and capital were avoided, Jefferson claimed, American democracy would *automatically* follow different laws from that of any previous human society, because all previous politics had grown up in consequence of a scarcity of land, and hence concentration of political power. But now all men could be free, he thought, just as long as they allowed their social and political lives to be the automatic expression of small ownership. On the other hand, there was the Hamiltonian school, which preferred to risk the automatism resulting from concentrations of men and capital in order to achieve the national power and private wealth which, in theory and in practice, would also follow automatically. The Jeffersonian path remained the national dream, and the Hearst press and the National Association of Manufacturers try to have it both ways. They talk Jefferson and follow Hamilton. Of course, Jefferson would have admitted at once the folly of trying to achieve his ends by Hamiltonian means. If the economic power were not actually distributed evenly among small owners and craftsmen, then it would be impossible to conduct political life on the assumption that human welfare could be attained by merely avoiding strong central government.

It is very noticeable that the Hearst press and the N.A.M. always talk the language of the little man, the Jeffersonian citizen. They are folksy by instinct, foxy by interest. They talk as if there were no such thing as economic power as a factor in human freedom. In this they are deeply muddled. To talk of freedom but never of power is partly, at least, the result of confusion and timidity of mind. Yet to have created a power which destroys freedom is alarming even to an industrialist. And that he should choose not to talk about the industrial power of regimentation but rather to exhort people to be free is, in the circumstances, just ordinary human weakness: "I didn't know it was loaded."

The problem, then, as to what it takes for a man to *stay* in business is not necessarily identical with what it takes for a society to stay in business. For it is no longer easy to see that in merely having something to sell a man is necessarily a producer or a useful member of society. Nor is it obvious any longer that a man who can discover or create a demand has thereby a social right to make himself rich.

Murder the Umpire

Modern business is a game just like philosophy or art, only more creative?

Please don't notice that the umpire is carrying the ball for the public?

The lunatic and the ordinary man use the same reasoning process, but it still does matter from where you start?

Is football a ritual drama enacting the state of mind of a specialized commercial audience?

THIS AD of the Electric Light and Power Companies appeared in *The American*. Like the Ringside Seat ad for Diesel engines, it illustrates how naturally the imagery of competitive sport is linked to much of our thinking and feeling about government and business. According to Noel Busch, Briton Hadden, co-founder of *Time*, dreamed of owning the New York Yankees. Waiting for that day, he ran the magazine on ball-club lines as far as he could.

More obviously than most entertainment, competitive sport is a direct reflex of the various motives and inner dramas of a society. But private games like chess, bridge, and poker are no less expressive. And for businessmen, golf is the recognized dramatization of the most immediate kind of personal competition. Thorstein Veblen's celebrated notion that sport is the degradation of the instinct of craftsmanship is useful as a pointer, but it fails to take into account the positive functions of sport as a kind of magical art in society. For sport is a magical institution, celebrating by a precise ritual the impulses that seem most necessary to social functioning and survival in any given group. (In the section "Love Novice" it is suggested how the sport ritual has come to be embellished by the figure of the drum majorette.)

Professional baseball, however, is a very different affair from college football. Baseball is a spectator sport, with much of its inner drama depending on close attention to league standings and complex batting and other averages. The mixture of gamble and skill, so necessary to spectator satisfaction, is kept within specific limits by a precise code. As interpreter of the code and of the action, the umpire stands for something like government interference in business and is just as popular. Masked, padded, and impersonal in policeman blue, he is the Supreme Court and human fate rolled into one. He calls the strikes, can bench a player, or wreck a club. His role is to appear ruthless, harsh, arbitrary, and dramatic. In its feature on George Barr's "School for Umpires," *Life* (March 10, 1947) pointed out that the school exists to teach the art of calling decisions with "the gestures that are . . . understood from the bleachers."

It is an important part of the enjoyment of the game that he should be cussed and resented by players and spectators alike. For he is the image of authority and decision. Few if any umpires have been killed, but the scream of "Moider da umpire" is well known. Leo "the Lip" Durocher is a popular hero who speaks with the voice of enterprise when he talks back to the big man in blue.

In goon sports like all-in wrestling, it is often part of the show to have the referee knocked out by "enraged"

What goes on here?

Referee makes first down — or did he really just miss it? Field judge blocks out the nearest tackler — or was it clipping? If the officials call 'em — and play too — what kind of a game is that?

You wouldn't stand for that sort of thing on a football field — but it happens every day in the electric light and power business. Government not only regulates the electric companies — but is in competition with them at the same time!

The catch is that government sets up two different sets of rules. The government's electric agencies pay little or no interest on the money they borrow, and pay no Federal taxes — but electric companies do, and expect to. When government-in-the-power-business can't make ends meet — it gets a handout of tax money from the U. S. Treasury. Who foots the bill? American taxpayers—of which you are one.

If government can get into the light and power business this way — it can get into every other business the same way.

In sixty-odd years, the self-supporting electric companies have built for America the most and the best electric service in the world. While costs of everything else are way up (including the costs of making and delivering electricity) electric service is still the best bargain in the American family's budget . . . it does so much, and costs so little.

This is a good record for the thousands of people who work in power companies, and for the millions of people who invest savings in them.

Don't you think these men and women deserve a fair break?

The answer is yours to make, for government money is your money.

It is to your benefit to know the facts about your electric service, and to ours to have you know them. That's why this advertisement is published by America's business-*managed, tax-paying* ELECTRIC LIGHT AND POWER COMPANIES★.

★Names on request from this magazine.

Hear famous stars in radio's great new dramatic show — THE ELECTRIC THEATRE . . . CBS, Sundays, 9 P. M., EST.

participants. But all-in wrestling has less the character of a magical art staged for spectators—who thus participate in the wider drama of the stock exchange—than a minor side show for bloodthirsty typists and debutantes who get a sex wallop from the mauling and groaning and gore.

The kind of spectator participation in baseball, the precise character of the evocation and discharge of feeling that is achieved, would be hard to pin down. As in most modern sports, the size of the crowd assisting at the ritual is an important ingredient in the effect achieved. To identify oneself with notable individual players while secure in the anonymity of the mass—that is part of the show.

Something of the character of baseball magic comes out in contrasting it with football. In the latter, as a college game, the spectators and players are in very different relations as compared with baseball. The players are college men, selected, as it were, from the audience. Identification of spectators and players is close. Moreover, football is less statistical than baseball. Its dramatic appeal, relatively, is to crude power rather than to skill and chance. It is a ritual celebration of college life as seen sentimentally through the eyes of the old boys, on one hand, and, on the other, it gives to the young a sort of foretaste of the world of real business. The spectator of the ball game is usually a mere *spectator* of the business world as well. But the spectator of college football is more typically an actual participant in the business game.

In England the same contrast may be seen between the rugger crowd and the soccer crowd. The latter is a professional game played to vast crowds who are on the sidelines of life as well as of sport. The rugger crowd consists of relatively privileged people who are spectators of sport but participants in business and society.

One fact worth attention out of many that cannot be introduced here is the way in which baseball and football more than maintained their positions during War II. It was partly because through these sports people in and out of the services could maintain an intimate link with ordinary social and business life. But also because of the close relation between competitive sport and the competition of war. War games, the business game, and sport are not directly or logically connected, but they belong within kindred frames of reference.

Sport, with its passion for victory, helps to stoke up the boiler that provides the steam for an activistic, extrovert way of life. The intensity of coaching and training procedures in sport reflect not only the passion for victory but the extreme to which we are prepared to go to control the outcome. And it is in this latter situation that the referee or umpire achieves his role as target for irrational abuse. Excitement, not fun, is the object or function of sport in a competitive industrial world. The passions which sport arouses systematically are much too intense to leave any scope for that element of detachment which provides fun in life and art. One has only to listen to the tense gunfire delivery of radio sports announcers to understand this.

The present ad, which is an excellent gauge of the way most fans feel about the umpire or referee who deprives them of victory, is just as indicative of how the private firms sponsoring the ad feel about the government, which, they consider, is carrying the ball for the opposition. But the ad fails to pick out the opposition. That is a considerable gap in its pictorial argument. The opposition is the public, the audience. This ad is like a slip of the tongue that reveals a hidden attitude.

I am the Bill of Rights

Why do big authoritative tones and gestures come so easily to the tycoon?

Why is Business so jealous of our right to listen—to Business?

You've heard money talking? Did you understand the message?

Is there any role left for the individual in a world of collective megaphone personalities?

THE PRESENT ITEM is like a hasty cartoon-warning tied to a brick and heaved through a window. It bristles with menace and adds up to the great impulse to "Moider da umpire!" We the people say to we the people, in Li'l Abner phraseology, "Yo' is all a lot of false gods." But it doesn't make sense, because it's like heaving a brick into one's own parlor.

We have seen how the Hearst press, employing the Jeffersonian arguments, really speaks for a great portion of America. Like the present ad of Revere Copper and Brass Incorporated, and with equal incoherence, unintelligibility, irrelevance, and total ignorance of the history of philosophy, politics, or economics, it rattles off the clichés and the postulates which were the intellectual currency of the philosophers of the Enlightenment of the eighteenth century. When Henry Ford pronounced that "History is bunk," he spoke for this great tradition of social mechanics of the eighteenth century, which was born in anti-history and was baptized by the doctrine of automatic progress. And the Hearst press is terribly embarrassing to the liberal, for he hears it uttering daily several of the commonplaces without which he could not carry on.

In the same issue of the *New York Sun* (January 5, 1948) as that which carried the present ad, there was another full-page advertisement sponsored by John R. Moroney of Dallas, Texas, which is worthy of notice. Presented in free-verse form, it embodies the highest rhetorical effort (*March of Time* tone) in the form of a sort of dialogue between the Bill of Rights and the stars on the flag. It is understood that the American people had better be listening in:

> I am the Bill of Rights—the Ten Commandments of our People to their Public Servants, saying "Thou Shalt Not!"

That is to say, the Bill of Rights is treated as a private revelation, somehow different from the Ten Commandments. However, the commandments are not quite so negative as is suggested. The "Public Servants" are classified as hired men—not representatives of delegated authority but of special interests. The business of government, it is implied, is not to govern. "Thou shalt not govern."

> I am the individual Man, Woman and Child, straight from the hand of God, and greater than any false god of government.

That is, Society is to be regarded as an aggregate of isolated units. All individual actions are accountable

"... Business profit, of course, is the keystone of our free enterprise system. It is the incentive that inspires individual business performance, high level employment, and the progressive improvement of business methods..."

As he addressed these words from the WHITE HOUSE to the Boston Distribution Conference, the voice of President Truman was indeed The Voice of Business.

REVERE COPPER AND BRASS INCORPORATED • 230 PARK AVENUE • NEW YORK 17, NEW YORK

Founded by Paul Revere in 1801

only to God. God alone can harmonize and order the conflicting appetites and passions of individuals. No man or no government, without the penalties of supreme presumption, dares to assist the work of social order which belongs to God alone. This doctrine is straight out of the absolute cosmology of Leibnitz, Newton, and Locke. It is based on the idea that the universe and society are self-regulating mechanisms. The laws of the market are God's providential and primary machinery for expressing His will to the people.

> I am Liberty—more than a principle—a Passion.

But a passion is much *less* than a principle. For passions are private emotions and appetites, or combinations of such, whereas a principle binds all men and all things. Therefore, principles must be superseded by passions in this scheme of utilitarian mechanism. Principles are intelligible and abiding aspects of reality. They bind men in mutual social obligations deriving from the very nature of man and his dignity as a rational creature. The grasp of principles assists men to resist private passions and order them to a rational good that is both private and social. But in this last excerpt, however, it is implied that only God can have principles, and that men must live only by blind passion in order to provide the dynamism for the big social machine which God directly governs in accordance with His own inscrutable plans. And that any effort to achieve a social order guided and restrained by human principles is, in this scheme, arrogant presumption derogatory to the Divine omnipotence. Such is the Leibnitzian mathematical code of eighteenth-century political enlightenment, and also the code of nineteenth-century economic liberalism as understood in terms of the self-regulating market in land, labor, and capital.

> I am God's mightiest effort, advancing on chaos and the dark.

"God" is no longer outside the machine. He is now inside. He is seen as trying to develop his personality by big dynamic efforts at extroversion in the domain of matter, energy, and industry. With the Bill of Rights, God gained yards. He began to see His goal. Up till then He had worked in murk and fog and slime.

> I am the pulse of Destiny.

At this point God gets the Hegelian brush-off. Merged in the cosmos, He is now felt only as a pulse in the big vibrating organism of matter and energy. Destiny is where He wants to go, what He wants to become. However, He still can't bear any false gods of social government even in His diminished stature.

> I am the Higher level, more often lost than found.

Higher level is not mystical contemplation but high production, high profits, high frequency of gadgets, perhaps high employment. Very incidentally it might be "high moral tone" or something ethereal like that. There then follows, much more briefly, a group of folksy items: the hum of cities, home and fireside, truth and honor, friendship, and,

> I am courage, the soul of all mighty achievement . . .

The moral is in this last line:

> Be ashamed to die unless you also strike a blow against Human Bondage!

And that means to strike at the false god of government shackles on the spirit of enterprise.

It is not by any means plain that there is a lack of good faith in all this. There is only the evidence of a painful confusion of mind and exuberant incoherence. The stereotypes to which such ads appeal are now embedded in the popular dreams of success and opportunity for all.

The Tough as Narcissus

LET JACK DEMPSEY SHOW YOU HOW TO FIGHT TOUGH

Police Tactics	*Disabling Blows*
Fighting Two Men at Once	Hack and Jab
Arm Twist	Rear Arm Strangle
How to gouge out an eye	Grab belt or Crotch
Attack from the ground	Chart of Disabling blows
Blocking kick to testicles	

MATCHING the quality of this ad is the appeal of the full-page ads in the kids' comics, such as this one from the back cover of *Plastic Man:*

> YOU TOO CAN BE TOUGH
> LEARN TO DEFEND YOURSELF!
> 55 Lessons worth $150
> When Given in Training!

In an emergency would your actions show the lady in your life

You are a *Man*? Sure you've guts—but is bravery alone enough to stand up against guns, knives, clubs while you have only your bare hands?

Is this little tough the twin brother of any self-patting, self-admiring deb?

Let's all concentrate on our own wonderful chemical factories so we can grow up and have energy to burn?

Is it an accident that the narcissistic heroes like Tarzan, Superman, cowboys, and sleuths are weak on social life?

Fear is the primary motive in toughness. Fear easily gives rise to hate, which intensifies brutality. And the numerous variants on straight-arm tactics, from lynch law to the third degree, all reduce to inner panic as their origin. It is the weak and confused who worship the pseudosimplicities of brutal directness. The terror inspired by wild beasts, which led tribal societies to get psychologically inside the tribal totem animal, is being repeated today to the degree that those who are confused or overwhelmed by a machine world are encouraged to become psychologically hard, brittle, and smoothly metallic. The slick-chick and the corporation executive, as they now register on the popular imagination, are already inside the totem machine.

This trek toward the voluntary annihilation of our individual humanity can be gauged in many ways, one of which is by the worship of "personal hygiene." Totemistic worship of mechanism is recorded not only in a dozen popular hygienic and social rituals for avoiding human contact, but the very word "contact" has come to mean getting a business prospect inside the network of one's private success mechanism.

The boy who worships "The Massive Massimo" is merely carrying out the instructions of the adult world, the basic sickness of which was publicly proclaimed by Thomas Carlyle in 1840. In that year he began to preach the idolatry of great men in his *Heroes and Hero-Worship.* For the growing sense of helplessness among the new urban masses he prescribed large doses of hero-worship. If you are a weak little man, get inside a big strong man. But we are not yet done with the long century of hero worship or self-worship which began with the popular enthusiam for Napoleon, "the little corporal," and which has seen the rise of the superman in theory, practice, and fantasy simultaneously.

The boy in the ad is engaged in the rituals of self-worship or disguised "hero worship" as much as the slick chick from the "love-goddess assembly line." He is hep to all those century-old psychological devices for transforming himself into a youthful and provisional facsimile of the adult world which he finds around him. The barbaric and nihilistic creed promoted by Thomas Carlyle in 1840 underwent a series of degradations with-

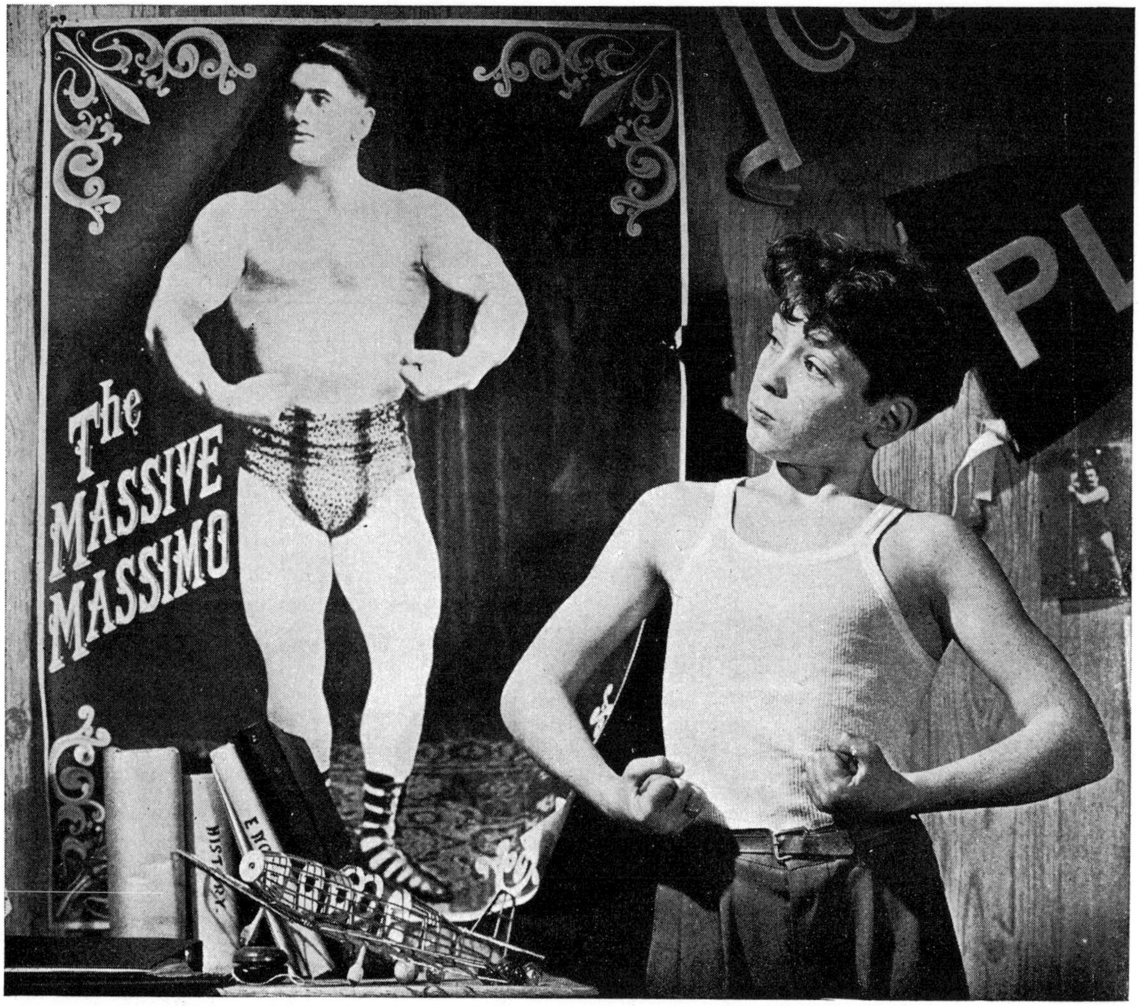

How to make a muscle

Our young friend has growing pains. He yearns to bulge a bicep. Although he doesn't know it, he's quite a man for his age—holds his own on the playground and in the classroom. *And at the dinner table.*

In wealth of food resources, this is a fortunate country.

But using those resources—making the most of them—is where America shows up best. We have good foods because we've learned more about how to grow and process, pack, ship and store them.

Another reason this is the best nourished nation is because we've taken foods apart, isolated their vital elements and applied this knowledge to feeding babies, growing children, mothers, workers everywhere.

National Dairy has had a large share in the progress of this country in foods, particularly in dairy products like milk, cheese, butter and ice cream. Some of the foods you'll eat today will bear the National Dairy labels shown on this page.

Many of the *new* foods you'll eat tomorrow will bear these labels, too. There is much progress still to be made in feeding America's millions. And National Dairy laboratories are dedicated to this endlessly important job.

Dedicated to the wider use and better understanding of dairy products as human food . . . as a base for the development of new products and materials . . . as a source of health and enduring progress on the farms and in the towns and cities of America.

in a few decades. But it has never lost its hold. That is not to say that we have remained consciously loyal to Carlyle, but only that Carlyle himself was unconsciously reacting to a situation he had never understood. Let us look at two striking instances of the subsequent degeneration of Carlyle's doctrine of self-worship. Defining "liberal education" in 1868, Thomas Henry Huxley, popularizer of Darwin, made the famous pronouncement about the liberally educated mind as "a clear, cold, logic engine, with all its parts of equal strength, and in smooth working order; ready like a steam engine to be turned to any kind of work . . . etc." Sherlock Holmes was invented only a few years later. But even before Holmes, it was the positive ideal of the eminent and representative Huxley that mechanization should take command of the training of the mind. And in "How To Develop Your Executive Ability" and "Know-How" it has been shown how many basic attitudes today are variations on this theme.

The present ad has been selected as a focal point for some further aspects of the attitude promoted by Huxley and others equally attuned to the *Zeitgeist*. R. M. Tisdall's *The Young Athlete* is written from an English point of view which tends to be more chummy and less mechanical and behavioristic than that of the United States, yet this is what he tells the young:

> Regard your body as the engine—far more wonderful than any man-made machine—and you will find you can derive endless pleasure from cleaning, fuelling, lubricating, tuning and testing it, as well as from actually racing it. And look upon your brain as the driver.

Taken with the present ad, that passage draws attention, for example, to the high degree of narcissism in the athletic ideal. And it should be noted that the perennial adolescence of the confirmed athlete matches up very well with the Baby Snooks mentality of the equally self- and body-centered "love goddess." Concentration on "scientific" hygiene and beauty aids do for the glamour girl what "scientific" muscle-building does for the athlete and scientific character-building for the executive. For each of these types there is an ever-present totem image equivalent to "The Massive Massimo" and his leopard-skin pants.

It should be noted in the passage from R. M. Tisdall that there is a quality in English body-machine worship that is alien to that of the United States. The English are much more self-conscious and sentimental about the romance of machinery, perhaps because less deeply committed than the Americans. They have a more organic approach than the Germans, whose attitude is closer to the psychological. The organic emphasis produces the totem ideals of Kipling's Mowgli and *The Jungle Book*, which in turn produced the Baden-Powell world of out-of-door scouting and troops of youth organized into wolf packs and cub packs. The English writer Harold Stovin, in his *Totem: The Exploitation of Youth*, gives an excellent account of the spread of this Darwinian primitivism not only via scouting but through a dozen other primitivistic schemes of organized camaraderie which have been tried in England. He sees quite clearly that they are not rooted in any concept of civilized society but are merely a blind drive toward the phantom security of subrational collectivism. But there are still prevalent in England remnants of genuinely rational and humanistic social traditions that reflect a bizarre light on the panic drive toward totemistic experiments. So that the Englishman cuts an awkward and uneasy figure when trying out his jungle capers.

The mechanisms of organic sentiment were being dropped as trite and unsatisfactory by the Germans as early as Darwin. They had had their romantic orgy of simple organicism in the early nineteenth century and passed swiftly to the more intense psychological emphasis with Nietzsche. By now, criticism of both the goose-stepping and the Nietzschean brands of nihilism amounts to a large library of books and articles. But few of these have done much to relate the German passion for mechanism to our own different variety. Most observers are agreed that there is a *total* commitment in the German brand that is frightening. And Wilhelm Reich, in *The Mass Psychology of Fascism*, links this passion at many points to führer-worship, which he rightly regards as narcissistic:

> It is this attitude of blind trust and of seeking protection . . . which gives the dictators the power to "do it all." . . . Even more important is the *identification* of the mass individual with the "Führer." . . . This tendency to identification is the psychological basis of *national narcissism*, that is, of a self-confidence based on identification with "the greatness of the nation."

Wyndham Lewis's novel *Tarr*, for example, is a study of the brittle and sentimental mechanisms of the Teuton Otto Kreisler, and the ways in which petty disappointments transform him into a lethal machine of self-destruction. As early as 1914, in *Blast*, Lewis set the international situation in the same light:

> It is commonly reported that the diplomatic impossibility of a visit to Paris, from time to time, darkens the whole life of the Kaiser. The German's love for

the French is notoriously *un amour malheureux*, as it is by no means reciprocated. And the present war may be regarded in that sense as a strange wooing. The essential German *will* get to Paris, to the Café de la Paix, at all costs, if he has to go there at the head of an army and destroy a million beings in the adventure.

It may be argued that the psychological type of mechanism tends to involve more of the human person than the organic end. So that the rigidity of the German psyche has become more complete than any other. Even the German peasant, the man of the soil, appears to be more psychologically inflexible than, say, the American urban dweller. And the ego-annihilating force implicit in this attitude brings on the joys and security of mass hysteria and collective consciousness with great speed. Again, it might be noted that, just as the English have avoided many of the final involvements in emotional totemism, thanks to a core of civilized tradition, so the individual German often tends to escape via Austrian tradition, with its taproot in French and Italian embodiments of European civilization.

It is surely thanks to the great diversity of civilized traditions and attitudes in the United States that the lad pictured before the mighty icon of "The Massive Massimo" is not likely to become either a Boy Scout, out-of-doors crank, nor yet a superman or tragic-history crank. He is committed only superficially and temporarily to mechanistic assumptions, not deeply and finally. It is this salutary diversity and confusion of attitudes which at present, at least, permits the boy in the ad to look a little sceptical both about "The Massive Massimo" and himself, and for the ad also to be intentionally humorous. It may also help to explain how the most mechanized country in the world is not a country of machine *lovers*. Not in the German nor English sense anyway. It may or may not be to our credit that we feel and express such a careless attitude toward the elaborate mechanisms which cost us so much time and money. But our casual indifference in managing and scrapping cars and equipment, which so shocks the European, may yet prove to be rooted in a complex of attitudes which can save us from the worst effects of mechanization.

This is said not to negate the points made in "Know-How" and elsewhere, but to suggest that we would do well to strengthen those inner resources, which we still undoubtedly exert, to resist the mechanism of mass delirium and collective irrationalism. But the unofficial nation-wide agencies of education, production, distribution, entertainment, and advertisement are friendly neither to diversity nor to inner resistance. The monopolistic trends of intense competition are unfavorable to local talent and tradition alike. And as for resistance, every success drive and sales drive is committed to erasing this in all its varieties. In short, the capital of individual resistance and autonomous existence is being used up at a very visible rate. Is it being replaced? Or is the power of inner renewal increasing in proportion to the increasingly numerous mechanisms for anticipating and controlling the thoughts and feelings of many millions with which the present book is much concerned? It is really impossible to say, but there is no room for complacency. At some point in the mechanistic drama of our time each individual experiences to some degree the attractions and even the fact of submission and surrender. The price of total resistance, like that of total surrender, is still too high.

Consequently, in practice, everyone is intellectually and emotionally a patchwork quilt of occupied and unoccupied territory. And there are no accepted standards of submission or resistance to commercially sponsored appeals either in reading or living habits. All the more, then, is it urgent to foster habits of inspection until workable standards of securely civilized judgment emerge from those habits. Nation-wide agencies of mental sterilization now make it impossible to repose in mere habits of *laissez faire*. The low quality of mental habit engendered thus far by universal literacy, when confronted with the extreme complexity of current affairs, cannot be said to produce thought. So that the exhortation to "think for yourself" is, in these circumstances, a cause of discouragement only. It positively encourages a plunge into any collective myth that happens to have appeal.

The dream of irresistible national might, for example, is achieved by the individual surrender to the totem of the war machine. (At the end of War II the *Fortune* survey editors [June, 1949] were surprised to find nearly all the vets in favor of getting inside a *big* business. Money was found to be a secondary consideration.) But national, economic, or social might achieved by this kind of cohesion of submissive, expendable units is of little human value or significance. For the worst of it is that such agglomerations are fatally disposed to destroy both others and themselves. Narcissism and self-worship are neither humanly tolerant nor productive.

Bogart Hero

Why so sad and corrugated, chum?

Is Bogart America's Shropshire Lad?

Does the glamorous but doomed gangster provide an escape valve for the guilt of the respectable?

Remove the films and novels of violence and how much entertainment is left?

Why is the killer a man of the big town and the Henry Fondas and Jimmie Stewarts men of the small town?

The Hollywood trend is fusing the good- and bad-girl types, hitherto kept rigidly apart, has been taken up by current sociological comment. More complex in some ways are the motives which have given rise to the bad man as hero. Bogart typically enacts the role of the puzzled man driven to crime or violence by the complexity of forces he cannot understand. And in this respect his role coincides with that of the Hemingway hero. His corrugated brow and eyes full of pain shed the light of human dubiety over all actions both "good" and "bad." Goaded by circumstances, he takes the vigorous, direct course calling for courage and daring and death, but he is usually doomed from the first frame on the reel. That is his role and business—to be doomed.

A commercial society dedicated to the smash and grab and one-man fury of enterprise has produced just one popular type of tragic hero—the gangster. Would it not be strange, therefore, if this gangster were not a sort of reversed carbon copy of the go-getter? If he were not at some level representative of accepted motivations and of the fatalities born of these motives, he could have none of the appeal which, in fact, he does have.

There is quite enough general uneasiness about the current motives and methods of the success drive to make the figure of the doomed gangster a very satisfactory scapegoat, a means of purging guilt feelings by evoking them in a context other than those of our own lives. Here, as previously, the testimony of Dr. Mead's *Male and Female* is welcome when, from her very different point of view, she takes up the same materials as are under scrutiny here. In the underprivileged parts of our cities, she points out, where the boys "are unable to take their fathers' failures as clues to a remote pattern of male success as reinterpreted by the mothers," they develop an asocial gang life which "provides a basis for the adult criminal world in America." In short, the gangster world is a kind of streamlined or short-circuited version of the usual success pattern.

It is the resulting freedom from the ordinary marks of respectability plus its desperate intensity which endow it with a kind of esthetic distance from "normalcy." But otherwise it reflects the forms and tensions of the average social pattern. Thus, *Life* (November 29, 1948) reviews the Chicago Capone crowd as a group of energetic and talented men who, but for the fates, might have been pillars of the board of trade. Respectability pays. Crime doesn't pay. That is the main difference between the two spheres. As for the arbitrary and precarious place one occupies in the respectable world or the gang world, that is a matter of calculated risks. But whereas the tycoon risks his money, the gangster risks his life.

THE BOGART HIT THAT LEAVES YOU GASPING FOR BREATH!

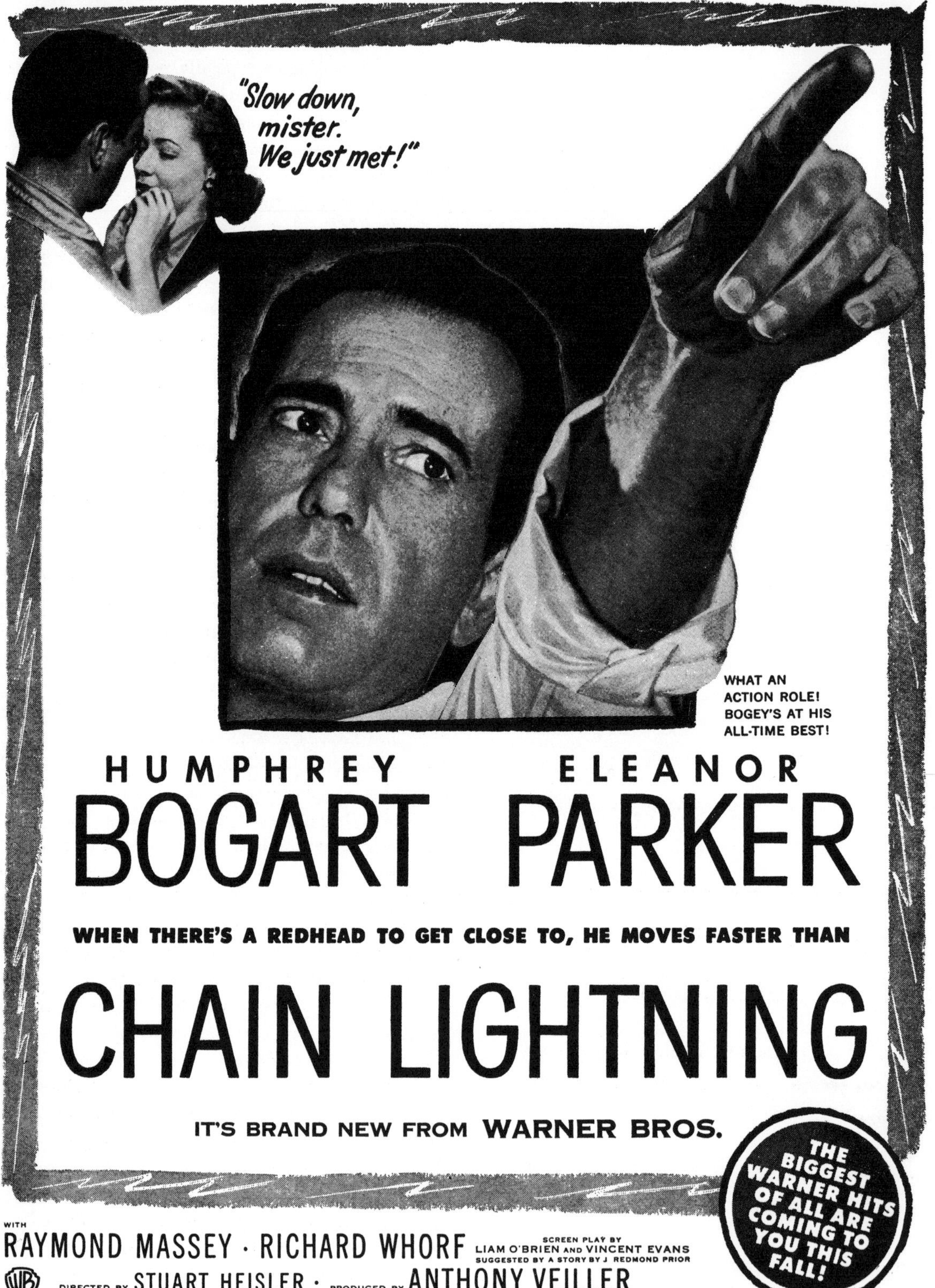

WITH RAYMOND MASSEY · RICHARD WHORF

SCREEN PLAY BY LIAM O'BRIEN AND VINCENT EVANS
SUGGESTED BY A STORY BY J. REDMOND PRIOR

DIRECTED BY STUART HEISLER · PRODUCED BY ANTHONY VEILLER

And so far as the screen is concerned, he is there to suffer and die rather than to act or succeed.

Like the tycoon, the gangster must be a man in a big town, and one skilled in its routines. His body gestures and speech must be rigid and precise, linked impersonally to all the elaborate mechanisms of a great industrial city. But he moves amid its wealth and gaiety, its stark jive and acrid sensuality, an alien and a stranger. This role—of the trapped spectator of a world he can never own—is usually heightened by bringing into his life some good girl who may even be from the respectable part of society. Or she may be a waif like himself.

That Bogart very well understands the roots of the role he has been elected to play appears in the first movie he sponsored on his own, *Knock On Any Door,* in which he plays the part of a crusading defense attorney who understands the big-city slums. It would seem that he finds his ordinary screen roles very distasteful with their advance copy: "He kisses so tenderly, he murders so carefully," though he may have little notion of the artistic catharsis which the screen (and real-life gangster, too) provides for a commercial society.

It would be instructive to study the Greek and Elizabethan tragic heroes in comparison with our own. Our relative crudity appears in the quality of the catharsis we demand. The gangster hero stands in relation only to the laws of land which he has defied. The Greek tragic hero stands in relation to a wider and more terrible law. He may be a most respectable citizen. The Greeks were prepared to admit that even a good family man who paid his bills and income tax might be offensive to the gods. Our entertainment shows few signs of any eagerness on our parts for that degree of catharsis.

On the other hand, we are ready to accept the redemption of gangsters "in the crucible of war," as Parker Tyler has said. But war itself has become a normal feature of industrial competition. Many popular pictures attest to our pleasure in seeing the gangster style of energy and toughness turned loose against "the common enemy." So, by and large, it would appear that the gangster hero provides us now merely with another stock mechanism of emotional evasion, much as the Oscar Wildes and the artists of his generation functioned as scapegoats or public victims for the grossness and hypocrisy of commercial Europe.

Pollyanna Digest

How quickly can you think?

Do you belong to the era of heavy reading and light anecdotes?

You prefer the trotting harness of *Time's* horse opera to the moon-calf ebullience of *Reader's Digest?*

Barnum rides again. But *Quick?*

Nickelodeon platter all samee as *Digest* yatter?

"UNPACK your suitcase and live!" Between the covers of the *Reader's Digest* the sky is officially not cloudy all day. Here again we are home on the range and away from the cold-groin and blue-armpit world of the daytime serial. Here we meet not the gothic gargoyles of the lonely hearts, but the pep and bounce of the ozone plains where the deer and the antelope play. But just as these cheerful words are set in the song to a most mournful air, so the "keep smiling" creed of the *Digest* gets its meaning from the joyless intensity of commerce.

Since the merely practical man lives so much in a world of risk capital, liquidity preferences, and uncertain probabilities, he craves many kinds of reassurance and a spate of encouraging words. Poised on the bubble of business confidence, panic easily rises in his heart, even as he keeps the bubble floating along. Those prayerful imperatives which decorate the walls of the private chapels of commerce are easily understood in this context: THINK. SMILE.

The success story in a hundred guises is the formula of the *Digest,* as in such items on the present cover as:

Blind, He Teaches Those Who See.

Marriage Control: A New Answer To Divorce

Take a Cow to College And Make It Pay

Human Engineering at Boys' Ranch

In "Sunny—The Spirit of '76" there is a story about a little ranch girl:

> The meanest old hammerheads under her tutelage became as cooing doves. All day long she worked with them and at night she sang about them. Sitting on the hearth, her blonde hair golden in the firelight, she'd cuddle the ranch guitar and croon heartbreakingly . . .
>
> "You ought to be on the radio," Noelke told her.

This is not just the *Digest* formula but will be found in most entertainment, business, and education. It can be stated very simply: Since there's a heap of goodness, beauty, and power in everybody and everything, let's extract it and then box it, bottle it, or can it, and hurry to market. The smart little pig went to market, the dumb little pig stayed home. But if some accident should keep the smart little pig at home, then bet your boots that little old home is going to bloom out into a $100,000 business, at least, and provide a lesson of comfort and solace to the entire community.

The endless use of the Barnum and Ripley technique of stressing the feasibility of the impossible as a challenge to curiosity and emulation results in the tediously terrific and the forcible feeble. If there is any harm done by the *Digest* or by any of the related entertainment industries, it is in supplanting better fare. It is the sheer presence of successful stupidity which commonly blocks and clutters the minds of those who might conceivably prefer something better. The *Digest* is also typical of all these agencies of mass diversion in eagerly creating an aura of intolerance around itself and its readers. Enfolded in its jovial, optimistic, and self-satisfied version of the higher things, the reader soon hardens into a man who "knows what he likes" and who resents anybody who pretends to like anything better. He has, unwittingly, been sold a strait jacket. And that is really as much as need be said about any of the effects of commercial formula writing, living, and entertainment. It destroys human autonomy, freezes perception, and sterilizes judgment.

The higher comedy is not to be found in the earnestness of *Digest* cheerfulness but in such displays as *The New Yorker* when attacking the *Digest*. In a book called *Little Wonder*, mainly reprinted from *The New Yorker*, the *Digest* was supposedly devastated. However, the author was much embarrassed at being unable to discover any sizable chinks in the moral armor of the *Digest* and its editors, and he was content to sneer at what was too evidently a lack of aesthetic dandyism in the earnest and convinced *Digest* makers. It was like a wrestling match between two men, each of whom was locked in a separate trunk. *The New Yorker* fan and the *Digest* addict are carried in different coaches through the same tunnel.

This fact is pointed out lest it be supposed that it has been argued here that there is value in merely attacking vulgarity and stupidity. Because today there is far too much of these commodities intermixed with valuable articles to make such a course desirable. What is needed is not attacks on obvious imbecility but a sharp eye for what supports and is now involved in it. It is from this habit of dissociation that the means of recreating shopworn values can come. As said earlier in "From Top to Toe," our situation is very like that of Poe's sailor in "The Maelstrom," and we are now obliged not to attack or avoid the *strom* but to study its operation as providing a means of release from it.

AUGUST 1947 25¢

THE Reader's Digest

ARTICLES OF LASTING INTEREST • 26th YEAR OF PUBLICATION

WRITER'S DIGEST

NOVEMBER, 1947 25c

Stan Lee

>> THERE'S MONEY IN COMICS!

By Stan Lee

How To Make a Fan -- Book

By William Lynch Vallee

The Truth About True Detectives

By R. J. Travers

Money in Comics

Seen any staggering figures lately?

Heard about the Colorado monument to Steve Canyon, the comic-strip hero of Milton Caniff? The pun that turned to stone?

Why aren't you interested in the private lives of the strippers and pulp artists who upholster our desert landscape?

Is folk art made by folk artists?

CONTRADICTING the maxim that "crime does not pay" is the fact that violence and crime in the comic-book industry alone is very big business. Just how tightly and bureaucratically this business is organized is plain from the fact that in the space of six months it recently shifted a large section of its enterprises from murder to love comics. The combined attacks of Dr. Frederic Wertham, Mr. G. Legman, and others suggested the advisability of a partial switch from Death to Love. English censors have urged that Disney's Donald Duck cartoons be banned as bad medicine because frequently loaded with mayhem and violence. And an A.P. report from Wethersfield, Connecticut (March 13, 1950) tells of the alarm and indignation of the convicts at the State prison over the spread of crime in radio programs and pulps.

In this last situation there is probably some jealousy that respectable citizens should be so well paid for acting and portraying the crimes for which the professionals are behind bars. In the same way a serious artist who might be glad to get twenty-five hundred dollars for a good portrait might feel some resentment at Norman Rockwell's receiving six thousand dollars a subject or Maxfield Parrish's getting from ten to twenty thousand for one of his creations.

A magazine like *Writer's Digest,* however, is surprisingly modest. It would seem to be written not so much to let the public in on the celestial know-how of the most successful as for those who barely scratch a living from the pulps by banging away on their typewriters sixteen hours a day. Stan Lee, writing "There's Money in Comics," warns copy writers for comic-book illustrators:

> DON'T WRITE DOWN TO YOUR READERS!
>
> It is common knowledge that a large portion of comic magazine readers are adults, and the rest of the readers who may be kids are pretty sharp characters. They are used to seeing movies and listening to radio shows . . . a great deal of thought goes into every story; and there are plenty of gimmicks, sub-plots, human interest angles. . . .

This happens to be true. In the matter of intellectual quality there is little to choose between *Dare Devil Comics* and *Gone With the Wind* and between the claims made for the romantic movie and novel of our day, just as in emotional pattern there is little or no difference between the "middle-brow" and the "low-brow." The difference is mainly in the amount of lush verbiage and opulence of turnout. There is no question of perception or taste in the genteel movie or novel or in the pulps.

But the superiority of the pulps is in their absence of pretentiousness, and the readers of this form of entertainment are altogether undeceived by it. They are never under the impression of having bought or read something with "class."

The basic criterion for any kind of human excellence is simply how heavy a demand it makes on the intelligence. How inclusive a consciousness does it focus? By this standard there is very little fiction in a century, very little music, and very little poetry or painting which deserves attention for its own sake. One function of the critic is to keep the best work free from the surrounding clutter. But, in order to free the mind from the debilitating confusion, it is not enough to claim priority for excellence without considering the bulk which is inferior. To win more and more attention for the best work it is necessary to demonstrate what constitutes the inevitably second-rate, third-rate, and so on. And in the course of doing this one finds that the great work of a period has much in common with the poorest work. The air of unreality which has hovered over the little-magazine coterie culture in general is due to their neglect of the close interrelations between the good and bad work of the same period. The result of this neglect is, finally, failure to see the goodness of the good work itself. The great artist necessarily has his roots very deep in his own time—roots which embrace the most vulgar and commonplace fantasies and aspirations.

Corset Success Curve

Is that photographer throwing a trick curve?

Why laugh and grow fat when you can experience anguish and success in a strait jacket?

How much self-pity is needed to put a spare tire on you?

Is it the unconfident male who contracts the feminine form?

Nobody has to be told that people who crave to be held tight, whether in somebody's arms or in a "foundation garment," are looking for extra security. And one of the paradoxes of modern feminine attire is the strange mixture of brevity and rigidity. When a woman wants to "look her best" today, she not only zips herself into a strait jacket but puts spikes under her heels to ensure that she will be incapable of a single free gesture of arm or leg. The whole forward thrust of her body then requires stiffening of neck and shoulders to prevent general collapse.

Yet, so far as general coverage is concerned, this same woman may be wearing a skirt which enforces semi-nudity if she ventures to be seated. Moreover, her transparent stockings are suspended at such high tension that she expects any sudden move to produce an

New Sensational Money-Saving Plan!

The Famous DuBarry Success Course

with Introductory Supply of DuBarry Beauty Preparations *Only* $12.95

Now—by a new plan—you can have the benefits of the DuBarry Success Course—the famous Course you have read and heard so much about—at the lowest price at which it ever has been offered: only $12.95. Yes—the same Course that 340,000 women and girls have taken at home, the same analysis of your beauty problems, the same easy-to-follow lessons, the same individual guidance in helping you to be the slender, attractive woman or girl you want to be.

How can we offer this Course at such a low price? Here is the answer: It has been the practice to furnish with the DuBarry Success Course an assortment of twenty DuBarry Beauty and Make-up Preparations and Richard Hudnut Hair Preparations. The tuition for the Course, including these Preparations, has been—*and still is*—$28.50. But hundreds of women have written to ask: "Isn't there some way I can have the Success Course on an easier plan? Why can't I just enroll for the Course and get the Preparations as I need them?"

Lowest Price Ever Offered!

Out of these suggestions has come this new plan: With your Course you receive not twenty, but the *three* preparations you start using at once in your daily beauty ritual—DuBarry Special Cleansing Preparation, Cleansing Cream and Skin Freshener. Then you also receive a DuBarry Beauty Guide, showing you what Beauty, Make-up and Hair Preparations you can purchase as you need them at your local store.

This plan makes it possible for *you* to have the DuBarry Success Course for only $12.95—a price so low that you can surely start right away.

The very day your lessons arrive, you start on the most exciting experience of your life. It's just like stepping into the famous Richard Hudnut Salon on Fifth Avenue, New York, where beauty-maker Ann Delafield has been working her "miracles" for years. You get an individual analysis of your needs—skin, hair, figure, posture, weight. You eat tempting, delicious foods while pounds fade away. You learn professional secrets for making your lips more alluring, your eyes more sparkling, your hair more beautiful.

It's a never-to-be-forgotten adventure in beauty. Keep it a secret if you wish, but you won't be able to keep it a secret long. For the rewards are wonderful—compliments of family and friends, tender attentions from the man in your life, and deep-down pride in what your mirror tells you.

Here's How Easy It Is to Start

Simply fill out and mail the special coupon below, indicating the plan on which you wish to enroll and how you wish to pay your tuition. (Yes, if you prefer, you may enroll for the Course with 20 Preparations for $28.50.) You'll be thrilled with what comes hurrying back to you: Your first lessons, your Success-O-Scope to enable the Salon to give you an individual analysis, and your supply of DuBarry Beauty Preparations (three if you enroll on Plan A; twenty, if you enroll on Plan B).

Don't miss this chance to have the famous DuBarry Success Course at the lowest price ever. Don't wait another day. The sooner you send this coupon, the sooner you will be started on your own exciting adventure in beauty.

Mrs. Inga Merriman, Portland, Maine, took the DuBarry Success Course, lost 15 pounds in 6 weeks. She says: "I never saw anything work so like magic. My skin glows like satin, my hair is soft and lustrous. Let the Success Course show you how to get slim and stay slim."

Before *After*

DuBarry Success Course

ANN DELAFIELD, *Directing*

Richard Hudnut Salon, Dept. SY-59, 693 Fifth Ave., N.Y.

Included with your Course when you enroll under PLAN A

DuBarry Special Cleansing Preparation
DuBarry Cleansing Cream
DuBarry Skin Freshener

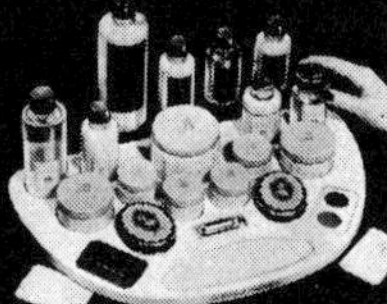

Included with your Course when you enroll under PLAN B

DuBarry Cleansing Cream
DuBarry Skin Freshener
DuBarry Special Cleansing Preparation
DuBarry Lubricating Cream
DuBarry Derma-Sec Formula
DuBarry Foundation Lotion
DuBarry Hand Beauty Cream
DuBarry Rose Cream Mask
DuBarry Eye Cream
DuBarry Make-up Base
DuBarry Lipstick
DuBarry Cream Rouge
DuBarry Eye Shadow
DuBarry Face Powder
DuBarry Lash Beauty
DuBarry Dainty-Dry

Also, Richard Hudnut Enriched Creme Shampoo, Creme Rinse, Creme Hair Dressing, Dandruff Lotion.

RICHARD HUDNUT SALON
Dept. SY-59, 693 Fifth Ave., New York 22, N. Y.

Please enroll me for the DuBarry Success Course on the plan before which I have marked X:

☐ **PLAN A**—DuBarry Success Course, with introductory supply of three DuBarry Beauty Preparations.

☐ I enclose $12.95 as payment in full.
☐ I enclose $6.95 and will send $6.95 in one month.

☐ **PLAN B**—DuBarry Success Course with twenty DuBarry Beauty and Make-up Preparations and Richard Hudnut Hair Preparations.

☐ I enclose $28.50 as payment in full.
☐ I enclose $7.50 and will send $7.50 a month for three more months.

(Send all payments by check or money order payable to Richard Hudnut Salon. Do not send currency).

Miss
Mrs. ______
Street ______
City ______ *Zone* ___ *State* ______

(If under 21, consult parent or guardian and have their consent before taking this Course.)

Accepted for advertising in publications of the American Medical Association

Whether you enroll under Plan A or Plan B, please let us have the following important information so that we may send you DuBarry Beauty Preparations for your type.

Color of Hair ______
Eyes ______
Lashes ______
Skin: Dry ☐ Oily ☐
Age ______
Height ______
Weight ______
Skin Color: Cream ☐ Fair ☐ Med. ☐ Dark ☐

outburst of "ladders." Is it strange, then, that the muscles of her face act rather mechanically when she smiles and thus produce a grimace rather like springing a trap?

The liberation of women from the tyranny of long dresses and the male-imposed modesty of the past would seem to be incomplete. For what avail bare thighs and plunging necklines and screaming lipstick if intense biological and psychological rigidity remain? The nudists are in the same dilemma. Theoretically freed from all restraints by their fanatical ideology, in practice they are puritanically rigid with fear of their own bodies. More obviously than most, they proclaim man's effort to rid himself of mechanized routines by plucking frantically at their restricting garments. But the ordinary glamour girl is a much more interesting case of mechanization. She accepts from a technological world the command to transform her organic structure into a machine. A love machine? It would seem so. At least she is told that the end of all the methodical processing will be love unlimited.

That is the meaning of "success" in the present ad. Not just a treatment but a *course.* Whereas the man takes a course to reshape his entire personality, the women are offered a new body as a success formula. New Bodies by Du Barry, "only $12.95." So far as the "before" and "after" photos are concerned, both show a "fine figger of a woman." And to get a similar difference between the same views of any person, no more is needed than to switch the camera angle from front to profile. Elementary dodges of this sort are reinforced here by giving the "after" shot a smile, a hair-do, and a tiptoe stance. All glamour photos of standing figures are tiptoe, because this not only creates the effect of a longer limb but also that muscular rigidity which is so necessary in making one "belong" in a world of machines. But biological rigidity in a mechanized world is as nothing to the overlayering of the mind with idea mechanisms which obliterate every spontaneous movement of thought and feeling.

The present ad says, as it were: "You are 39 and nothing ever happens? Natch. But leave it to us to put your old jalopy back on the road to romance. For only $12.95 we can soup up the engine, take off the spare tires and fenders, install a supercharger, and send you to screaming heights of man-woman madness just like the ads for your favorite movies."

However, it might be timely to recall the story of the plump wife who went off for a prolonged slimming course and came home to find that her husband had vamoosed with a woman much plumper than she had ever been.

Horse Opera and Soap Opera

You have been told that these popular art forms are inferior to the glossy guff from the book clubs?

How long can the urban male live imaginatively on the frontier of eighty years ago?

Why is the American heart split between the frontier and the small town?

Got any light on why our intellectuals take such a dark view of pop kulch?

In The John Ford Tradition of Greatness
John Ford and Merian C. Cooper
present
JOHN WAYNE
JOANNE DRU
JOHN AGAR
BEN JOHNSON
HARRY CAREY, Jr.
in
She Wore a Yellow Ribbon
JOHN WAYNE
in his most heroic role as Captain Brittles of the U.S. Cavalry.
with VICTOR McLAGLEN
MILDRED NATWICK · GEORGE O'BRIEN
ARTHUR SHIELDS
Directed by JOHN FORD
Story by JAMES WARNER BELLAH
Screen Play by FRANK NUGENT and LAURENCE STALLINGS
COLOR BY TECHNICOLOR
Produced by ARGOSY PICTURES CORPORATION
Distributed by RKO RADIO PICTURES
JOANNE DRU as Olivia
JOHN AGAR as Lt. Cohill
BEN JOHNSON as Tyree
HARRY CAREY, Jr. as Lt. Pennell
VICTOR McLAGLEN as Sgt. Quincannon
GEORGE O'BRIEN as Maj. Allshard

LIKE THE home town, the world of the frontier is a focus of numerous feelings and emotions which make it every year a bigger and bigger fact of industrial folklore. As the frontier recedes historically, it looms larger and larger imaginatively. When movies for a paying public began on Broadway in 1894 at the Kinetoscope Parlor, major attractions there that year were two Westerns, "Annie Oakley" and "Buffalo Bill." Fifty years later Horse Opera is just getting into stride with John Ford's top direction and with department stores running full-page ads when Hopalong Cassidy duds hit town.

Soap opera tends to have its center in the home town as much as horse opera is located on the frontier. But there are many links between the two. And not least of these is the similarity between the barrels of woe which flood the daytime serials and the slow-paced and monotonous melancholy of cowboy lyrics. "Home on the Range," one of President Roosevelt's favorites, in which the Pollyanna sentiment is contradicted by the doleful music, is an instance of the larger paradox of horse opera itself.

The public has never been home on the range, and the frontier disappeared before this generation was born. It lives in a crowded, peppy, optimistic world of business bustle and systematic change. Why should it be obsessed with an archaic past in which there was no commerce, no routine, no change? For horse opera is a stylized world of timeless properties. Men, women, horses, guns, dresses, and ranch houses there are beyond the reach of fashion or the Sears Roebuck catalogue. Industrial progress has no part in this world. Hygiene and plumbing have never come near it.

Is it an ideal past specially constructed to justify the ideal future? Or is it just an ideal contrast to a present reality? Certainly the West of Buffalo Bill which attracted movie patrons in 1894 was not the same as the one that appeals to suburban kids today. The frontier as presented to the contemporary child is a world full of lessons in citizenship and business enterprise. Roy Rogers portrays a combination of Quaker Oats salesman and Mr. District Attorney. On the other hand, the idea of the West that appealed to the patrons of 1894 and still lives in the imagination of French, German, and English boys is the West not of Gary but James Fenimore Cooper; that is, a world of fantastic adventures and noble savages. It was directly related to the romantic ideals of revolutionary France and the attack on feudal civilization.

The celluloid West still plays something of that role in our imaginations. It offers equestrian dash and characters of ruthless and exuberant individualism to a population bedraggled by mechanical routine and befuddled by complex economic and domestic changes. The old enemy was a slick feudal aristocracy. The new enemy is the slick and anonymous machine. To people overwhelmed by industrial scale, the West restores the image of the human dimension. To a commercial society far advanced along the road of monopolistic bureaucracy, the West holds up the primordial image of the lonely entrepreneur. That is why the celluoid image becomes more and more vivid as the historical actuality gets dimmer.

Closely associated with these cultural dynamics is the deep nostalgia of an industrial society, a nostalgia bred by rapid change. Obsolescence is a major reality in this kind of world of business turnover. Competitive machine processes are often out of date before they can be widely applied. Books are discarded before a fraction of the potential readers have heard of them. Hair, clothes, educational, and hit-parade patterns are switched faster than the young can grow into them. And record albums of the songs of 1930 or 1935 do a roaring trade as quaintly sentimental revivals of forgotten eras. A twenty-five-year-old can get wistful about reminiscences of ten years ago. In such a world the lasting qualities of horse opera with the fringe on top have great appeal.

Again, under complex conditions of rapid change, the family unit is subject to special strain. Men flounder in such times. The male role in society, always abstract, tenuous, and precarious compared with the biological assurance of the female, becomes obscured. Man the provider, man the codifier of laws and ritual, loses his confidence. For millions of such men horse opera presents a reassuringly simple and nondomestic world in which there are no economic problems. In that territory mating, likewise, is a simple affair without elaborate courtship and dating preliminaries.

Part of Hemingway's popularity rests on his agreement with the American male that mating should be uncomplicated. And James Michener's *Tales of the South Pacific* embodies this attitude (as does Melville's *Typee*) in the idyll of Cable and Liat, the marine and the half-caste. Horse-opera heroes aren't expected to be imaginative or eloquent. In horse opera particularly, as in Hollywood in general, suave manners are the sign of the treacherous heart and selfish lust. This great dogma was transferred to horse opera from Victorian melodrama. But it dates back to the eighteenth-century middle-class envy and resentful admiration of aristocratic Lovelaces. The heroines of horse opera are waxwork Victorian dolls as simple and true as the heroes. They don't get candy, flowers, compliments, or kisses. They don't get the Boyer treatment.

Even a casual glance at horse-opera heroes suggests that they share with the ideal businessman and the athlete certain qualities of muscular asceticism and harshness. The puritanical rigor of the celluloid frontier appeals to those who have espoused other kinds of rigor in their business and social lives. So the cowboy is as non-erotic as the hard-driving executive. He is emotionally hardened and unresponsive to any but a tiny area of experiences. He can act, but he cannot feel. Therefore he cannot be cast in a lover role any more than the businessman. Both are rigidly adolescent and non-receptive to experience. So Hollywood has to import its screen lovers, and often the women to whom they make love, as well.

Horse opera, like the sports page, is a man's world, free from the problems of domesticity. Soap opera is a woman's world, laden with personal problems. It is an intimate home-town world, not the harsh frontier. Add the interests of horse opera and soap opera together, and you get the ingredients of Elizabethan domestic drama à la Dekker and Heywood, or the eighteenth-century novel à la Richardson and Burney. In a word, you have *Jane Eyre, East Lynne* and nineteenth-century melodrama. But by themselves soap-opera serials are short on action, long on situations. The pace is slow. Suffering is intense and prolonged. The voices are mournful with sympathy and understanding. Here, in short, is that woman's world which in our industrial society has been so sharply split off from the business world.

From nine to five the housewife is usually separated from her husband, a situation glanced at in the current lyric:

> I don't care if the sun don't shine,
> I get my lovin' in the evening time.

There is no sunshine in soap opera, but anxiety and woe, and even common sense, are plentiful. Yet these interminable dramas, with their theme that "life *can* be beautiful" but never is, are much more nearly adult affairs than horse opera, just as the American woman is typically more emotionally mature than the man. These dramas are more realistic than horse opera, since the situations they present are often very close to ordinary domestic experience. Moreover, they suggest that the bogus cheerfulness of business bounce and optimism "where never is heard a discouraging word" doesn't quite overpower the millions of housewives who are daytime serial fans. The Pollyanna philosophy of the *Reader's Digest* and the *Saturday Evening Post* simply doesn't impress the home-town scepticism of the soap-opera adherent. Cheerfulness as normal extrovert behavior, necessary for keeping things humming, is not very appealing to American women, it would seem.

In addition, when you consider that soap operas are written and acted quite as well as the ordinary evening radio drama, it will appear that they have been the object of a good deal of irrelevant criticism. The fact that evening shows feature well-known stars in radio versions of Broadway or Hollywood successes seems to have beguiled a number of critics into quite pointless abuse of the daytime serials. In the same way, the minor but real excellence of much horse opera, as of much detective drama, such as the Philip Marlowe program, is overlooked simply because it is popular. Just so, the crudity, violence, and morbidity, and, at times, illiteracy in some of the work of Charles Dickens was very plain to the educated taste of his day, and it took longer for his excellencies to be appreciated. Dostoevski or Conrad saw and utilized the best of Dickens while it was neglected by his countrymen.

Horse opera and soap opera, then, embody two of the most important American traditions, the frontier and the home town. But the two traditions are split rather than fused. They show that radical separation between business and society, between action and feeling, office and home, between men and women, which is so characteristic of industrial man. These divisions cannot be mended until their fullest extent is perceived.